INCLUSIVE EDUCATION

Perspectives on pedagogy, policy and practice

Edited by Zeta Brown

Routledge
Taylor & Francis Group

LONDON AND NEW YORK

First published 2016
by Routledge
2 Park Square, Milton Park, Abingdon, Oxon OX14 4RN

and by Routledge
711 Third Avenue, New York, NY 10017

Routledge is an imprint of the Taylor & Francis Group, an informa business

British Library Cataloguing in Publication Data
A catalogue record for this book is available from the British Library

Library of Congress Cataloging in Publication Data
Names: Brown, Zeta.
Title: Inclusive education : perspectives on pedagogy, policy and practice / edited by Zeta Brown.
Description: First published 2016. | New York : Routledge, 2016. | Series: Routledge Education Studies Series.
Identifiers: LCCN 2015042643| ISBN 9781138913899 (hardback) | ISBN 9781138913905 (pbk.) | ISBN 9781315691152 (ebook)
Subjects: LCSH: Inclusive education.
Classification: LCC LC1200 .I5185 2016 | DDC 371.9/046–dc23
LC record available at http://lccn.loc.gov/2015042643

ISBN: 978-1-138-91389-9 (hbk)
ISBN: 978-1-138-91390-5 (pbk)
ISBN: 978-1-315-69115-2 (ebk)

Typeset in News Gothic
by Wearset Ltd, Boldon, Tyne and Wear
Printed in Great Britain by
Ashford Colour Press Ltd, Gosport, Hants

For Christopher, Mia and Damie

CONTENTS

TABLES

CONTRIBUTORS

Vernie Clarice Barnes is Principal of the Montserrat Community College. Previously Professor of Education and Psychology at the College of Education, William V.S. Tubman University, Liberia and founder of the Pupil Support Unit, Montserrat, she has worked with students on the psycho-social effects of natural disaster and war. Her research interests are natural disasters and their impact on learners, and strategies for working with traumatised learners.

Kay Bennett is a Lecturer in Childhood, Family and Community Studies at the University of Wolverhampton. She has a background in health and her current research interests are early child development and education. She is currently studying for an EdD in Early Childhood Education.

Stephanie Brewster is Senior Lecturer in the Institute of Education, University of Wolverhampton, teaching Special Needs and Inclusion Studies and Education Studies. Part of her role also entails working towards equality of university experience for disabled students. Her current research interests include inclusive teaching and learning in higher education.

Zeta Brown is a Lecturer in Childhood, Family and Community Studies at the University of Wolverhampton. She is leader of the Childhood, Youth and Families research cluster for the Centre of Developmental and Applied Research in Education. She is an executive member of the British Education Studies Association and the International Society for the Scientific Study of Subjectivity. Her research interests include the practical implementation of inclusion and standards in early childhood and primary education.

Tracey Edwards is a Lecturer in Childhood, Family and Community Studies at the University of Wolverhampton. She is a course leader of the BA Honours in Childhood Studies with Early Years Teacher Status. Her research interests are placement experiences of childhood students and students developing professional identity.

Suanne Gibson is an Associate Professor of Education at Plymouth University, where she teaches and manages the BA Education Studies degree. Her specialist areas of teaching and research are 'disability', 'special educational needs' (SEN), 'inclusion' and critical pedagogy. She has published widely in the area of SEN and teaching and learning in higher education. Suanne has been awarded four teaching fellowships at Plymouth University, in 2011 she was named 'Outstanding Personal Tutor' by Plymouth University's Students' Union and in 2012 her work was recognised at a national level when she received her National Teaching Fellowship from the HEA. In May 2013, she was awarded an International Scholarship with the HEA for the purposes of carrying out a project with six different centres (USA, Europe and New Zealand) to: 'Develop a critically inclusive pedagogy of relationship for the retention and success of "diverse" undergraduate students or "undergraduate students at risk of exclusion"'. She has been a fellow of the RSA since 2014.

Alan Hodkinson was a teacher and SENCO in the state schooling system and is an Associate Professor in the Centre for Cultural and Disability Studies at Liverpool Hope University. He is co-author, with Phillip Vickerman, of the best-selling book *Inclusion and Special Educational Needs* and has authored many research papers that critically explore the concepts and ideologies of inclusion and inclusive education.

Graham Jones is Senior Lecturer in Childhood, Family and Community Studies at the University of Wolverhampton, where he is course leader for the Childhood Studies degree programme. He previously qualified as a secondary school teacher and spent 15 years teaching psychology at a sixth form college. He had various roles during his time teaching in the 16–19 sector, including head of department, careers advisor and personal tutor.

Mike Lambert writes on education and educational research (http://wlv.academia.edu/Mike Lambert). Previously, he taught in a variety of schools, with particular interest in the education of students with special educational needs and disabilities, and worked internationally for voluntary organisations in this field. Subsequently, he was Principal Lecturer in Education at the University of Wolverhampton; his doctorate focused on pedagogy for gifted students.

Sarah Mander is Senior Lecturer in Childhood, Family and Community Studies at the University of Wolverhampton. Sarah also leads the joint award undergraduate programme for Special Needs and Inclusion Studies and Childhood, Family and Community Studies. Her research interests lie in the well-being of children, young people and families and in particular early intervention and prevention within emerging early help service provision.

Catherine Meehan is the Director of Early Childhood at Canterbury Christ Church University, Kent. She has worked in a range of early childhood educational settings and teacher education in Brisbane, Australia before moving to the UK. Catherine is on the OMEP UK committee and her research interests include children's voice in research, children's rights and participation in education and care. Catherine is a Principal Fellow for the Higher Education Academy.

Ioanna Palaiologou has worked as lecturer and researcher in HE for the last 20 years and is now returning to her career as a child psychologist. She is a Chartered Psychologist with the British Psychological Society with specialism in child development and learning theories. During her time in HE education, she has worked for five universities and among her main responsibilities was to supervise postgraduate research students, as well as mentoring early career researchers. Her research interests are focused on ethics in research, child development and implications for pedagogy and the epistemic nature of pedagogy. Her recent books include *Early Years Foundation Stage: Theory and Practice* (3rd edn, SAGE, 2016), *Doing Research in Education: Theory and Practice* (SAGE, 2016), *Child Observation in Early Childhood* (3rd edn, SAGE, 2016).

Nektaria Palaiologou is Associate Professor of Intercultural Education at the Department of Early Childhood Education, School of Education of the University of Western Macedonia in Florina, Greece. From 2006, she was Associate Editor on the journal *Intercultural Education* (Taylor and Francis) and since 2015 has been the journal's Editor-in-Chief. In 2010, she was elected as a board member of the International Association for Intercultural Education (IAIE). Nektaria has published four books in Greek, two books in English, 30 articles as journal publications and about 70 articles as conference proceedings. Prior to her current position, Nektaria was teaching the Intercultural Education modules on a part-time basis at seven Greek universities. Her research interests focus on educational policy issues for immigrant children in Greece, on teachers' education and training in the field of intercultural education and currently on citizenry issues for migrants.

Gavin Rhoades is Senior Lecturer in the Institute of Education at the University of Wolverhampton, where he teaches on a range of undergraduate and postgraduate courses. Prior to joining the university, he was an Assistant Headteacher at secondary schools in Staffordshire and Cumbria. His research interests include inclusion, effective teacher behaviours and online dialogic learning.

Lynn Richards is Course Leader of the Family and Community Studies undergraduate degree programme at the University of Wolverhampton. Her background is in working with children, young people and their families in a variety of provisions: early years settings, play schemes, youth clubs and community projects. She is currently studying for a Professional Doctorate seeking to gather a storied account of students' sense of belonging at the university. Her research interests include student engagement and the attitudinal dispositions that the workforce brings to bear on the educative process.

Tunde Rozsahegyi is Senior Lecturer and Subject Leader for Special Needs and Inclusion Studies at the University of Wolverhampton. Previously, she trained and worked as a 'conductor', specialist educator of children and adults with disabilities through Conductive Education at the Petö Institute in Budapest, Hungary, then played a key role in establishing the National Institute for Conductive Education in Birmingham. Tunde has a strong interest in early pedagogical support for disabled children, their families and professionals; her doctorate examined outlooks on the early development and learning of young children with cerebral palsy.

Philip Vickerman is Professor of Inclusive Education and Learning at Liverpool John Moores University. He works nationally and internationally in areas including Special Educational Needs (SEN) and Disability, Physical Education (PE) and Sport. He has advised agencies, including the Department for Education and the Equality and Human Rights Commission on best practice training materials for teachers. His research interests focus around the training of PE teachers for the inclusion of children with SEN. He also has an interest in research on gaining insights into children with SEN and their experiences of PE.

Stephen Ward is Emeritus Professor of Education, Bath Spa University, formerly Dean of the School of Education and subject leader for Education Studies. A founder member of the British Education Studies Association, he has published on the primary curriculum, primary music teaching and Education Studies. His research interests are education policy and university knowledge.

Jo Winwood is Senior Lecturer and team leader for the MA at the University of Wolverhampton. Her background is in teaching in mainstream and special provision. Her current research interests revolve around the development of inclusive provision, with a focus on the role of the Special Educational Needs Coordinator (SENCO).

SERIES EDITOR'S PREFACE

Education Studies has become a popular and exciting undergraduate subject in some 50 universities in the UK. It began to develop across the sector in the early 2000s. At that time, Routledge published one of the first texts for undergraduates, *Education Studies: A student's guide* (Ward, 2004), now in its third edition. It comprises a series of chapters introducing key topics in Education Studies. There is always discussion about what Education Studies should include, and the three editions of this book have contributed to the thinking and development of the subject. Intended for second- and third-year undergraduates, this book is the first in a series of Routledge publications which builds on the introductory guide and looks in depth at a current priority in education: inclusion.

Education Studies is concerned with understanding how people develop and learn throughout their lives, the nature of knowledge and critical engagement with ways of knowing. It demands an intellectually rigorous analysis of educational processes and their cultural, social, political and historical contexts. In a time of rapid change across the planet, education is about how we both make and manage such change. So Education Studies includes perspectives on international education, economic relationships, globalisation, ecological issues and human rights. It also deals with beliefs, values and principles in education and the way that they change over time.

It is important to understand that Education Studies is not teacher training or teacher education. Its theoretical framework in psychology, sociology, history and philosophy is derived from teacher education, and undergraduates in the subject may well go on to become teachers after a PGCE or school-based training. However, Education Studies should be regarded as a subject with a variety of career outcomes, or indeed, none: it can be taken as the academic and critical study of education in itself. At the same time, while the theoretical elements of teacher training are continually reduced in PGCE courses and school-based training, undergraduate Education Studies provides a critical analysis for future teachers who, in a rapidly changing world, need so much more than training to deliver a government-defined curriculum.

Our first book, by Zeta Brown and her contributors, fully meets the needs of the serious student of education. The approach does not address a single phase in education. Instead, it sweeps across the full range of education from early years to further and higher education. While those students interested in a single phase, such as primary or secondary, might dip into those chapters, the point about Education Studies is that we should have a grasp of the nature of provision overall.

While it was derived from the theory for teaching in schools, Education Studies in recent years has broadened its scope beyond teaching and schools to the broader analysis of childhood and the family in society. This is richly explored in the book with examples and recommendations for good practice in the relationship between education professionals and communities.

Probably the strongest and most distinctive feature of Education Studies is its potential to apply critique to policy and practice: that we should not take the status quo or government policy for granted. Each chapter in the book applies a critique to the area discussed, raising questions about the claims made for inclusion and presenting alternative possibilities. Activities interspersed through the book raise such questions and enable us to reflect on our own understanding and assumptions.

The book deploys the academic disciplines of Education Studies to raise and answer questions about the nature of inclusion in education today. The historical dimension to chapters shows how the use of the term has grown and how practice has changed over the years. There is philosophical analysis of the nature of inclusion and its use as a term, and the psychology of learning and pedagogy in inclusive practice is explored. Of course, education is essentially a political activity and contributors use sociological methods to expose the political nature of inclusion as one of the latest drives in education.

As noted above, Education Studies must include a global perspective, and the final chapters of the book offer fascinating accounts of the development of inclusive education across four continents. These are powerful in the ultimate aim of critical analysis, offering contrasts with the UK and helping us to think beyond the immediate locale in which we work and think.

Stephen Ward
October 2015

Note

The academic network for tutors and students in Education Studies is the British Education Studies Association (BESA). It has an annual conference that shares academic practice and research in Education Studies and to which students are welcome. There are two e-journals, one designated for students and early researchers: www.educationstudies.org.uk.

Reference

Ward, S. (2004) *Education Studies: A student's guide.* London: Routledge.

ABBREVIATIONS

The following abbreviations are used in the text:

ABS	Australian Bureau of Statistics
ACARA	Australian Curriculum, Assessment and Reporting Authority
ALFIE	Alliance for Inclusive Education
ALPP	Accelerated Learning Program for Positive Living and United Service
ALS	Additional Learning Support
ARC	Aimhigher Research and Consultancy Network
ATSI	Aboriginal, Torres Strait Islander
AVCE	Advanced Vocational Certificate of Education
BIS	(Department for) Business Innovation and Skills
BME	Black and Minority Ethnic
BTEC	Business Technology and Education Council
COAG	Council of Australian Governments
CPAG	Child Poverty Action Group
CSIE	Centre for Studies on Inclusive Education
DCSF	Department for Children, Schools and Families
DDA	Disability Discrimination Act
DfE	Department for Education
DfEE	Department for Education and Employment
DfES	Department for Education and Skills
DSA	Disabled Students' Allowance
EAL	English as an Additional Language
EBD	Emotional and Behavioural Difficulties
ECB	European Central Bank
ECU	Equality Challenge Unit
EC$	East Caribbean Dollar
EFA	Education for All
EFA	Education Funding Agency
EHC	Education, Health and Care Plan
ELSTAT	Hellenic Statistical Authority (Greece)
EPPSE	Effective Pre-School, Primary and Secondary Education

EQUIP	Educational Quality Improvement Programme
ESP	Education Sector Plan (Liberia)
EYFS	Early Years Foundation Stage
FE	Further Education
FEFC	Further Education Funding Council
FSM	Free School Meals
GCSE	General Certificate of Secondary Education
HE	Higher Education
HEA	Higher Education Academy
HEFCE	Higher Education Funding Council for England
HMG	Her Majesty's Government
IEP	Individual Education Plan
IMF	International Monetary Fund
IOM	International Organisation for Migration
IPODE	Institute for Paideia, Omogeneia and Diapolitistik (Intercultural) Education (Greek)
JRF	Joseph Rowntree Foundation
LDDC	Learning Difficulties and Disability Committee
LEA	Local Education Authority
LGBT	Lesbian, Gay, Bisexual and Transgender
NCB	National Children's Bureau
NCERT	National Council of Educational Research and Training
NDIS	National Disability Insurance Scheme (Australia)
NEET	Not in Employment, Education or Training
OECD	Organisation for Economic Cooperation and Development
OFFA	Office for Fair Access (to universities)
Ofsted	Office for Standards in Education
ONS	Office for National Statistics
RTTI	Rural Teacher Training Institutes
SALT	Speech and Language Therapy Team
SAT	Statutory Assessment Test
SDAC	Survey of Disability, Ageing and Carers (Australian)
SEN	Special Educational Needs
SENCO	Special Educational Needs Coordinator
SEND	Special Educational Needs and Disability
SENDA	Special Educational Needs and Disability Act
SEYS	Specialist Early Years Service
SLT	School Leadership Team
TA	Teaching Assistant
TLR	Teaching and Learning Responsibility
TLRP	Teaching and Learning Research Project
UCAS	Universities and Colleges Admissions Service
UN	United Nations
UNESCO	United Nations Educational, Scientific and Cultural Organisation
UNHCR	United Nations High Commission on Refugees

UNICEF	United Nations International Children's Emergency Fund (known as United Nations Children's Fund)
UPIAS	Union of Physically Impaired People Against Segregation
USAID	United States Agency for International Development
WP	Widening Participation (in higher education)
YTS	Youth Training Schemes
ZPD	Zone of Proximal Development

Introduction

Zeta Brown

Inclusive education is complex, multi-faceted and ever-changing. To date there has been no fixed definition of what is meant by the term 'inclusion' and this has led to confusion about what inclusive education means in practice. There are multiple definitions of inclusion, which make it unclear whether inclusion is intended solely for children with SEN or for all learners (Fredrickson and Cline, 2009). As such, Clough and Nutbrown (2006) consider inclusion to be operational as opposed to conceptual due to its many present versions. This has led to the need for differing stakeholders, including practitioners, teachers, lecturers and members of the government to decide what inclusion means to them. In the first chapter of this book, Hodkinson and Vickerman detail differing definitions of inclusive education and how these definitions impact on who is 'included' in inclusion. It is therefore important that we discuss the position this book has taken and the definition of inclusive education that has influenced each of its chapters. The book considers inclusive education in its broadest sense: by referring to 'inclusion' as considering the educational needs of all learners. It is a participatory approach and is comparable to the *Index for Inclusion* as it focuses on the need to value all learners and view difference as a resource to support learning (Booth *et al.*, 2000; Booth and Ainscow, 2004).

Inclusive education is an ongoing process of development and can be seen as ideological. Many definitions focus on the projected future of education in which learners can be fully included in their educational experiences (Booth *et al.*, 2000; Winter, 2006). It can be argued that inclusion focuses more on what can happen in the future than what is happening in today's educational practice. In order to be fully inclusive, educational settings need to adapt their provisions, resources, methods and implementation of the curriculum to accommodate the needs of all learners in their setting (Fredrickson and Cline, 2009). Throughout the book, contributors have considered this broader concept to critically evaluate the realities of practically implementing inclusive objectives. Some contributors highlight differing groups of individuals; this is not to categorise, or to say that individuals can be represented in one categorised group. Instead, groups are mentioned to provide detailed accounts of individual experiences within inclusive practice and to represent the complexity of inclusion that goes beyond a focus on special educational needs. The way this has been achieved varies between chapters, providing contributors with the opportunity to focus on the inclusion of all learners in the context of their specific chapter. For instance, Rhoades, in Chapter 8, focuses on inclusive practice in secondary schools and considers groups that are seen as marginalised in education, including Roma/travellers, refugees/asylum seekers, young carers and 'looked-after children'. Brewster, in Chapter 10, reviews inclusive practice in higher education (HE) and critically considers those who are under-represented because of socio-economic status, gender, ethnicity and disability. In Chapter 5, Bennett, Mander and Richards discuss the need for families, including families seen as hard-to-reach and in poverty, to be involved in the inclusion of their children and young people.

The book's structure has been designed to introduce readers to the underlying knowledge and wider complexities of inclusion and how this can relate to practice. For example, Rozsahegyi and Lambert in Chapter 2 consider what pedagogy means in education and what it means for inclusive pedagogy. In Chapter 3, Winwood considers the influences on inclusive practice of leadership and management. The chapters in Part I of the book provide the knowledge and critical reflection that then can be applied to the chapters in Part II. This part focuses on the experiences that children, young people and adults may encounter across their time in education, from early education to HE. The format has been used so that readers can either focus on a particular stage of learning or compare and contrast experiences across differing education institutions. Links can be made across these chapters, including conflicts between inclusive theory and practice, practical barriers to inclusion and difficulties with balancing the need for standards alongside inclusion. Part III of the book details international examples of inclusive practice to provide a global perspective and comparison with the education systems in the UK. There is information on the meaning, importance and implementation of inclusive practice in the changing society and struggling economy of Greece (Palaiologou and Palaiologou, Chapter 11), in the perceived 'lucky country' of Australia (Meehan, Chapter 12), in the context of conflict and natural disasters in Montserrat in the Caribbean (Barnes, Chapter 13) and in Liberia in the continent of Africa (Barnes, Chapter 14).

The book has been written to support the learning of Levels 5 to 6 for undergraduate students studying relevant degrees including Education Studies, Childhood, Disability Studies and Special Needs/Inclusion Studies. It is also relevant for practising teachers, practitioners, tutors and students in primary, secondary, FE and HE teacher training. However, the structure of each chapter has been designed to provide students with the opportunity to critically develop their thinking about inclusive practice, by providing moments of reflection. Contributors have illustrated broad theories and concepts with individual and group tasks, case studies, discussion questions and recommended reading. Importantly, contributors are writing either about their own experiences in practice or from their research and highlighting other perspectives from literature, which provide students with a variety of evidenced perspectives and contrasting ideas throughout. Examples of chapters that provide findings to a recent study include Chapter 4 by Gibson, who details the experiences and views of undergraduate students who have disabilities to illustrate a time for change in HE inclusive practice. 'Students as core' is conceptualised as involving students in the development of university policy and pedagogic practice. Another example is Chapter 7, where I focus on a study investigating teachers' positions on the practical implementation of the inclusion and standards agendas, and whether these agendas can be implemented simultaneously. Specific case studies are included in Chapter 6 on early years inclusive practice. In this chapter, Palaiologou and I use case study examples from Ofsted and one early years advisor to illustrate inclusion in practice. Chapter 9 by Edwards and Jones also details a case study by explaining the practices of one FE college as an example of inclusive practice in further education.

Overall, this book has uniquely brought together contributors, including noted and international academics who have either practically experienced and/or researched into inclusive practice in differing contexts and places. By bringing these individuals together in one book, readers are encouraged to consider chapters in relation to one another and critically question the practical implementation of inclusive practice.

 Individual/group task

Before and after task: consider how you define inclusive education and how much you think we can practically include all learners in a variety of settings – for instance, the early years, primary education, secondary schools, further education and/or higher education. Once you have read the relevant chapters, reflect back on your original comments. Has your perception changed? Whether you have the same or a changed perspective, write down three or four reasons for this perspective from theory.

  Whilst reading the book: critically consider questions such as:

What does inclusion mean?

How inclusive is today's education system?

Are there any developments that are needed to further enhance the practical implementation of inclusive practice?

Summary points

- Inclusive practice is complex, multi-faceted and ever-changing.
- There is no fixed definition of inclusion; instead there are multiple definitions and this leads to confusion in defining inclusion.
- It is left to stakeholders, such as teachers, practitioners, lecturers and members of the government, to decide what inclusion means to them.
- Inclusive education is an ongoing process of development and can be seen as ideological.
- In order to be fully inclusive, practitioners, teachers and tutors in settings need to adapt their provisions, resources, methods and implementation of the curriculum to accommodate the needs of all learners.

References

Booth, T. and Ainscow, M. (2004) *Index for Inclusion: Developing learning, participation and play, in early years and childcare*. Bristol: CSIE.

Booth, T., Ainscow, M., Black-Hawkins, K., Vaughan, M. and Shaw, L. (2000) *Index for Inclusion. Developing learning and participation in schools*. Bristol: Centre for Studies on Inclusive Education.

Clough, P. and Nutbrown, C. (2006) *Inclusion in the Early Years*. London: Sage.

Fredrickson, N. and Cline, T. (2009) *Special Educational Needs, Inclusion and Diversity* (2nd edn). Maidenhead: Open University Press.

Winter, E. (2006) Preparing new teachers for inclusive schools and classrooms. *Support for Learning.* **21**(2), 85–91.

Part I
The wider complexities of inclusive practice

1 Inclusion

Defining definitions

Alan Hodkinson and Philip Vickerman

Introduction

Special education over the last 25 years has been subject to major advances, not least in the development of inclusive education, and inclusion has become the new orthodoxy. 'Inclusion' is a high-status buzzword that has acquired international currency within educational and social policy initiatives. To some it is an uncomplicated concept: a bedrock to equality in learning communities where all pupils are welcomed and valued by all people, at all times for all that they do. It is important to recognise, though, that whilst inclusion might have a commonly accepted theory, its operation has varied at differing times and in different contexts. In theory, inclusion might appear straightforward, but in the harsh reality of educational practice it is not an uncomplicated ideological construct. The question that has come to dominate educational discourse and praxis is what is this 'inclusion' of which we all speak?

This chapter analyses the 'politico-philosophical' and 'co-construction of contemporary meaning and values' that ground the term 'inclusion'. Dictionary definitions are employed to provide a theoretical lens for the analysis of inclusion policy and its associated discourse. We aim to reframe inclusion with its associated 'expertism' and to disrupt the 'decidability within texts' that have plagued attempts to operationalise inclusive education (Allan, 2008: 71).

✎ **Individual/group task**

Before you commence reading the next section, consider how you would define inclusion and inclusive education. What children and young adults would or indeed should be included in mainstream classrooms? At the end of this chapter, you may wish to revisit your definitions. You will need to employ your definition of inclusion to fulfil the task laid out in Chapter 7 of this book.

Definitions of 'inclusion'

Let us commence with the Oxford English Dictionary. It observes inclusion operating within a triumvirate of meaning (Hodkinson, 2012). First, it may be employed as a singular noun, the object in a sentence. Here the object, a person or thing, is included into an environment. For example, 'the pastel study of a little boy was included as an exhibition in an art gallery'. Second, inclusion may be the noun of the Many. In such formulations, it is the *process* of including or of being included within and by the group. Third, inclusion may be defined as a geological composite. In this formulation, distinct and distinctive particles become incorporated within an amalgam of rock. These three types of meaning place inclusion upon a continuum, blurring the distinction between object and process. *Being* inclusive 'forces' the location and participation of the chosen one; in *becoming* inclusive, the Many control a process of inclusion, and to have *become* inclusive involves the symbiotic relationship between the individual identity of the included and those who seek to include. Through these characterisations, it will be demonstrated how inclusion can be distilled down to an essence of the control and of controlling individual identity in schools.

Inclusion as a singular noun

In the Green Paper *Excellence for All* (DfEE, 1997: 44), the UK government defined inclusion as:

> [seeing] more pupils with SEN included in mainstream primary and secondary schools ... For example, we believe, that ... children with SEN should generally take part in mainstream lessons rather than being isolated in separate units.

And in India:

> all learners, young people – with or without disabilities being able to learn together in ordinary pre-school provision, schools and community educational settings with appropriate networks of support services.
>
> (NCERT, 2006: 4)

From the late 1990s, educationalists have employed statements, such as the ones above, with an almost missionary zeal to demonstrate how governments worldwide had accepted the new orthodoxy of inclusive education. We must, though, be circumspect, noting perhaps the employment of phrases such as 'seeing more pupils', 'generally take part in' and 'appropriate networks of support' and question these governments' theory of inclusion. Indeed, we might first argue that these texts reveal a reality where government did not want all children to be educated together, but rather equality could only operate if 'appropriate' systems and processes were in place. In addition, if we examined other definitions of inclusion from this period – for example, those which require that all pupils in a school 'regardless of their weaknesses or disabilities should become part of the school community' (Judge, 2003: 163) – we might question whether inclusion policy was built upon the bedrock of equality at all.

What these definitions highlight is the categorisations and language of medical deficit. We might suggest that definitions employing 'language and categorisations' shackle an individual's inclusion to entrenched societal attitudes. For example, take society's employment of the words 'weakness' and 'disability'. In the context of the disability rights movement, the application of these words is both patronising and degrading to the very pupils governments were seeking to include. The employment of such terminology reveals a conceptual naivety in its operation of inclusive education.

To illustrate the point,   you will, the current Prime
Minister, David Cameron,   ng and asked to discuss the
merits of quantum physi   This word, like 'disability', is
subjective and bound w   ility. Inclusion located within
these literacy frameworks
   To further the analysi   posed 'inclusive school':

   Sometimes it is dif   cess, especially children in the
   learning centre her   ainstream but we always try to
   access areas wher   t go out for a lesson you know
   they are particular   vhat they can cope with and ...
   so we do seek to   ever possible.

Or this comment from

   They [children labelled as SEND] have full inclusion for assemblies, playtimes and dinners so
   they are very much part of the school.

These comments reveal the control mechanism and object of the singular noun: teachers decide
who can and who cannot be included. Interestingly, research demonstrates that, despite little or no
training in special educational needs and/or disability (SEND), teachers have the responsibility for
deciding who can and who cannot be included in mainstream classrooms (Hodkinson, 2009).

   In this formulation, inclusion empowers decidability over definition and dominance over subordination. We might also observe how it invests power in those who are to *include* and how it
removes power from those who are to be *included*. In line with art critics, this picture of inclusive
practice reveals the empowerment of the 'Grand Masters' to become judge and jury as inclusion
policy leads inclusive education to be but a gallery of the 'best' exhibits. Children in this characteri-
sation are reformed as commodities, scrutinised through professionals' notions of societal good
taste. Notions of sensibility and conformity override children's rights and social justice.

 Individual/group task

Reconsider the definition of inclusion you formulated at the outset of this chapter. Carefully
consider if inclusion and inclusive education should be solely controlled by teachers and
educational professionals. Should inclusion only exist for those children who teachers decide
are capable of being 'successful' in mainstream classrooms?

Inclusion as a noun of the Many

Where all children are included as equal partners in the school community the benefits are felt
by all. That is why we are committed to comprehensive and enforceable civil rights for disabled people. Our aspirations as a nation must be for all our people.

(DfEE, 1997: 5)

The participation of all pupils in the curriculum and social life of mainstream schools; the participation of all pupils in learning which leads to the highest possible level of achievement; and the participation of young people in the full range of social experiences and opportunities once they have left school.

(DfEE, 1998: 23)

Inclusion in the above statements is enshrined within the principles of social justice. Phrases such as 'join fully', 'take part', 'equal partners', 'enforceable civil rights', 'all pupils' and 'participation' create an image of an inclusion process which truly values and welcomes all into mainstream schools. However, we should pause here to reconsider these definitions and analyse how they represent inclusion as mediation. In examining the first definition closely, another elusive and more 'slippery' definition materialises. The employment of phrases such as 'wherever possible' (p. 6) and other words employed elsewhere in government discourse, such as a 'neighbourhood of schools', suggests that the process of inclusion was always intended to pursue a 'twin-track system' where segregation of some pupils in special schools was acceptable. Pupils were to be placed *there* but not allowed *here*, present in an inclusive process but absent from mainstream classrooms. In this *becoming*, inclusion, we suggest, is nothing more than spectacle: process over person. It could not be described as equality because the Many control a process of location and subordination of individual identity. In the second quote, inclusion is defined as a right to be extended to all children. This statement, though, seems at odds with the first, where any form of 'exclusion' is deemed morally indefensible. Inclusion here seemingly is not a right but becomes a *duty*. The pupil's duty is to participate. This form of participation makes inclusion an obligation and not a right. Žižek's (2009) notion of a 'paradox of forced choice' is useful to underpin this analysis. Inclusion's obligation is 'freedom to do what is necessary', so long as pupils 'do exactly what they are expected to do'. Inclusion here is defined neither by choice, nor as a human right, but rather becomes en*forced* participation.

✎ Individual/group task

In thinking about how we might define inclusion, consider the following statement:

> 'Inclusion, manifested here is defined neither by choice, nor as a human right, but rather becomes placed upon the continuum of definition as *enforced* participation.'

In producing your definition of inclusion, consider whether a child should have the right not to be included in a mainstream school if that is their wish.

Interestingly, inclusion was also defined by agents of accountability and standards. Note, for example, Ofsted's definition of inclusion.

An educationally inclusive school is one in which the teaching and learning, achievements, attitudes and well-being of every young person matter. Effective schools are educationally inclusive schools. This shows, not only in their performance, but also in their ethos and their willingness to offer new opportunities to pupils who may have experienced previous difficulties. This does not mean treating all pupils the same way. Rather it involves taking account of pupils' varied life experiences and needs.

(Ofsted, 2000: 3)

Despite Ofsted stating that inclusion was 'more than a concern about any one group of pupils' and that 'its scope is broad', they formulated a set of inclusive principles with which to judge the processes schools adopted.

The question we must ask at this point is whether inclusion is a summative measurable entity determined by academic standards, or indeed one that can be 'forced' by the process and metrics of accountability? What we do know is that, during this period in the harsh reality of practice, schools whose reputations depended upon success in pupil achievement became wary of accepting those children whose low attainment and discipline might have depressed examination scores (Frederickson and Cline, 2002).

Within this process, power was held by the Many and identity location became policed by those who would include. 'All can be included' became the mantra of the late 1990s, but this was inclusion on society's terms. All could participate, but 'not here, not where they wanted to'. The spaces created by these processes were in reality manifestations of extant ghettos. Inclusion was bounded by limiting frontiers and policed by sometimes 'well-meaning' but often bigoted border guards.

Furthermore, within these processes of inclusion, governments also wanted us to believe that inclusion offered an opportunity for all children to achieve their full potential. Indeed they stated that:

the education of children with special educational needs ... is vital to the creation of a fully inclusive society ... We owe it to all children ... to develop to their full potential and contribute economically and play a full part as active citizens.

(Blunkett, 1998: 4)

Interestingly, this quote contains three references to full – 'fully inclusive', 'full potential' and 'play a full part'. It would seem that the more the idealist renderings promote greater levels of participation, the more we encounter growing levels of difference as competition and economics force the survival of the fittest. Consider how this statement links inclusion with economics and employs 'active citizens' without a sense of irony. Inclusion in these terms, whilst promoting 'a route to equality of opportunity for all', would appear to also be about providing support for 'a productive economy and sustainable development'.

What these statements reveal is inclusion's contradictions. As a process, inclusion does not ensure equality but rather invokes multiple ideologies of academic achievement, functionalist ideology and enforceable civil rights. Inclusive education formulated in this controlling process becomes conflictual. Children who want to take a *full* part must be able to *fully* compete, *fully* contribute economically and be 'active' in these ideals. This discourse promotes winners and losers as the cloak of inclusion disguises market economics. In this process, inclusive education compromises the ideal of inclusion and renders it as 'a mask of its exact opposite' (Žižek, 2009: 210).

Through the noun of the Many, inclusion subsumes individual identity totally within a process of control. Process not the person holds importance and individual identity is assimilated into a homogeneous structure. Here, we might employ Foucault's theory of the modern Western state with its techniques of 'subjective individualisation' and processes of 'objective totalisation' to demonstrate how the process of inclusive education creates 'docile bodies' and where individualisation competes with the totalising structures of modern power (Agamben, 1998: 5). Children in this process are not valued and welcomed into mainstream, but rather are forced to conform to processes of society's norms. It is perhaps interesting here to note the Latin origin of the word 'inclusion', which is literally to 'shut in'. This has resonance in how inclusive education is operated as a process of the Many within the commodification of education.

Conclusion

Inclusion, we might conclude, has a particular view that is built upon absolute presence of all children. However, in attempting to define inclusion, we started with the premise that in mainstream classrooms 'either a thing is here or it is not' (Chiesa, 2009: 201). However, analysis of this inclusion concept has led us to believe that 'in all kinds of ways absent things leave traces of their presence and a thing can be present while being partially absent' (ibid.: 201). Inclusion, then, may be represented as a very simple concept operating merely as a series of dictionary meanings, but in the reality of practice it is actually a construct that is defined by presence and absence and one where there is a continuum of blurred boundaries with no sharp distinctions in educational practice.

At the crossroads of policy initiative where we now find ourselves, perhaps it is time to stop focusing on the processes of inclusion or upon professionals recreating inclusion in line with societal sensibilities and educational commodification. Instead, we should adopt a different vision and formulate inclusive education on the basis of individual identity and to ensure individual children and their families can choose when, where, how and even indeed *if* they want to be included at all.

Summary points

The chapter has demonstrated that inclusion:

- is a concept that relies on complex ideology that makes it difficult to operationalise in applied educational settings;
- within the United Kingdom's educational policy, always intended to pursue a 'twin-track system' where segregation of some pupils within special schools was acceptable;
- invests power in the state, education authorities and education professionals to control the lives of children and their families;
- must be reconceptualised so that individual children and their families choose when, where, how and even indeed *if* they want to be included at all.

Further reading

Frederickson, N. and Cline, T. (2009) *Special Educational Needs, Inclusion and Diversity: A textbook* (2nd edn). Buckingham: Open University Press.

Peer, L. and Reid, G. (Eds) (2012) *Special Educational Needs: A guide for inclusive practice*. London: Sage.

Slee, R. and Allan, J. (2005) Excluding the included. In J. Rix, K. Simmons, M. Nind and K. Sheehy (Eds), *Policy and Power in Inclusive Education: Values into practice*. London: RoutledgeFalmer.

References

Agamben, G. (1998) *Homo Sacer – sovereign power and bare life* (trans. D. Heller-Roazen). Stanford, CA: Stanford University Press.

Allan, J. (2008) *Rethinking Inclusive Education: The philosophers of difference in practice*. Dordrecht: Springer.

Blunkett, D. (1998) Foreword to SEN Action Programme, in DfEE (1997). *Excellence for All Children: Meeting special educational needs*. London: DfEE.

Chiesa, L. (2009) The world of desire: Lacan between evolutionary biology and psychoanalytic theory. *Yearbook of Comparative Literature*, 55, 200–225.

DfEE (1997) *Excellence for All Children: Meeting special educational needs*. London: DfEE.

DfEE (1998) *Meeting Special Educational Needs: A programme for action*. London: DfEE.

Frederickson, N. and Cline, T. (2002) *Special Educational Needs, Inclusion and Diversity: A textbook*. Buckingham: Open University Press.

Hodkinson, A. (2009) Pre-service teacher training and special educational needs in England, 1970–2008: Is government learning the lessons of the past or is it experiencing a groundhog day? *European Journal of Special Needs Education*, 24(3), 277–289.

Hodkinson, A. (2012) Illusionary inclusion: What went wrong with New Labour's landmark educational policy? *British Journal of Special Education*, 39(1), 4–11.

Hodkinson, A. (2015). *Education Studies Essential Issues: Inclusion and special educational needs* (2nd edn). London: Sage.

Judge, B. (2003) Inclusive education: Principles and practices. In K. Crawford (Ed.) *Contemporary Issues in Education*. Norfolk: Peter Francis.

NCERT (2006) *National Focus Group on Children with Special Educational Needs: A position paper*. New Delhi: NCERT. Available at: www.ncert.nic.in/new_ncert/ncert/rightside/links/pdf/focus_group/special_ed_final1.pdf (accessed 29 September 2015).

Ofsted (2000) *Evaluating Educational Inclusion: Guidance for inspectors and schools*. London: Ofsted. www.naldic.org.uk/Resources/NALDIC/Teaching%20and%20Learning/EvaluatingEducationalInclusion.pdf (accessed 29 September 2015).

Žižek, S. (2009) *In Defense of Lost Causes*. London: Verso.

2 Pedagogy for inclusion?

Tunde Rozsahegyi and Mike Lambert

Introduction

Education systems which aspire to respect and address equally and inclusively the developmental, educational and social ambitions of all learners require strengthened understanding of the notion of 'pedagogy'. This chapter explores this concept: What does pedagogy mean? What does it entail? In particular in relation to the focus of this book: What is the relevance of pedagogy to potentially disadvantaged groups within values, policy and practice for all learners? Issues considered are whether there can be 'pedagogy for inclusion' and, if so, what kind of conflicts and questions this needs to address. In examining these issues, the chapter invites readers' engagement in pedagogical discourse, a process which has the potential to inform educators' thinking and activity and thereby strengthen learning for all learners.

What is 'pedagogy'?

Pedagogy was memorably defined by Gage (1978, cited in Galton *et al.* (1999: 189)), as 'the science of the art of teaching'. The phrase suggests that, while much of teaching is a creative process (the 'art'), there are firm principles which lie behind it (the 'science'). These principles inform the structure of education and help to determine its practical activity. They can be formulated and argued over, but in general are accepted as the basis for educational work by policymakers, researchers, practitioners and wider society.

Over many years there have been other, more extended definitions of the 'pedagogy' term and varied explanations of what it involves. Alexander (2004: 11) focused on an integrated process of what is done and how theories, beliefs, policies and controversies about what is done are discussed:

> [Pedagogy is] the act of teaching together with its attendant discourse. It is what one needs to know and the skills one needs to command, in order to make and justify the many different kinds of decisions of which teaching is constituted.

Daniels (2001: 1) related the concept to a broad view of human development: 'Pedagogy should be construed as referring to forms of social practice which shape and form the cognitive, affective and moral developments of individuals'. Leach and Moon (1999: 268–269) emphasised the notion of social approval for educational practice, seeing pedagogy as a 'view of mind, of learning and learners, of the kind of knowledge that is valued and above all by educational outcomes that are desired'. Both Daniels and Leach and Moon imply a 'mindset', an attitudinal stance, where commitment to children's overall development, attributes and personality are a vital addition to concern for formal learning outcomes normally associated with education.

We should not be surprised at the existence of a range of perspectives related to pedagogy. With its close connection to social values and practice, its nature is likely to vary according to the cultural context in which education takes place. Different international settings may have differing values and principles, as well as differing views on their importance – indeed, study of these 'can jolt us out of the familiar mentalities shaped by habitual practices, national obsessions, taken-for-granted discourses and culturally-specific curricula' (Leach and Moon, 2008: xi). Thinking and practice may also change over time, with different eras reflecting and producing divergent ideas. Importantly too, the nature of pedagogy may reflect the age, range or nature of students being taught and the contexts in which their education and development are pursued.

What is common, however, for all situations where pedagogy is a prominent element is the idea that there is some kind of shared formulation and understanding of educational ideas, even beliefs, which underpin both policy and practice. Determining what these might be for inclusive contexts, where the aim is that the rights and needs of all children or students should be respected and addressed, is the focus of this chapter.

 Individual/group task

Find a book, chapter or article with 'pedagogy' in its title. What definition is given for this concept? If there is no clear definition, what understanding of this term is evident in the text as a whole?

Three questions about pedagogy

We can see that the notion of 'pedagogy' has no easy explanation or definition. A range of ideas can be applied both to its meaning and its implications for educational practice. Let us now look more closely at three particular aspects of this variability.

Science or art?

The first relates to differing perceptions of the nature of teaching which the concept of pedagogy seeks to encompass. As seen in Gage's definition, there are attempts to balance ideas of principle and structure: pedagogy as the 'science' of teaching, with those of flexibility and idiosyncrasy: pedagogy as teaching's 'art'. Watkins and Mortimore (1999: 3) noted a much older, nineteenth-century citation, which characterised 'pedagogics' as 'the science, art or principles of pedagogy'. Mitchell (1999: 45) also found room for both of Gage's concepts:

> Improving classroom learning requires both craft and scientific knowledge, but the complexities of classroom teaching mean that it also has elements of an art. There are some aspects and examples of skilled teaching that are highly creative and cannot be codified and taught in advance.

Discussion

In your view, is teaching and other educational or developmental activity more of a 'science', or more of an 'art'? If both elements are present, how might the two come together in a notion of 'pedagogy'?

Theory or practice?

A second area where differing perspectives can be found concerns application of pedagogy – to what exactly does it refer? Is it more about theory or about practice? Does it arise from what we believe in our minds to be right from a social and moral point of view, or from what we see in educational practice to be successful? Does it emerge from social principles and ideas or from evidence of daily educational and developmental work?

Simon's (1981: 142) concern was mainly at a theoretical level: he wanted 'means and principles which underlie specific methodological (or experiential) approaches'. Bruner (1999: 5) wrote in a negative tone about 'folk pedagogy', with educationalists 'equipped with notions about how the child mind works and even what makes it grow', but without ability to verbalise pedagogical principles. Watkins and Mortimore (1999: 9), citing McNamara (1991), were similarly concerned about 'vernacular pedagogy' – the views of practitioners rather than those of theoreticians. Teachers, they claimed, 'simplify the goals in order to cope with the demands ... simplify practice in order to cope with the complexity of the classroom' (1999: 11). They cited also a suggestion by the American educationalist Roland S. Barth that researchers' knowledge may be a mile wide and an inch deep, whereas that of classroom practitioners is an inch wide and a mile deep. Leach and Moon (1999: 268–269) called for developments in thinking all round:

> Pedagogy is more than the accumulation of techniques and strategies ... It is informed by a view of mind, of learning and learners, of the kind of knowledge that is valued and above all by the educational outcomes that are desired.

Alexander (2004: 10) brought both perspectives together, seeing pedagogy as sourced both by principles and by practical knowledge. In his view, the notion of pedagogy 'brings together within one concept the act of teaching and the body of knowledge, argument and evidence in which it is embedded and by which particular classroom practices are justified'.

 Individual/group task

Make two columns, with these titles: 'Pedagogy as Theory' and 'Pedagogy as Practice'. List ideas from the literature (those presented here and others found from your own reading) under the appropriate title. Which column seems stronger? Which seems more persuasive as an explanation of what pedagogy means for you? In what ways might items in both columns be dependent on or connected with each other?

Education, development or society?

The third variation is in the term's coverage, its scope. Does pedagogy relate just to education or does it encompass more wide-ranging development? Is it concerned with organised educational settings, or with the values and practices of broader social processes, even of society as a whole?

The focus of some writers has been on ideas and activity related to the classroom. Hewston *et al.* (2005: 6) saw it as 'the set of principles upon which effective teaching in classrooms is based'. In relation to the education of children under the age of five, Siraj-Blatchford *et al.*'s (2002: 28) study (which was influential in recent growth of pre-school education in England) associated pedagogy with 'the different assumptions that are held about learning, child development, appropriate styles of instruction and curricula'.

In the 1930s, however, the Soviet psychologist Lev Vygotsky provided a wider outlook: pedagogy as *'nauka o vospitanii detyei'*: 'the science of the upbringing of children' (Vygotskiĭ, 1991: 37). Note how this definition encompasses much wider processes than those occurring in organised educational settings. It extends much beyond curricular objectives and activity to concern for the nurturing of children's all-round growth and development by family, educators, even society as a whole, together with strengthening of the many contexts in which this takes place. Daniels (2001: 1) also focused on wider activity when claiming that pedagogy should refer to 'forms of social practice which shape and form the cognitive, affective and moral development of individuals', to construction of a child's identity as well as to formal learning outcomes.

Q **Discussion**

Where do you stand on the three questions posed above?

1   Is teaching better seen as a science or an art – or as a combination of the two?
2   Is pedagogy about theory or practice – or both?
3   Should the notion of pedagogy focus on education, or should it encompass wider processes – for example, upbringing and overall human development?

Examples of pedagogy

While pedagogy is manifested in various forms, it is also possible that in some contexts the notion may have little or no presence at all. Indeed, Watkins and Mortimore (1999) noted how rarely, and Daniels (2001) how uncomfortably, the term was employed in England. Before then, Simon (1981) famously asked, 'Why no pedagogy in England?', concluding that traditional public-school concern for children's character development had resulted in a lack of prestige for enquiry into the values and principles of instruction itself. More than twenty years later, Alexander (2004) found the concept still lacking, this time asserting that overriding importance in the English system was given to issues of curriculum, rather than to pedagogical thinking. Leach and Moon (1999) felt the notion of pedagogy was out of step with England's individualistic and pragmatic traditions.

In other international contexts, however, the notion has been more clearly and readily accepted as a fundamental element of educational and social discourse. Here are some examples of well-developed pedagogical thinking from which educational practices have emerged:

- The American psychologist John Dewey was concerned with the interaction of society and individuals: 'If we eliminate the social factor from the child we are left only with an abstraction; if we eliminate the individual factor from society, we are left only with an inert and lifeless mass' (1964: 429–430). School as an institution should 'simplify social life, should reduce it, as it were, to an embryonic form' (1964: 430).
- Originating in Italy, Maria Montessori's 'scientific pedagogy' embraces the liberty of young children to pursue spontaneous activity in child-centred, child-sized learning environments (Montessori, 1912), while in the Reggio Emilia approach the growing understanding of young children is guided through facilitative activity and discussion: 'It is not the answers that are important, it is the process that you and I search together' (Carlina Rinaldi, quoted in Boyd Caldwell, 1997: 63).
- The pedagogy of Conductive Education, developed in Hungary for learners with disabilities such as cerebral palsy, prioritises the influential role of the child or adult group, its educators or 'conductors', and its integration of developmental activities. Learning experiences are designed to be heterogeneous in relation to individuals, but homogeneous in relation to the group's common tasks (Hári and Ákos, 1971).
- The 'critical pedagogy' of the Brazilian Paulo Freire is overtly radical and political, preserving the teacher as a source of knowledge, but promoting the freedom of students to reflect on, question, reject and refashion the understandings gained. His thinking is *pedagogia do oprimido*, 'pedagogy of the oppressed', whereby students are 'actively involved, through *praxis* [political practices] in controlling their own education' (Aronowitz, 1993: 11).
- At a different level, Leach and Moon (2008) describe a range of educational contexts which reflect specific pedagogical values relevant to local circumstances. These include parental involvement to re-fashion pre-school education after the fall of socialism in Albania; a developed sense of community in a small North American high school; and support for teachers in strengthening their own intellectual curiosity and collegial work in a cosmopolitan secondary school in London.

Q **Discussion**

How clearly do you recognise the concept of 'pedagogy' in relation to your own current and past experiences? To what extent do common values and principles underlie thinking and practice in the context or contexts with which you are familiar?

Inclusive pedagogy?

We can ask one more question, particularly pertinent to the focus of this book. To what extent does the nature of pedagogy apply in the same way to all learners, and to what extent might it differ between them? To what extent is pedagogy 'shared'? To what extent is it 'differentiated'?

At first sight, the notion of 'inclusive education' implies a common pedagogy, one which incorporates thinking, policies and practices for all learners. This pedagogy would say that all people, no matter who they are, have the same rights to fruitful development and education. However, this may be seen as too simplistic, or incomplete. Learners facing individual difficulties – social or developmental – may require different policies and different practices if their rights to learning are to be fulfilled. 'Policies should specify the optimal circumstances in which successful learning and teaching can take place' (Wedell, 2008: 130).

Norwich (2008: 1) has helpfully explicated this position in his notion of 'dilemmas of difference'. This is the predicament, which many in education will recognise, whereby practitioners and others find themselves having to choose between emphasising similarity or dissimilarity amongst the learners they serve. If we emphasise similarity, we facilitate integrated educational settings, strengthen pursuit of a common curriculum and increase recognition of every human being's right to learning and development. This sense of communality, however, may not help us to provide distinctive help for individuals or for specific groups based on actual need. On the other hand, if we emphasise difference, we may be able more readily to access specialist support and pursue differentiated approaches in order to make learning successful, but can then find ourselves having to segregate some learners from others in order to accomplish this. While Norwich's main focus is on children with special educational needs and disabilities, the dilemma is applicable much more widely: whether to recognise differences or not to recognise them, 'as either option has some negative implications or risks associated with stigma, devaluation, rejection or denial of opportunities' (Norwich, 2008: 448).

Q Discussion

Where do you stand on Norwich's 'dilemmas of difference'?

- To what extent should pedagogy for inclusion recognise differences in learners?
- How should this influence policy and practice?
- To what extent should pedagogy for inclusion promote shared characteristics amongst learners?
- In what ways should this idea of shared characteristics influence learning and teaching?

There are also other problems to resolve when trying to fashion pedagogical thinking related to inclusion in the real world. A 'raising-standards' agenda, accompanied by growing accountability of agencies, schools and teachers themselves, has produced in many contexts a keen focus on output measures, a move towards, in the words of Bernstein (1993: xxi), 'performance and the graded child'. For instance, Broadfoot *et al.*'s (2000: 3) comparative study found in England 'a discourse rooted in a rationalist vocabulary of scientific measurement – of standards and scales; of objective judgements and comparisons', and the persistence of tests, inspections and school league tables has provided little alleviation in the years since then.

The question here is how these two differing agendas – inclusion and raising of academic standards – might exist side by side. Florian and Rouse (2005) have argued that they should do so – if inclusion does not improve outcomes for all, it can hardly deserve to be promoted as a central premise for education. We might, however, question what kind of outcomes are sought: better examination grades, or less tangible attitudinal, social and emotional benefits for growing children, or indeed both and more of these? The aims of teaching and learning are in themselves an important aspect of education, and the standards agenda emphasises the need within inclusive pedagogy for resolution here too.

Ultimately, systemic development may be needed if segregated systems of education are to become inclusive, both in values and in practical activity. In relation to special educational needs in the English context, Pollard and James (2004: 25) advocated 'new forms of learner-aware pedagogy', while Wedell (2008: 128), drawing from this concept, argued for greater recognition of diversity in learning needs and a continuum of flexible provision, incorporating close professional understanding of the child and environment and 'compensatory interaction' between the two. Florian and Black-Hawkins (2011: 826) examined more pragmatically how educators might 'extend what is ordinarily available in the community of the classroom as a way of reducing the need to mark some learners as different … providing rich learning opportunities that are sufficiently made available for *everyone*'.

✎ **Individual/group task**

Taking the final point from Florian and Black-Hawkins (2011), devise and outline some opportunities for learning which would be meaningful for everyone in an inclusive classroom or other educational context.

Conclusion

As can be seen, seeking pedagogy for inclusion is a motivational challenge for everyone who has a concern for learning and development. We could start with an assumption with which few might disagree:

> All children should be not just educated but educated *well*, in ways that are educationally appropriate and offer families a reasonable degree of choice, to match their children's education to their goals and values; this in full recognition that children change over the course of childhood, with any upbringing and education worth their salt playing a prime role in this.
>
> (Sutton, 2000: 32)

To achieve this, we might also approve of the views of Lindsay (2003), who argued for closer consideration of children's needs, rather than legislation. Nevertheless, Leach and Moon (2008: 6) warned against looking too narrow-mindedly at specific features of individuals: 'Learning is a social process … any attempt to influence learning has to go beyond the characteristics of any individual learner to embrace all the influences that impinge on learning in their social settings'. Finally, Simon's (1981: 141) long-standing dictum warns against differentiating too much and too early in any pedagogically oriented discourse of this kind:

To start from the standpoint of individual differences is to start from the wrong position. To develop effective pedagogic means starting from the opposite standpoint, from what children have in common as members of the human species; to establish the general principles of teaching, and in the light of these, to determine what modifications of practice are necessary to meet specific individual needs.

Q Discussion

What are your views on pedagogy in relation to inclusive education? Can there be an inclusive pedagogy which encompasses all learners? Before you read other chapters in this book, what are your initial thoughts about the values and principles which might reflect this most clearly?

Summary points

- The notion of 'pedagogy' encompasses deep thinking about the values and principles of education and wider social activity.
- It also provides a basis for manifestation of these in educational and social policy and practice.
- In considering an ideal of inclusive education, we therefore need to consider the idea of 'pedagogy for inclusion' – values and principles, locally or nationally determined, which can be discussed, determined, refined and used to guide policy decisions, organisation and delivery of services and the actual processes of teaching and learning.
- The issues and questions raised in this chapter will inform critical scrutiny of the wide-ranging ideas and examples presented in this book.

Further reading

Hart, S., Dixon, A., Drummond, M.J. and McIntyre, D. (2004) *Learning Without Limits*. Maidenhead, UK: Open University Press/McGraw Hill.
Swann, M., Peacock, A., Hart, S. and Drummond, M.J. (2012) *Creating Learning Without Limits*. Maidenhead, UK: Open University Press/McGraw Hill.
Sheehy, K. and Rix, J. (2009) A systematic review of whole class, subject-based pedagogies with reported outcomes for the academic and social inclusion of pupils with special educational needs. *Research Evidence in Education Library*. London: EPPI-Centre, https://eppi.ioe.ac.uk/cms (accessed 22 September 2015).

References

Alexander, R. (2004) Still no pedagogy? Principle, pragmatism and compliance in primary education. *Cambridge Journal of Education*, **34**(1), 7–33.
Aronowitz, S. (1993) Paulo Freire's radical democratic humanism. In P. McLaren and P. Leonard (Eds) *Paulo Freire: A Critical Encounter*. London: Routledge.
Bernstein, B. (1993) Foreword. In H. Daniels (Ed.) *Charting the Agenda: Educational Activity after Vygotsky*. London: Routledge.

Boyd Caldwell, L. (1997) *Bringing Reggio Emilia Home: An Innovative Approach to Early Childhood Education*. New York: Teachers College Press.

Broadfoot, P., Osborn, M., Planel, C. and Sharpe, K. (2000) *Promoting Quality in Learning: Does England Have the Answer?* London: Cassell.

Bruner, J. (1999) Folk pedagogies. In J. Leach and B. Moon (Eds) *Learners and Pedagogy*. London: Paul Chapman.

Daniels, H. (2001) *Vygotsky and Pedagogy*. London: RoutledgeFalmer.

Dewey, J. (1964) My pedagogic creed. In R.D. Archambault (Ed.) *John Dewey on Education*. Chicago: University of Chicago Press.

Florian, L. and Black-Hawkins, K. (2011) Exploring inclusive pedagogy. *British Educational Research Journal*, **37**(5), 813–828.

Florian, L. and Rouse, M. (2005) Inclusive practice in English secondary schools. In M. Nind, J. Rix, K. Sheehy and K. Simmons (Eds) *Curriculum and Pedagogy in Inclusive Education*. London: RoutledgeFalmer.

Galton, M., Hargreaves, L., Comber, C. and Wall, D. with Peel, A. (1999) *Inside the Primary Classroom: 20 Years On*. London: Routledge.

Hári, M. and Ákos, K. (1971) *Konduktív Pedagógia*. Budapest: Tankönyvkiadó. Translation published as: Hári, M. and Ákos, K. (1988) *Conductive Education*. London: Tavistock/Routledge.

Hewston, R., Campbell, R.J., Eyre, D., Muijs, D., Neelands, J. and Robinson, W. (2005) *A Baseline Review of the Literature on Effective Pedagogies for Gifted and Talented Students*. Occasional Paper 5. Warwick: National Academy of Gifted and Talented Youth.

Leach, J. and Moon, B. (1999) Recreating pedagogy. In J. Leach and B. Moon (Eds) *Learners and Pedagogy*. London: Paul Chapman.

Leach, J. and Moon, B. (2008) *The Power of Pedagogy*. London: Sage.

Lindsay, G. (2003) Inclusive education: A critical perspective. *British Journal of Special Education*, **30**(1), 3–12.

Mitchell, I. (1999) Bridging the gulf between research and practice. In J. Loughran (Ed.) *Researching Teaching: Methodologies and Practices for Understanding Pedagogy*. London: Falmer Press.

Montessori, M. (1912) *The Montessori Method*. Translated by Anne E. George. New York: Frederick A. Stokes.

Norwich, B. (2008) Dilemmas of difference and the identification of special educational needs/disability: International perspectives. *British Educational Research Journal*, **35**(3), 447–467.

Pollard, A. and James, M. (Eds) (2004) *Personalised Learning: A Commentary by the Teaching and Learning Research Project*. Swindon: Economic and Social Research Council.

Simon, B. (1981) Why no pedagogy in England? In B. Simon and W. Taylor (Eds) *Education in the Eighties: The Central Issues*. London: Batsford.

Siraj-Blatchford, I., Sylva, K., Muttock, S., Gilden, R. and Bell, D. (2002) *Researching Effective Pedagogy in the Early Years*. Research Report 356. Norwich: HMSO.

Sutton, A. (2000) Transforming choice. *Managing Schools Today*, March 2000, 31–33.

Vygotskiĭ, L.S. (1991) Pedagogika i psikhologiya. In V.V. Davydova (Ed.) *Pedagogicheskaya psikhologiya*. Moscow: Pedagogika.

Watkins, C. and Mortimore, P. (1999) Pedagogy: What do we know? In P. Mortimore (Ed.) *Understanding Pedagogy and Its Impact on Learning*. London: Sage.

Wedell, K. (2008) Confusion about inclusion: Patching up or system change? *British Journal of Special Education*, **35**(3), 127–135.

3 Leading and managing for inclusion

Jo Winwood

This chapter will explore how the Special Educational Needs Coordinator (SENCO) can support the development of inclusive provision for all. The role of the SENCO will be critically examined within the changing legislative context before considering how this role could be reconceptualised in order to support inclusion, developing the SENCO as a 'knowledgeable guide' and leader for inclusion. Whilst most practitioners are committed to the ideal of inclusion, many are concerned about how to respond to the increasingly diverse needs of the pupils in their care. By adopting the knowledgeable guide approach, the SENCO would act as advocate for the pupils and a critical friend for staff, enabling opportunities to share good practice, try new approaches to learning and reflect on outcomes.

What are leadership and management?

Other chapters in this book consider what inclusion is (see Chapter 7), but it is important to clarify some key terms for this chapter, starting with 'leadership' and 'management'. Distinctions between these two terms often refer to issues surrounding vision and strategic development (leadership) and the practical, operational objectives which follow on from this vision (management). Bush (2011) refers to Bolam's definition of leadership as the formulation of any organisation-wide 'policy', whereas management implements these policies. From this perspective, leadership can be seen as the creation of aims for an establishment and management as the achievement of objectives developed from the broader aims. The author stresses the importance of clear links between the two, otherwise staff tend to focus on achieving shorter-term goals, which can be at the expense of wider educational aims and purposes. An example of this is the production of education plans for children with special educational needs (SEN). Computer-based packages were seen by many schools as an efficient way to produce targets for pupils to work towards. This meant that Individual Education Plans (IEPs) were completed quickly and by all staff; they no longer had to write targets for each child but could instead choose one from a range offered within the package. However, many of the targets were a 'best fit' and did not always reflect the precise needs of each child. Furthermore, although children had targets, often they were not used to inform or guide learning for the majority of lessons. This example illustrates how the management of learning targets was governed by process (completing the form of every child who needed one) rather than educational aims (leading for learning).

Traditional perspectives on leadership often refer to a specific job role, such as head teacher. From this perspective, those holding the position were automatically seen as a leader, regardless of how they might operationalise the role. Earley and Weindling (2004: 3) define this as the 'great man' notion of leadership, where one person guided and influenced the organisation from the apex position. However, more modern notions of leadership linked to vision, ethos and transformation through team work are perhaps more relevant to modern educational settings. Within this, the concept of inclusion works in partnership with key educational aims, enabling all participants (pupils and staff) to learn, a willingness to try different approaches, valuing diversity and difference rather than 'aiming at the middle', a supportive, reflective environment where everyone can contribute and develop. As stated previously, most if not all teachers advocate inclusion, but translating this belief into practical action within a classroom can be challenging. By developing the role of SENCO as a 'knowledgeable guide' it would be possible to address the challenge of inclusion by moving away from traditional deficit responses to SEN by enabling staff to work collaboratively on inclusive practice.

✎ **Individual/group task**

Consider what the terms leadership and management mean to you. You might want to reflect on your own professional experiences and that of those you work with. What makes an effective leader or manager? Are you either or both, and how does this influence your work?

Roles, responsibilities and influences on the SENCO

The SENCO role: policy definitions

Many authors (Oldham and Radford, 2011; Wedell, 2012) have recognised that the SENCO could have a pivotal role to play in developing inclusive provision, but this notion has not always been supported by policy, and many SENCOs report being a manager of the paperwork which surrounds SEN provision (Winwood, 2013).

The revised Code of Practice (DfES, 2001: 50) outlined the following areas as key responsibilities for SENCOs in a primary school:

- overseeing the day-to-day operation of the school's SEN policy
- coordinating provision for children with special educational needs
- liaising with and advising fellow teachers
- managing learning support assistants
- overseeing the records of all children with special educational needs
- liaising with parents of children with special educational needs
- contributing to the in-service training of staff
- liaising with external agencies, including the LEA'S support and educational psychology services, health and social services, and voluntary bodies.

This highlighted the essentially managerial nature of the role, also seen in the 1994 version, in that the majority of roles outlined above revolve around ensuring children receive the support required. Supporting and leading other members of staff on professional development are mentioned, but under the original Code of Practice (DfE, 1994) the huge amount of administration required by the role effectively prevented SENCOs from taking on this leadership role.

Within the revised Code of Practice (DfES, 2001: 51), the leadership element of the role was stated as: 'In terms of responsibility the SENCO role is at least equivalent to that of curriculum, literacy or numeracy coordinator.... Many schools find it effective for the SENCO to be a member of the senior leadership team.' Very similar definitions of the role relating to early years and secondary settings were also outlined in the Code of Practice (DfES, 2001). However, as various authors (Szwed, 2007; Garner, 2001; Rose, 2003) have highlighted, whilst the role might have been defined in the Code of Practice, the interpretation within individual schools varied considerably, and this impacted on what was expected of a SENCO. Furthermore, although the Code of Practice referred to the SENCO in a leadership role, it did not explain how this related to practice or how it might be implemented in schools.

Government documentation (House of Commons Education and Skills Select Committee, 2006) emphasised the increasing gap between policy and practice for the role, stating that SENCOs had essentially lost any strategic leadership role, despite what the Code of Practice suggested. Furthermore, the SENCO Update (2008) argued that the introduction of Teaching and Learning Responsibility (TLR) payments led to further downgrading of the role because, as the above definitions demonstrate, the SENCO role does not include any reference to teaching and learning, only training of staff, coordinating provision and record keeping. Regulations issued by the DCSF (2008) meant that all SENCOs had to be qualified teachers and the postgraduate-level National Award for all new SENCOs was introduced. Drafts of these regulations had required the SENCO to be a part of the school leadership team (SLT), but following consultation this requirement was altered, so that if the SENCO was not part of SLT, a champion of SEN would represent them, meaning that the role retained a focus on coordination and not leadership, nor teaching and learning. Hallett and Hallett (2010) compared these requirements to other roles within schools and noted that the only other role that requires statutory qualification is that of head teacher. The authors claim that the changes support the view of the SENCO as working with pupils with SEN, but also as an agent for change across the whole school, working at a strategic leadership level and influencing the learning opportunities of all pupils, whilst maintaining a focus on the specific needs of individuals.

In 2015, a new SEND Code of Practice was published which maintained many of the areas of responsibility outlined in previous versions (see page 108 of the code for details). However, the document supports the notion of SENCO as a leader by stating:

> The SENCO has an important role to play with the head teacher and governing body, in determining the strategic development of SEN policy and provision in the school. They will be most effective in that role if they are part of the school leadership team.

And:

> The SENCO provides professional guidance to colleagues and will work closely with staff, parents and other agencies.
>
> (DfE, 2015: 108)

✎ **Individual/group task**

Download the latest version of the SEN Code of Practice and reflect on the details outlined about the SENCO role and that of teachers. How useful is this for you? Is there any additional information and guidance you would like to have?

SENCO as leader or manager?

The above definitions of the SENCO role, from the Code of Practice (DfE, 2015), make reference to the role having both management and leadership elements. Bush and Bell (2002: 3) claim that leadership is about 'vision, mission and purpose coupled with a capacity to inspire others to work towards the achievement of these aims', whereas management is concerned with the implementation of the vision at a much more practical level. Day et al. (2000: 17) support this view, claiming that leadership is 'strategic', whereas management is 'operational'. Whilst much of the research into the role of the SENCO (Pearson et al., 2015) suggests that a leadership approach would be beneficial to both staff and students, research by Szwed (2007) suggested that SENCOs continue to spend significant amounts of time fulfilling roles that are operational rather than strategic, which limits opportunities for SENCOs to work at a strategic level, meaning that a SENCO is more likely to be part of middle management and senior leadership teams (Layton, 2005). More recently (Lindqvist, 2013), the role has been seen as bridging both leadership and management elements, so that the SENCO is still involved with the administrative aspects of SEN, whilst at the same time having opportunities to work with colleagues in order to contribute to the development of teaching and learning for all (Pearson et al., 2015).

Busher and Harris (2000) described the role of the SENCO as diffuse, in that it is cross-curricular and needs to involve a number of staff, many of whom are likely to have additional roles and responsibilities in other subject areas. One of the challenges this presents is that the SENCO cannot be responsible for and manage every aspect of SEN provision; it needs to be distributed to a team of staff across the school. Blandford and Gibson (2000: 13) support this view, stating that 'SEN should have a figurehead, a visionary providing leadership, but he/she should not necessarily be the sole manager of all SEN issues within the school', an approach also advocated by Norwich (2010), who questioned whether it is realistic for one person to be responsible for so many tasks. Blandford and Gibson (2000) use the term leadership to refer to the development and guidance of the subject area, making a clear distinction between that and management. Being part of the leadership team or having the support of senior leaders has been identified as a key component in raising the status of SEN and the SENCO within schools. Liasidou and Svennson (2014) take this further, suggesting that systemic change is needed, with the SENCO being empowered to develop inclusive practice within schools and thus being seen as a key part of any school leadership team in the same way as core curriculum coordinators.

School structures have tended to follow a traditional model of leadership, with the head teacher as a leader. Kugelmass and Ainscow (2004: 133) define this as leadership due to 'behaviour rather than action, as having to do with persons rather than ideas, and the emphasis on bureaucratic'. This suggests that the position of head teacher has traditionally been the pinnacle of a hierarchical structure for staff, with the head teacher taking responsibility for much of the decision-making processes within all areas of the school. However, as schools become increasingly complex in organisation, structure, staffing and students, it is questionable whether this traditional approach to leadership is suitable or sustainable. Thus the notion of 'distributed leadership' has become increasingly popular. Harris (2001: 11) defines distributed leadership: '[distributed leadership] incorporates the activities of multiple groups of individuals in a school who work at guiding and mobilising staff ... and implies inter-dependency rather than dependency'. This approach mirrors Blandford and Gibson's (2000) approach to leadership with a figurehead working with others to develop the subject area, rather than a single person completing all tasks related to the area. The fundamental difference between the traditional approach to leadership and distributed leadership is that the latter advocates a shared responsibility rather than responsibility being assumed through the position of head teacher or subject leader. In this way, SENCOs would maintain overall responsibility for the SEN department, but also actively involve others in issues relating to SEN. Collaboration and the ability to make a vision real are two key elements of distributed leadership. Through this, other members of staff could participate with the SENCO, making clearer links between learning in their own subject area and SEN, to develop inclusive practice. Furthermore, by becoming actively involved in the decision-making processes, staff can be seen as part of the community of a school rather than reacting to directions from a leader. This is particularly relevant to issues related to SEN, as Jordan *et al.* (2009) suggested that many teachers feel that they lack the necessary skills to work in inclusive classrooms and can see SEN as an additional responsibility that is outside their role, despite the SEN Code of Practice stating that children with SEN are the responsibility of every teacher.

✎ Individual/group task

Consider your own experiences of work (not just school based). To what extent did the leadership styles reflect the distributed approaches outlined above? What was the impact of this?

  Make a list of potential benefits and limitations of this approach.

Developing the SENCO role as a leader could enable schools to support the development of inclusive practices. Dyson and Millward (2000) highlight the fact that schools have faced the dilemma of trying to value students' differences and diversity whilst still responding to the needs of individuals if they are to access all aspects of the curriculum. The authors stress the dichotomy between inclusive education for all, regardless of need and the substantive differences between students within one classroom. This difference is fundamental to any discussion of SEN provision as it raises questions about how teachers address individual needs within a mainstream setting without disadvantaging others and by using limited resources effectively. Student differences have not disappeared, they have simply been accommodated, and staff need to receive training if they are to balance inclusive practices with ensuring all pupils can and do access the curriculum.

The role of the SENCO and inclusion

The role of the SENCO is linked to the development of inclusive practice in the same way that every teacher is expected to respond to the needs of the children in their class and to ensure that any barrier to learning is removed (DfE, 2013). Furthermore, the Code of Practice (DfE, 2015) outlines the importance of SENCOs developing provision for pupils with SEN, which would enable inclusion to occur.

Whilst the SENCO role might focus exclusively on SEN, the school ethos needs to value inclusion, which is then supported and nurtured in classrooms and actively put into practice, alongside achievement. Every school is unique and thus the teaching and learning needs to reflect this, but many teachers are not sure what inclusion looks like at a practical level when planning and delivering lessons. Responses tend to be located within existing practice – for example, the use of TAs to support particular groups of pupils in lessons – rather than changing planned activities and learning opportunities. Schools need to consider the various elements of their community, such as ethnicity and socio-economic background, if they are to develop inclusive provision which is relevant to their setting. Many recent policy documents (*Help Children Achieve More*, DfE, 2010; *SEND Code of Practice*, DfE, 2015) have acknowledged the diversity which is apparent within and between schools, but this has tended to focus on each learner as an individual. However, in order to develop inclusion for all, teachers need to consider how they might develop their pedagogy if they are to provide learning experiences which acknowledge the cultural, social, academic and personal diversity of pupils in their class. One way to achieve this would be to encourage professional learning and development within the staffroom. Hansman (2008) suggests that by providing supportive and safe environments staff are enabled to question current practices and to have the confidence to 'play' with new approaches to learning. Although this can be a challenging process, by using the SENCO as a support mechanism to encourage staff to reflect on their work, as well as providing an opportunity to discuss alternative ways of enabling learning through collaborative approaches, inclusion can be translated into practical solutions. Jacobson (1996) and Hansman (2008) suggest that, through collaboration, staff have opportunities to learn from the expert (SENCO) but also through the conversations and interactions with each other, which encourage an ownership of the learning. This can lead to changes in classroom provision which are high impact but not time- or work-demanding and are thus more likely to be transferred into lessons.

The approach advocated above would be a move away from the traditional deficit model of SEN, which starts from a child with a problem in that it recognises both the diversity of students and a curriculum which includes elements of skills, knowledge, understanding and attitudes, thus making educational achievement about much more than scores in national tests. This type of approach would allow schools to focus on the needs of the pupils in their classrooms, such as social and behavioural, as well as developing what could be termed academic skills and achievement that specifically relate to learning. This type of approach has enabled schools to develop inclusive practice and has had positive effects on both learning and relationships. Furthermore, greater involvement of the SENCO at the classroom level could further enhance inclusive practice and develop the professional skills of all practitioners involved.

✎ **Individual/group task**

Many of the debates above suggest that the ethos of the setting is essential in developing inclusive provision. Consider, interpret and understand the term and how this might influence practice.

For example, a supportive leadership style which sees staff as partners in facilitating and owning change might be seen as part of an inclusive ethos. Within this, people feel confident to question and disagree, rather than simply 'do as they are told'.

Developing inclusive provision: SENCO as knowledgeable guide

Having explored the role of the SENCO and how this continues to develop in conjunction with the changing demands placed on it by policy initiatives, expectations from staff, pupils, parents and other external agencies, a logical next step might be to move away from an association with SEN and instead reconfigure the role so that it supports the development of inclusive provision for all. This would be one way to support staff in order to translate the theory of inclusion into practical solutions and strategies and at the same time challenge traditional approaches to SEN.

Debate about the SENCO role often explores the different dimensions which create the whole, such as coordination responsibilities, liaison with staff or external agencies and working with pupils, as well as the leadership or management elements of the role. Another approach has been to explore the way SENCOs have responded to the role and the elements they have chosen to focus on. Both approaches have offered insights into how the SENCO role has developed, areas for future development and what matters to SENCOs in terms of their professional values and priorities. They reveal that conflicting demands on SENCO time need to be managed in some way, perhaps with a reconceptualisation of how the SENCO role can be operationalised in relation to other subject areas and the professional skills that many SENCOs have. One option would be to develop the SENCO post around two key areas, in order to start to define it further and position it within the context of other subject areas and responsibilities within schools. The development of SENCO as an inclusion leader, which could incorporate the relational aspects of the SENCO role (working with pupils, staff, parents) could be integrated to form the SENCO as 'knowledgeable guide'. This would ensure that staff have support from an inclusion and SEN expert when it is required, and the SENCO maintains responsibility for specialist areas within the field of SEN, but at the same time the role moves away from SEN exclusively and instead is linked to pedagogy for all pupils, developing inclusion across the whole school.

Developing the SENCO as a leader would enable them to focus on strategic developments within the SEN department, delegating administrative duties to other members of staff, such as class or subject teachers. The SENCO would still be available to staff to support their professional development in relation to SEN and inclusion issues, but not be directly responsible for the planning of day-to-day support for children with SEN. Norwich (2010) debated some of the key tensions that surround different elements of the SENCO role and how these impact on provision within school. He concluded that whilst SENCOs do have skills and knowledge that are unique and valuable to their role, many of the tasks they complete are somewhat generic. These could be taken away from the SENCO and incorporated into subject coordinator roles and responsibilities, encouraging the ownership of issues related to SEN in all teachers, not just the SENCO. Layton (2005) and Szwed (2007) note how the SENCO is more likely to be a part of middle management, because the role requires a variety of operational tasks to be completed before the SENCO can move onto more strategic roles and responsibilities. However, if some tasks which have traditionally been completed by the SENCO are distributed to other subject coordinators and class teachers, this has the potential to enable the SENCO to concentrate on strategic development of inclusion across the school. Due to the diffuse nature of the SENCO role, it must involve other staff because it is cross-curricular. This type of approach, reflecting principles of distributed leadership, would force the SENCO role to move away from administrative tasks. Although the initial change might mean that SENCOs continue to be actively involved with administration, such as IEP writing, it would be in collaboration with other staff, so that they develop the skills and knowledge to take responsibility for these areas in the longer term. This reflects the concept of 'connective specialisation', coined by Norwich (1996) as a way to describe the integration of generic skills into the workloads of other subject coordinators, ensuring that SEN and inclusion are seen as an essential element of them. Adopting this type of approach would also go some way towards strengthening the notion that teachers have a responsibility to support the needs of all children, including those with SEN, supporting the development of inclusive practice.

Developing the role of SENCO as a knowledgeable guide would allow the SENCO to be part of the leadership team of the school but also to work closely with teachers, enabling them to promote the cultural values of the school through practice in classrooms. The SENCO can be seen as the representative for matters relating to SEN, and as an enabler through whom the staff team share good practice, as well as offering support and professional guidance. Additionally, the SENCO could act as a part of a transformational team that has opportunities to reflect on practice and work in consultation with other members. By adopting this style of leadership, the SENCO would be able to maintain an overview of the daily issues within classrooms, as well as the strategic role which enables whole-school progression towards inclusion, developing effective pedagogy for all children. The SENCO role would then be about how to develop effective provision, reflecting Dyson's (1990) original vision of the SENCO as a pedagogy expert. Maintaining links with pupils, parents and external agencies would be a part of the 'expert' leadership element of the SENCO role, and further build the reciprocal relationship between the SENCO, other staff members and the pupil.

The approach outlined above would encourage staff to develop individual strengths, but this does not remove the need for ongoing staff development and training in the area of SEN provision. This includes training that involves all staff, which encourages individuals to actively participate. Staff also need opportunities to reflect and analyse current practice and to develop alternative approaches which are similar to the key themes associated with distributed leadership. These include encouraging staff to actively take part in decision-making, considering what the implications mean for themselves and the pupils in their class and the ethos that they are trying to develop within school. This would enable staff to change practice in line with changing values and priorities. By adopting this type of process, SENCOs would be able to involve staff in the development of an inclusive system within school, move away from a traditional deficit model which focuses on diagnosis and adopt a leadership approach that uses what York-Barr et al. (2005: 211) term 'leadership through horizontal channels.... Keeping a vision or goal in clear focus while observing the details.' By distributing leadership and having opportunities to debate the issues, reflect on practice and receive professional training and development, staff should no longer feel isolated and ill-prepared to support children with a variety of needs within a mainstream classroom. They would also be aware that colleagues, including the SENCO, are available to guide and support, maintaining and extending professional relationships between staff and pupils.

Conclusion

The SENCO role has the potential to influence the development of teaching and learning for all pupils, as well as support teachers and teaching assistants so that they are more able to respond to diverse leaning needs within their classrooms. School staff need a commitment to the ideals of inclusion but they also need to know how to transfer this into practical responses. By adopting a knowledgeable guide approach, the SENCO can encourage staff to reflect on current provision and consider how to develop pedagogy in order to enable all pupils to learn. At the same time, pupils, parents and external agencies continue to work alongside the SENCO, ensuring that additional support and resources are available to those requiring them.

Note: This chapter referred to the SENCO, which reflects a traditional view of SEN. With a move towards a 'knowledgeable guide', a more suitable title might be INCCO, or Inclusion Coordinator.

Summary points

- Leadership is much more than a title and all members of the school community can be leaders.
- The SENCO can contribute to all aspects of school life, but needs to be supported to achieve this.
- Limiting the role of SENCO to managerial tasks, such as paperwork, limits opportunities for professional development and learning.
- Inclusion is not an easy option and demands additional effort from staff, but this leads to effective teaching and learning for all.

Further reading

These articles offer interesting insights into the SENCO role.

Morewood, G. (2012) Is the 'inclusion SENCO' still a possibility? A personal perspective. *Support for Learning*. **27**(2), pp. 73–76.

Oldham, J. and Radford, J. (2011) Secondary SENCO leadership: A universal or specialist role? *British Journal of Special Education*. **38**(3), pp. 126–134.

Pearson, S., Mitchell, R. and Rapti, M. (2015) I will be 'fighting' even more for pupils with SEN: SENCOs' role predictions in the changing English policy context. *Journal of Research in Special Educational Needs*. **15**(1), pp. 48–56.

Tissot, C. (2013) The role of SENCO as leader. *British Journal of Special Education*. **40**(1), pp. 33–40.

This chapter has recognised the importance of the ethos of the setting, if inclusion is to be fostered. The following chapters explore this issue further:

Busher, H. (2006) *Understanding Educational Leadership*. Buckingham: Open University Press. Chapter 6: Creating cultures.

Haydon, G. (2007) *Values for Educational Leadership*. London: Sage. Chapter 5: School ethos and culture.

References

Blandford, S. and Gibson, S. (2000) *Middle Management in Schools: A Special Educational Needs Perspective*. www.leeds.ac.uk/educol/documents/00001621.htm (accessed 17 November 2009).

Bush, T. (2011) *Theories of Educational Leadership and Management* (4th Edn). London: Sage.

Bush, T. and Bell, L. (2002) *The Principles and Practice of Educational Management*. London: Paul Chapman.

Busher, H. (2005) Being a middle leader: Exploring professional identities. *School Leadership and Management*. **25**(2), pp. 137–153.

Busher, H. and Harris, A. (2000) *Subject Leadership and School Improvement*. London: Paul Chapman.

Day, C., Harris, A., Hadfield, M., Tolley, H. and Beresford, J. (2000) *Leading Schools in Times of Change*. Buckingham: Open University Press.

DCSF (2008) *SENCO Regulations – Explanatory Memorandum*. London: DCSF.

DfE (1994) *Special Educational Needs Code of Practice*. Nottingham: DfE.

DfE (2010) *Help Children Achieve More*. London: DfE.

DfE (2013) *The National Curriculum in England Framework Document*. London: DfE.

DfE (2015) *Special Educational Needs and Disability Code of Practice: 0 to 25 Years*. London: DfE.

DfES (2001) *Special Educational Needs Code of Practice*. Nottingham: Department for Education and Skills.

Dyson, A. (1990) Effective learning consultant: A future role for special needs co-ordinators. *Support for Learning*. **5**(3), pp. 116–127.

Dyson, A. and Millward, A. (2000) *Schools and Special Needs; Issues of Innovation and Inclusion*. London: Paul Chapman.

Earley, P. and Weindling, D. (2004) *Understanding School Leadership*. London: Paul Chapman.

Garner, P. (2001) What's the weight of a badger? Teachers' experiences of working with children with learning difficulties. In Wearmouth, J. (Ed.) *Special Educational Provision in the Context of Inclusion*. London: David Fulton.

Hallett, F. and Hallett, G. (2010) Leading learning: The role of the SENCO. In F. Hallett and G. Hallett (Eds) *Transforming the Role of the SENCO: Achieving the National Award of SEN Coordination*. Berkshire: McGraw-Hill/Open University Press.

Hansman, C.A. (2008) Adults learning in communities of practice. In C. Kimble, P. Hildreth and I. Bourden (Eds) *Communities of Practice: Creating Learning Environments for Educators*. Charlotte, North Carolina: Information Age Publishing.

Harris, A. (2001) Reflections on distributed leadership. *Management in Education*. **19**(2), pp. 10–12.

House of Commons Education and Skills Select Committee (2006) *Special Educational Needs, Third Report of Session 2006. Volume 1: HC478–1*. London: Stationery Office.

Jacobson, W. (1996). Learning, culture, and learning culture. *Adult Education Quarterly*. **47**(1), pp. 27–41.

Jordan, A., Schwartz, E. and McGhie-Richmond, D. (2009) Preparing teachers for inclusive classrooms. *Teaching and Teacher Education*. **25**(4), pp. 535–549.

Kugelmass, J. and Ainscow, M. (2004) Leadership for inclusion: A comparison of international perspectives. *Journal of Research in Special Educational Needs*. **4**(3), pp. 133–141.

Layton, L. (2005) Special educational needs coordinators and leadership: A role too far? *Support for Learning*. **20**(2), pp. 53–60.

Liasidou, A. and Svennson, C. (2014) Educating leaders for social justice: The case study of special educational needs co-ordinators. *International Journal of Inclusive Education*. **18**(8), pp. 783–797.

Lindqvist, G. (2013) SENCOs: Vanguards or in vain? *Journal of Research in Special Educational Needs*. **13**(3), pp. 79–87.

Norwich, B. (1996) Special needs education or education for all? Connective specialization and ideological impurity. *British Journal of Special Education*. **23**(2), pp. 100–104.

Norwich, B. (2010) What implications do changing practices and concepts have for the role of SEN coordinator? In F. Hallett and G. Hallett (Eds) *Transforming the Role of the SENCO: Achieving the National Award of SEN Coordination*. Maidenhead: McGraw-Hill/Open University Press.

Oldham, J. and Radford, J. (2011) Secondary SENCO Leadership: A universal or specialist role? *British Journal of Special Education*. **38**(3), pp. 126–134.

Pearson, S., Mitchell, R. and Rapti, M. (2015) I will be 'fighting' even more for pupils with SEN: SENCOs' role predictions in the changing English policy context. *Journal of Research in Special Educational Needs*. **15**(1), pp. 48–56.

Robertson, C. (2012) Special educational needs and disability co-ordination in a changing policy landscape: Making sense of the policy from a SENCO's perspective. *Support for Learning*. **27**(2), pp. 77–83.

Rose, R. (2003) Ideology, reality and pragmatics. In C. Tilstone and R. Rose (Eds) *Strategies to Promote Inclusive Education.* London: RoutledgeFalmer.

SENCO Update (2008) Children's Plan aims to strengthen SENCO's role. *SENCO Update.* **92**, pp. 1–2.

Szwed, C. (2007) Remodelling policy and practice: The challenge for staff working with children with special educational needs. *Educational Review.* **59**(2), pp. 147–160.

Wedell, K. (2012) SENCOs supporting each other: The SENCO forum. *Support for Learning.* **27**(2), pp. 67–72.

Winwood, J. (2013) *Policy into Practice: The changing role of the SENCO.* Unpublished EdD Thesis. University of Birmingham.

York-Barr, J., Sommerness, J., Duke, K. and Ghere, G. (2005) Special educators in inclusive education programmes: Reframing their work as teacher leadership. *International Journal of Inclusive Education.* **9**(2), pp. 193–215.

4   Students as core

A time for change in the higher education discourse of 'widening participation' and 'inclusion'

Suanne Gibson

Introduction

Over the past 20 years, the world of higher education (HE) in the UK has experienced many changes, not least those linked to the ubiquitous term 'inclusion'. This chapter addresses this, questioning what 'inclusion' is, what discourses form and frame it and the impact it has upon students, academics and the HE sector in general. The work will introduce you to new concepts and language, engage you with activities, reading and tasks to support your thinking and develop new critical insights into this area of HE.

In language terms, you will first note how 'inclusion' has been placed into quotation marks. This is to acknowledge how in education contexts it has various definitions, some convoluted and arguably incorrect linking it to practices of integration, some developed to fit within government policy and manifesto language and others connecting it to its orthodox origins – i.e. emergent from pressure groups and grass-roots movements regarding the political issue of human rights and equal opportunities, with a particular emphasis on the rights of those with disability. Examples of these groups are:

- The Alliance for Inclusive Education (www.allfie.org.uk)
- Centre for Studies on Inclusive Education (www.csie.org.uk)
- Union of the Physically Impaired Against Segregation (UPIAS: http://disability-studies.leeds. ac.uk/files/library/UPIAS-UPIAS.pdf)
- Parents for Inclusion (www.parentsforinclusion.org)

These organisations and other social movements argue for parity of access to education, the rights of 'disabled' or 'diverse' learners, independent living, relationships and employability. Their views, and those of others on issues of access and equality, stem from the 'social' model of disability. This model asserts the disabled are oppressed by society and this is tied up in relations of power: who has power and who has not (Barnes *et al.*, 2002; Swain *et al.*, 2003; Thomas, 2004). The model argues that barriers and exclusion for the disabled person are caused externally, i.e. the 'problem' or deficit is not located via a medicalised view of disability where the deficit is the medical label or disability, and the person is perceived as suffering from it. The social model assumes that the problem is created by external barriers, both visual and invisible – for example, a building without access to lifts or social and individual prejudices, assumptions or unconscious bias. Oliver provides a comprehensive definition (2009: 45):

First it is an attempt to switch the focus away from the functional limitations of individuals with impairment on to the problems caused by disabling environments, barriers and cultures. Second, it refuses to see specific problems in isolation form the totality of disabling environments [. . .] Third, endorsement of the social model does not mean that individually based interventions in the lives of disabled people are of no use or always counterproductive.

 Individual/group task: defining what you understand as 'inclusion'

Place the word 'inclusion' into a sentence.

In pairs, locate and discuss examples of your experiences or observations in education regarding 'inclusion'.

History and locating 'inclusion': a word, a political movement, a policy?

The term 'inclusion' is a reference used regularly and can be located in many sources within and throughout the university landscape/community, from degree curricula, to policies, library books and website resources, university committees and students' union activities. It is a term that is used outside the university setting, e.g. mainstream education, further education colleges, sports clubs, youth clubs, residential homes and the workplace. As an academic word, it is complex and sparks varied reactions when brought into conversation. It is a term which many people will have had direct experience of, either through their own education or that of others, family and/or friends.

'Inclusion' and practices of 'inclusive education' signified a departure in government policy terms from the late 1990s and a new direction for mainstream education provision. Tony Blair's New Labour government of 1997 and its 'Education, Education, Education' manifesto were seminal to this departure. Defining 'inclusive education' as a dominant theme of policy and practice from that time, Armstrong (2005: 135) summarises it:

> New Labour has placed inclusion at the centre of its educational agenda. Its policies have been characterised by an attempt to include disabled children, together with others identified as having 'special educational needs', within the ordinary school system and the shifting of responsibility for meeting their needs to teachers in the ordinary classroom.

'Inclusion' became the government's buzzword; it denoted a popular form of provision for learners who experienced exclusion from the mainstream or failure in education linked to matters of 'disability'. This quickly evolved to become a matter of 'social inclusion', meaning other excluded groups of students also became a focus, and matters of 'gender', 'race', 'ethnicity', 'sexuality' and social class soon became wrapped up in government and education discourses regarding 'inclusion' (DfEE, 1997, 1998; DfES, 2001). Policy and practice reflected on how causes of, or reasons for, student exclusion were linked to the culture and/or traditional forms of education practice and curriculum. 'Inclusion' became an ethical and political matter for policy makers, practitioners and of course recipients.

The following box provides examples of definitions of 'inclusion'.

Definitions of inclusion

UNESCO (1994):

> Inclusion and participation are essential to human dignity and to the enjoyment and
> exercise of human rights. In the field of education this is reflected in bringing about a
> 'genuine equalisation of opportunity'.

Barton (1998: 60):

> IE is about the education of all children, which necessitates serious change in terms of
> society and its economic, social conditions and relations and in the schools of which
> they are a part.

Centre for Studies on Inclusive Education (CSIE) (2013):

> Arguments for inclusive education are well documented and rest on notions of equality
> and human rights. Much more than a policy requirement, inclusion is founded upon a
> moral position which values and respects every individual and which welcomes diver-
> sity as a rich learning resource.

Gibson (2014):

> Inclusive education is political, a transformatory process for all participants. Social
> justice, acceptance and promotion of diversity inform its practices. Political in nature
> and purpose, institutionalised binaries of 'normal' and 'other' are critically explored and
> related outcomes or changes in practice regularly reviewed.

It has been argued that 'inclusion' became colonised by government policy makers in the mid-1990s, losing its more radical and orthodox ideological basis (Gibson, 2015). It was a very popular buzz-word; due to its wider social appeal as linked to notions of 'humanism' and 'social justice', it was a vote winner, particularly in its early policy manifestations. Once colonised by policy makers and polit-ical parties vying for government power, much of its radical emphasis on significantly changing the schooling and education system became lost in layers of government department bureaucracy, administration and deficit approaches towards the teaching of students with disabilities in main-stream schools, e.g. their education taking place away from their peer group in special educational needs departments (Carrington, 1999; Booth, 1999; Arnot, 2010; Blatchford *et al.*, 2012).

It has been argued that 'inclusion' became something it was never meant to be; a government representing paternalism and benevolent attitudes established their role and subsequently that of others as one which was to do good to the 'disabled', the 'other', to integrate them into traditional ways of working and learning as best possible with additional resources where needed. Such beliefs and practices were never part of inclusion's ideology as understood by its originators (UPIAS, 1976).

Education's traditional culture or ways of doing things were not significantly challenged; it did not make room for difference. That which challenged the status quo was to be managed and made secure within the system, not enabled to change the way things were done. Traditional practices of segregation through the withdrawal of disabled pupils and streaming of learners in setting practices continued. 'Scientific' approaches to assessing ability is ongoing today, a medicalised view of learners with disabilities exists and a related labelling culture is endemic (Avramidis *et al.*, 2000; Brownlee and Carrington, 2000; Anderson, 2009; Gibson, 2015).

Regarding 'inclusion's' various permutations, Gibson (2015) notes its origins within the disability rights movement of the 1970s/80s where exclusion from education, work and independent living was clearly seen as something done to the disabled community due to societal prejudice, traditional practices and policy which did not listen to or take account of diversity. In academic language, this type of world is informed by and retained via 'hegemony'. Hegemony means: the dominance of one cultural group over all others; its particular value set and view of truth informs wider social practices and institutions; it establishes insiders and outsiders and re-establishes them through forms of cultural reproduction. An example of this can be seen in the ways schools can replicate insiders and outsiders through their uses of Teaching Assistants (TAs). In some cases, this results in children sitting detached from the rest of the classroom, being educated by their TA in the SEN department or office and not engaging in peer group work. Further examples are peer bullying of students with special educational needs or those for whom English is an additional language. Other examples of groups who experience various forms of exclusion are travellers, 'Gypsy Roma', students from ethnic minority communities and/or LGBT students. This is not a complete list and it is important to note the complexities and tensions involved when attempting to locate, define or label groups of people, which can be perceived and experienced as an ostracising activity, i.e. reinforcing this person's or people's already excluded form (Ahmed and Swain, 2006).

'Inclusion' and widening participation in higher education

In relation to HE, the 2001 Special Educational Needs and Disability Act (SENDA) introduced 'inclusion' as statutory, i.e. a matter of law. Universities and faculties established committees and offices, e.g. 'Disability Assist office'. These offices address the matter across the curriculum and work to ensure outreach takes place – for example, applicants with disability are contacted in advance of their studies so appropriate provision is set up, e.g. laptop equipment or note takers. Universities were thus required to show clearly where and how they were opening their doors, planning and providing for disabled students. For the first time, universities were to come under statutory control and inspection in relation to their policies, practices and procedures regarding students with disabilities. SENDA moved the 1997 Education Act on from a focus of inclusion and equality in mainstream schools to addressing similar questions within HE (Burke, 2002; Armstrong, 2005).

Policy and related national developments connected to inclusion in HE

Special Educational Needs and Disability Act (SENDA) (2001)
Disability Rights Commission (2006)
Disability Equality Duty Act (2006)
Equality Act (2010)

Due to academic interest in this field many universities established new posts, e.g. lecturers or researchers in SEN, disability studies and/or inclusive education. This has led to much rich critical work addressing questions of inclusion, access and widening participation (Ahmed, 2012; Allan, 2010; Burke, 2002, 2012; Gibson, 2015).

As noted, the term 'social inclusion' became popular during Labour's second term of office; this was to further develop the idea that effective 'inclusive' practice was not just about students with disability. It is important we are aware there are complexities and blurring of lines when we speak of 'inclusive' education.

Current HE policies and practices connected to the reference 'inclusion' are usually linked to the widening participation (WP) policy drive of UK governments (HEFCE, 2001; DFES, 2003). WP was a flagship education policy under New Labour, connected to Blair's' emphasis on 'education, education, education'. Inclusion and WP were core elements of their manifesto. Blair maintained their policies would result in a 50 per cent increase in undergraduate students by 2010 and, whilst there has been an increase since 2001, the current figure of 43 per cent is far off the 50 per cent. The WP agenda aimed to encourage and increase both numbers and retention rate of traditionally under-represented groups. The following overview from ARC (2013: ii) provides clarity regarding what or who is being referred to when policy discusses under-represented student groups:

'Widening participation students' are not a homogeneous group. They may have a range of identities, diverse social characteristics and come from a variety of backgrounds [...] the following key target groups were identified:

- People from lower socio-economic groups
- Mature students
- Part-time learners
- Learners from ethnic minority groups
- Vocational and work-based learners
- Disabled learners
- Care leavers

These various conceptualisations of groupings in our society are termed in the literature as 'intersections'. They represent intersections of our world, groups in society who have experienced various forms of exclusion and oppression. There are debates within and between these various intersections as to where, why or indeed *if* they should all be linked to debates regarding inclusion (Liasidou, 2014). There is general consensus that matters and questions of social justice and equality are common across these intersections.

The next box draws on a research study working with undergraduate students who have disability (Gibson and Kendall, 2010). Their words highlight their experiences and views regarding 'inclusion' and 'exclusion'.

> At university it helped having a key contact on the course, a tutor you felt was approachable, someone you could actually share your concerns with, somebody you felt understood and who responded positively to your needs.

In the small groups at university there is this connectedness with other students and you get to know them as friends almost and therefore you feel more secure perhaps in sharing things or asking questions.

I can arrange one to one support so that you get taught how to use your equipment before you even start your degree so that you can navigate around it, that was a huge bonus.

I was diagnosed when I was at university, but I have struggled all my life and looking back over all my primary school reports and secondary school reports we can see the theme throughout all of it, which is quite interesting, but although I call it a learning difficulty I am quite passionate about the fact that it's been created because of the educational system ... The one way street and how they teach.

[...] my friends they all helped me but people who weren't really my friends weren't very nice. They just use to say that BTECs are dumb and that I was thick and stuff which, obviously, I didn't feel very good about myself then and stuff.

I found it hard and nobody would listen because the teachers kept saying either I was lazy, my grammar structure was poor [...] I think it is my determination to do well and it was trial and error on how do I learn because I knew I didn't learn the same as anyone else.

As noted, inclusive education in essence means wider access to education for those who have been 'traditionally' excluded due to societal practices, cultures or ways of doing that result in inequality, a series of processes or experiences which occur externally to the individual which they have no power or control over. This results in potential student transformation through learning at HE presenting itself as a closed door.

Such external experiences or processes which cause exclusion may be: matters of 'ability' as determined by mainstream education assessment practices, economic background, ethnicity, disability, gender or sexuality. Whilst many hold the view that wider access to HE for our society is a good thing, we are sometimes perplexed or confused by the purpose of that wider access. Is it for self-benefit and growth, self-transformation, community transformation, economic benefit to student and her country, all of the above or none of the above?

This is part of a bigger debate regarding the purpose of the university. Is its main purpose for economic sustenance of a nation or self-fulfilment and learner transformation plus learner benefit, or in establishing communities of education enabling learner transformation which subsequently impacts on society's transformation, making a difference in the real world? Of course, what you see as making a difference and for what purpose will be dependent on your values, beliefs and political views, i.e. the ideological basis upon which you view and interpret the world.

✎ Individual/group task

It is worthwhile having a discussion about this, to reflect on why you came to university and your experiences thus far. What do you see as the purpose of HE? How, if at all, do your values fit with that view? What, if any, political issues come into play and is 'ideology' linked to this view?

Another way we can construct inclusion in our minds and see the barriers to education is in relation to the discourses that surround 'inclusion', informing and determining it. One might operate from a view that it is all about social justice at an individual, institutional and social level, where transformation is furthered for all and rights to access leads to rights to choose what to study, where and why. An alternative discourse which arguably frames most of the WP policy discussion and subsequent provision is the 'neo-liberal'. Larner (2000: 5) provides a clear definition of 'neo-liberal':

> The term 'neo-liberalism' denotes new forms of political-economic governance premised on the extension of market relationships [...] neo-liberalism is associated with the preference for a minimalist state. Markets are understood to be a better way of organizing economic activity because they are associated with competition, economic efficiency and choice.

Apple (2001: 410) highlights how such views reinforce and recreate traditional groups in society.

> While there are clear tensions and conflicts within this alliance, in general its overall aims are in providing the educational conditions believed necessary for increasing international competitiveness, profit and discipline and for returning us to a romanticised past of the 'ideal' home, family, and school.

The alliance he writes about comes from various sections of capital; social and economic groupings that merge over a common ideology; aims, objectives and outcomes, where a successful future is located in the furtherance of a strong global capitalist market. It has been argued that notions of diversity, enabling education for all, responding to different 'voices' and promoting a politics of IE do not fit in such a world (Davies and Bansel, 2007).

Arguably, the discourse of WP is informed by neo-liberalism, where questions of employability, profit and 'graduateness' are the dominant ways in assessing impact, not questions of social justice or minority group histories (Burke, 2012).

Taylor (2012: 12) argues that the failure of current equality legislation is due to its not seeing or understanding where difference exists and how it becomes silenced, stating 'strands of equality and diversity are threatened in a climate of welfare cut-backs, economic crisis and an overhauling higher education system.... Diversity stories are told despite the reality of unequal opportunities.'

Thus inclusion's contemporary interpretation, as in that which has evolved from pressure groups to government policy then practice, seems to be framed within a neo-liberal discourse. The impact is that there has not been a significant increase in the numbers of 'diverse' students in HE. Yes, there has been some improvement, but not to the extent of what was anticipated in the ideological drivers of inclusion's grass-roots movements, nor in Labour's re-visioning of 'inclusion' in its flagship WP policy.

In relation to the continued under-representation of students with disabilities, Madriaga *et al.* (2011: 209) state that normalcy 'is equated ... with an everyday eugenics, which heralds a non-disabled person without "defects", or impairments, as the ideal norm'. As noted in the UK's Social Mobility and Child Poverty Commission report (2013: 5):

> Those in the most advantaged areas are still three times as likely to participate in HE as those in the most disadvantaged areas [...] There has been no improvement in participation at the most selective universities among the least advantaged young people since the 1990s [...]

From a wider European perspective, an independent report discovered six factors causing student 'drop out': socio-cultural, structural, policy, institutional, personal and learning factors (Quinn, 2013). All factors were seen as interrelated and, whilst WP policy was not seen as the source of the problem, the matter of massification as the major informant to evolving WP practices was. Clarifying this point, Quinn, states (2013: 71):

> Widening participation is when those accessing and succeeding in HE are fully representative of the diversity of the population and when there is equality of outcome across these groups. Massification can occur without the changes in the system that would actually widen participation and can also lead to a stratified system.

Thus, whilst numbers have increased significantly across the sector they are not fully representative at either uptake or graduate achievement sources. This, one might argue, is due to the discourse of 'normalcy' operating throughout the HE sector, creating a binary, i.e. the 'traditional' or 'non-diverse' student and the 'diverse' or 'WP' student. Such a sense of normalcy – one might call it the workings of hegemony – replicates thinking about the 'non-traditional' student, resulting in their continued suppression and marginalisation.

The impact of 'inclusion' and widening participation on higher education: what has it achieved?

Some have argued that WP has resulted in a social justice imaginary (Gale and Hodge, 2014), suggesting it was always, consciously or not, about the general growth of the HE sector, i.e. more student numbers, more graduates, a sustainable economy, more profit. Furthermore, that our society's dominant and traditional culture tied to our capitalist economy, i.e. the neo-liberal world in which we reside, has overridden any social justice aims which WP, policy and practice, claimed it would achieve. The neo-liberal reframing of 'inclusion' via widening participation policy did not take account of deeply embedded and complex histories of exclusion, inequality and misrecognition. The colonisation of inclusion's original ideas and ideological driver, its re-visioning by the establishment into an acceptable framework, has failed the very groups within society it claimed it would aid. WP was about the massification of HE, new degrees were developed, matters of 'employability and profit' tied more deeply to the undergraduate curriculum, further routes into HE were established and numbers of undergraduate students rose; these numbers were not representative.

Policies and practices in the name of 'inclusion' continue to emerge, whilst there is growing recognition that much more is needed to establish and sustain education spaces and practices that are positively responsive to the many histories, backgrounds and cultures of our students. Griffiths (2010: 4) highlights that:

> The UK is far from achieving social balance in access to the benefits of a university education (Department for Business Innovation and Skills, 2010) [....] Socio-economic background, gender, ethnicity and place of residence all influence the likelihood of an individual attending higher education, primarily because of their effect on attainment at school.

Adding further to this debate, giving insight into the experiences of these students, Gibson asserts (2015: 875): 'With high dropout rates, university transfers and negative student feedback [...] the world of many "included" students is one of trial and error, frustration and failure [...] as opposed to inclusion and academic success.' Burke provides a comprehensive account of WP. She highlights how, as a driver, it has resulted in a furthering of inequality across the sector, deeper divisions between traditional old universities and the post-1992 sector, where the reproduction of social inequalities continues, albeit through new forms of HE labelled as promoting equality, e.g. foundation degrees, part-time study, yet reproducing old binaries which add to *the re-privileging of certain institutions, courses, academics and students* (Burke, 2012: 32).

✎ Individual/group task

What issues do you think there are regarding the task of inclusion in HE?

What experiences have you had in relation to inclusion in HE?

What practices might be developed to address inclusion more effectively?

On the surface, much so-called 'inclusion' policy, stemming from government or other established sources, fails to fulfil its aims. This failure is due to the continuation of hegemony in our universities without time or space being given to challenging it in overt ways. Overt ways may be through dialogue, pressure groups and direct engagement with 'excluded' groups. How can such ideas or practices be taken forward?

Some suggest that, for more effective inclusive practices, the answers must be found from within the student body itself rather than from without (Beauchamp-Pryor, 2012; Vickerman and Blundell, 2010). Furthermore, it is suggested that university policy development and related pedagogic practices should emerge from conversations held with our students. In attempting to know what works, questions need to be asked 'with' – rather than policies and 'tool-kit' practices devised externally to and 'for' – the 'diverse' student body. Carrington (1999: 258) has argued 'by recognising and understanding social responses to difference and establishing "cultures of difference" [...] equity and the inclusion of all students could be promoted'. Furthermore, Thomas suggests (2013: 486) that 'the future contribution of inclusive education hinges on its ability to retreat from histories of identify-assess-diagnose-help and to examine the ways in which schools enable community and encourage students' belief in themselves as members of such a community'. Whilst writing about inclusion in schools, the premise and the argument regarding HE is similar and, it is suggested, applicable at this level too.

What for the future of 'inclusion' and HE? Changes to improve inclusive practice

'Rights' and 'statutory provision' have gone some way towards meeting the aims of 'inclusive' and social justice drivers, but at their core lies a conflict preventing institutions from fulfilling their surface-level aims and objectives. The conflict is a clash of cultures: one culture or group sits comfortably within this traditional way of being and doing replicated in hegemonic form; the other group is external migrants holding passports, but without any prior historic citizenship they struggle. After much reshaping and loss, what might be perceived as the squeezing of a migrant square box into a hegemonic round hole will work for some. However, for many it results in further exclusion, failure and frustration (Lewis *et al.*, 2007; Gibson, 2015).

The following citations are from students in the UK, New Zealand, Cyprus and the USA involved in an international study into questions of 'diversity' and inclusion in HE (Gibson, 2014).

- There isn't one answer [. . .] how to solve issues [. . . .] Listening to other people's stories, even when they are completely different to yours, just makes you realise you're not the only one having problems.
- The personal tutor is the face of the university to you. If you're going to university there's a million and one people who work here, so your personal tutor, your lecturer is the person you see the most, so having a strong relationship with them is really key.
- I don't feel connected to the uni [. . .] it's like there is no flow to things [. . .] this dept does this and this dept does this [. . .] there needs to be more connectivity between them.
- Everyone seemed to have the experience of being ignored/not listened to by someone.
- It's weird, because I don't like labelling. But when sexuality isn't on the form I feel 'oh, pah, I'm being ignored' and then when it's on the form it's like 'well, why is it any of their business?'
- It is a matter of culture (mentality) and it is not just school.

Their views and experiences highlight the complexities, paradoxes and frustrations with 'inclusive' HE provision. Their insights and the questions they raise corroborate much of the contemporary critical work on 'social inclusion' and widening participation as noted earlier. As part of this study, time was given to discuss alternative forms of provision or ways in which universities might be more effective in meeting 'inclusive' aims. The following box provides a summary (Gibson, 2014).

Suggestions from students for more effective forms of inclusive provision

Scheme in place to ensure tutors know about students with additional needs and students know that their tutors know.

Place value on the importance the relationship student holds with personal tutor and lecturers.

Need for all degree programmes to address the question of diversity and rights as part of their curriculum.

Suggestion of a transition process.

Need for 'diversity' to have a more visual presence on campus.

A student buddy system in the first year.

University needs to consider the changing student culture.

Alongside these practical suggestions, their desire for change centred on the 'university' hearing their stories, being proactive in listening to them and empowering them to become core change agents for effective inclusive provision. This sits well with much current research into effective pedagogy for students in HE which argues for 'relational' or 'student-centred' forms of engagement

(Beauchamp-Pryor, 2012; Gibson, 2012; Griffiths, 2010; Murphy and Brown, 2012). That being the case, how might such practices evolve?

Vickerman and Blundell, conducting research into questions of HE access and disabled students, suggest the following practical activities may enable a levelling of the barriers (2010: 21): 'pre-course induction support, commitment by HE institutions to facilitating barrier free curricula, consultation with disabled students, institutional commitment to develop support services and embedding of personal development planning'. These reflect some of the suggestions in the HEFCE and OFFA report (2014: v), which asserts that:

> retention and success are best addressed by approaches which seek to develop: supportive peer relations; meaningful interaction between staff and students; knowledge, confidence and identity as successful HE learners; and an HE experience that is relevant to students' interests and future goals.

These are all worthwhile suggestions, but I would argue are meaningless and likely to become merely reactionary practices if cultural barriers are not first considered. This, I suggest, takes place through cross-stakeholder dialogue about hegemony, how it manifests, operates and is experienced in both subtle and overt forms. Without this prior platform of questions and dialogue, HE will fall back into its neo-liberal hegemonic trap, providing set answers which fail as they do not come from an understanding of students' rich and varied histories.

A fresh political discourse in the university is needed, one which not only allows for conflict but actively seeks it as an essential ingredient in its future ways of working with all students. This fresh political discourse needs to challenge the 'pathological gaze' (Slee, 2001: 171) emergent from labelling and HE's hegemonic lens. Such a discourse provides space for educator political engagement, where the complex processes of inclusion and exclusion can be openly discussed. This discourse needs to set itself apart from institutionalised bureaucracy and procedures which may result in its colonisation and revisioning into a more traditional form. The end result is arguably a state of being where difference becomes ordinary and empowered students are the epicentre: from where change emerges. A quixotic vision for some, but one which is happening in small but effective measures where educators are taking seriously their commitment to and belief in social justice. Examples of this can be seen in programmes where:

- students give input into curriculum content and planning
- students take part in teaching
- students are encouraged during induction weeks and thereafter to share aspects of their individuality and individual education stories
- space is given to engage with all our journeys to higher education and thereafter, i.e. 'becoming student'
- assessment is more than examination or traditional forms of writing
- students and academics co-design, carry out and present education research projects
- focus is made to value student writing and connections made with undergraduate and education journals for their publications
- graduates return to share their graduate stories encouraging and inspiring students
- in sum, *relationship and knowing you* is both valued and clearly experienced in ways which can be observed by others looking in.

It is a proactive choice which needs energy from those educators who chose it, but is energy-giving in its form. Burke and Crozier's (2013) *Teaching Inclusively: Changing Pedagogical Spaces* connects to this argument. Their work, guided by the principle of 'praxis', serves through reflective pieces and group activities to support academics as they challenge practices and discourses that reinforce 'other' and serve to further exclude.

 Individual/group task

How might you take some of these ideas forward, e.g. in your students' union, your social groups, with your tutors?

Conclusion

This chapter has presented a historical and critical overview of 'inclusion' in HE. Government policy has been engaged with and research suggesting the impact of policy presented. Stories, experiences and future ideas have been shared by students who are linked to the WP discourse. It has been argued that cultural divisions and hegemony replicating exclusion are the key reasons why 'inclusion', mis-interpreted in WP policy, has not succeeded.

The arguments raised in this chapter suggest revisiting traditional, more radical views on inclusion and through conscious decision-making, not enforced by institutional policy or spin, choosing to know our students, their various histories and their aspirations. There is a need to work collectively across and with various stakeholders in higher education to create changes that are student-centred in design and transformational in effect. For this process to be effective, resulting in significant inclusive results, reflection is firstly required on how the university – its cultural ways of being and doing – has greatly aided certain groups over others.

> When will people who feel rejected [...] when will they feel accepted? When are they going to be able to participate equally? When will the society be ready to accept them? But these are theoretical questions with no clear answer.
>
> (Jody, in Gibson, 2014)

Summary points

- Inclusion in higher education is connected to government and university policy called 'widening participation'.
- The WP agenda has created some change but it has not resulted in inclusion; it has not achieved its original aims.
- The barriers have been noted as cultural and historic.
- WP and inclusion can be understood or viewed through different lenses: 'social justice' or 'neo-liberal'.
- Students are core to knowing and understanding what is necessary for their learning to be effective.

- Educators need to see the student stakeholder as central to future effective developments towards inclusion HE.
- A fresh political discourse, working outside of university bureaucracy, has been suggested as necessary for HE educators to take inclusive thinking and practices forward.
- Students need to be central change agents working with the university as part of this fresh political discourse.

Further reading

Ahmed, S. (2012) *On Being Included*. Durham: Duke University Press.
Allan, J. (2010) The inclusive teacher educator: Spaces for civic engagement. *Discourse: Studies in the Cultural Politics of Education*, 31(4): 411–422.
Burke, P.J. (2012) *The Right to Higher Education*. London: Routledge.
Gibson, S. (2013) Disability matters: The role of the personal tutor for inclusive teaching and learning. In T. Bilham (Ed.) *NTF collection: For the Love of Learning*. Basingstoke: Palgrave.
Gibson, S. (2015) When rights are not enough: What is? Moving towards new pedagogy for inclusive education within UK universities. *International Journal of Inclusive Education*, 19(8): 875–886.

References

Ahmed, S. (2012) *On Being Included*. Durham: Duke University Press.
Ahmed, S. and Swain, E. (2006) Doing diversity. *Policy Futures in Education*, 4(2): 96–100.
Allan, J. (2010) The inclusive teacher educator: Spaces for civic engagement. *Discourse: Studies in the Cultural Politics of Education*, 31(4): 411–422.
Alliance for Inclusive Education (ALFIE) www.allfie.org.uk (accessed 25 July 2015).
Anderson, R. (2009) They're telling me what I already know instead of what I don't know: Dyslexic pupils' experiences of withdrawal tuition during the later primary years. *Support for Learning*, 24(2): 55–61.
Apple, M. (2001) Comparing neo-liberal projects and inequality in education. *Comparative Education*, 37(4): 409–423.
ARC (2013) Literature Review of Research into Widening Participation to Higher Education, Report to HEFCE and OFFA by ARC Network.
Armstrong, D. (2005) Reinventing 'inclusion': New Labour and the cultural politics of special education. *Oxford Review of Education*, 31(1): 135–151.
Arnot, M. (2010) (Ed.) *The Sociology of Disability and Inclusive Education*. London: Routledge.
Avramidis, E., Bayliss, P. and Burden, R. (2000) A survey into mainstream teachers' attitudes towards the inclusion of children with special educational needs. *Educational Psychology*, 20(2): 191–211.
Barnes, C., Oliver, M. and Barton, L. (Eds) (2002) *Disability Studies Today*. Cambridge: Polity Press.
Barton, L. (1998) Sociology, disability studies and education. In T. Shakespeare (Ed.) *The Disability Reader: Social science perspectives*. London: Cassell.
Beauchamp-Pryor, K. (2012) From absent to active voices: Securing disability equality within higher education. *International Journal of Inclusive Education*, 16(3): 283–295.
Blatchford, P., Russell, A. and Webster, R. (2012) *Reassessing the Impact of Teaching Assistants: How Research Challenges Practice and Policy*. London: Routledge.
Booth, T. (1999) *National Policies on Inclusion in England: How Well Are We Doing?* www.eenet.org.uk/resources/docs/tbooth.php (accessed 15 December 2012).
Brownlee, J. and Carrington, S. (2000) Opportunities for authentic experience and reflection: A teaching programme designed to change attitudes towards disability for pre-service teachers. *Support for Learning*, 15(3): 99–105.
Burke, P.J. (2002) Accessing *Education: Effectively Widening Participation*. Stoke on Trent: Trentham Books.
Burke, P.J. (2012) *The Right to Higher Education*. London: Routledge.
Burke, P.J. and Crozier, G. (2013) *Teaching Inclusively: Changing Pedagogical Spaces*. Roehampton: University of Roehampton and HEA.

Carrington, S. (1999) Inclusion needs a different school culture. *International Journal of Inclusive Education*, 3(3): 257–268.

Centre for Studies on Inclusive Education (CSIE) (2013) www.csie.org.uk (accessed 25 July 2015).

Davies, B. and Bansel, P. (2007) Neoliberalism and education. *International Journal of Qualitative Studies in Education*, 20(3): 247–259.

DfEE (1997) *Circular 10/9*. London: DfEE.

DfEE (1998) *White Paper: Meeting Special Educational Needs*. London: DfEE.

DfES (2001) *Special Educational Needs Code of Practice*. London: DfES.

DfES (2003) *Widening Participation in Higher Education*. London: DFES.

Disability Equality Duty (2006) http://bit.ly/1KyZIA5 (accessed 25 July 2015).

Disability Rights Commission (2006) *Disability Equality Duty*. London: Disability Rights Commission.

Gale, T. and Hodge, S. (2014) Just imaginary: Delimiting social inclusion in higher education. *British Journal of Sociology of Education*, 35(5): 688–709.

Gibson, S. (2012) Narrative accounts of university education: Socio-cultural perspectives of students with disabilities. *Disability and Society*, 27(3): 353–369.

Gibson, S. (2014) *Listening to our 'Diverse' Students and Preparing Learning Futures to Enhance the Retention and Academic Success of All. Reflections on a HEA International Scholarship 2013–2014*. Paper presented at Higher Education Association Annual Conference, York, July 2014.

Gibson, S. (2015) When rights are not enough: What is? Moving towards new pedagogy for inclusive education within UK universities. *International Journal of Inclusive Education*, 19(8): 875–886.

Gibson, S. and Kendall, L. (2010) Stories from school: Dyslexia and learners' voices on factors impacting on achievement. *Support for Learning*, 25(4): 187–193.

Griffiths, S. (2010) *Teaching for Inclusion in Higher Education: A Guide to Practice*. York: HEA.

HEFCE (2001) *01/36 Strategies for Widening Participation in HE: A Guide to Good Practice*. Bristol: HEFCE.

Larner, W. (2000) Neo-liberalism: Policy, ideology, governmentality. *Studies in Political Economy*, 63(Autumn): 5–25.

Lewis, A., Parsons, S. and Robertson, C. (2007) *My School, My Family, My Life: Telling it like it is*. London: Disability Rights Commission.

Liasidou, A. (2014) Critical disability studies and socially just change in higher education. *British Journal of Special Education*, 41(2): 120–135.

Madriaga, M., Hanson, K., Kay, H. and Walker, A. (2011) Marking-out normalcy and disability in higher education. *British Journal Special Education*, 32(6): 901–920.

Murphy, M. and Brown, T. (2012) Learning as relational: intersubjectivity and pedagogy in higher education. *International Journal of Lifelong Education*, 31(5): 643–654.

OFFA/HEFCE (2014) *Outcomes of Access Agreement, Widening Participation Strategic Statement and National Scholarship Programme Monitoring for 2012–13*. Bristol: OFFA/HEFCE.

Oliver, M. (2009) *Understanding Disability: From Theory to Practice*. London: Palgrave Macmillan.

Parents for Inclusion, www.parentsforinclusion.org (accessed 25 July 2015).

Quinn, J. (2013) *Drop-out and Completion in Higher Education in Europe among Students from Under-Represented Groups, European Commission by the Network of Experts on Social Aspects of Education and Training*. NESET, European Union.

Slee, R. (2001) Social justice and the changing directions in educational research: The case of inclusive education. *International Journal of Inclusive Education*, 5(2/3): 167–177.

Social Mobility and Child Poverty Commission (2013) *Higher Education: The Fair Access Challenge*. London: Social Mobility and Child Poverty Commission.

Swain, J., French, S. and Cameron, C. (2003) *Controversial Issues in a Disabling Society*. Buckingham: Open University Press.

Taylor, Y. (2012) (Ed.) *Educational Diversity*. Basingstoke: Palgrave Macmillan.

Thomas, C. (2004) Disability and impairment. In J. Swain, S. French, C. Barnes and C. Thomas (Eds) *Disabling Barriers: Enabling Environments*. London: Sage.

Thomas, G. (2013) A review of thinking and research about inclusive education policy, with suggestions for a new kind of inclusive thinking. *British Educational Research Journal*, 39(3): 473–490.

UNESCO (1994) *The UNESCO Salamanca Statement*. Paris: UNESCO.

Union of the Physically Impaired Against Segregation (UPIAS) (1976) http://disability-studies.leeds.ac.uk/files/library/UPIAS-UPIAS.pdf (accessed 25 July 2015).

Vickerman, P. and Blundell, M. (2010) Hearing the voices of disabled students in higher education. *Disability and Society*, 25(1): 21–23.

5   Inclusive practice for families

Kay Bennett, Sarah Mander and Lynn Richards

Introduction

Family experience of high-quality inclusive practice at an early stage significantly influences the understanding and expectation of inclusion within learning environments. Parents/carers, children and young people possess personalised, unique expertise regarding their own service requirements. This has the potential to support educational institutions in their quest to successfully implement inclusive practice. It is particularly relevant for families who may be marginalised through poverty, or cultural or social factors, where reluctance to engage in and secure support from professional services offers a challenge to organisations to reflect upon and review the effectiveness of their inclusive practice.

The impact of parental involvement in their children's education is well documented; it has a positive influence on future educational attainment and therefore an integrated approach to parental engagement is advocated to build solid lifelong foundations for learning. This chapter will discuss the importance of user voice and associated participation strategies which are genuine and realistic, and also consider current service provision for excluded families with reflection upon the qualities and competencies required to firmly embed inclusion throughout all strands of these services. We shall use examples from the context of education as a way of exploring issues of inclusion with regard to children, young people and their families. The chapter is in three sections: poverty and inclusion, 'hard-to-reach' families: acknowledging diversity and complexity, and a case study example of effective consultation with parents of young children who experience disability. It is a salient point that families from minority ethnic groups and families with adults and/or children with disabilities are both more likely to experience poverty and disadvantage (Gupta and Blewett, 2008; Lansley and Mack, 2015) and so it is the issue of poverty that we focus on in the first instance.

Poverty and inclusion

In this section, we wish to consider how poverty is discursively constructed, and how lived experiences of 'poor' families might usefully be valued as a way of building a more cohesive and hopeful society for the future. While models of inclusion are traditionally based on such aspects to do with 'race'/ethnicity, gender and disability, public perceptions of poverty are arguably shaped by the definitions attributed to it.

✎ **Individual/group task**

How many children are currently living in poverty in the UK?
To what extent do you see this as a problem, and why?

Definitions of poverty can often be seen to incorporate 'absolute' and 'relative' measures; the former focuses on the needs for survival and basic subsistence, while the latter takes account of the economic and social conditions reflected within contemporary society (Lansley and Mack, 2015). A current standard of relative poverty within the UK is defined as 'people living in households with income below 60 per cent of the median for that year' (Joseph Rowntree Foundation, 2012), although the Organisation for Economic Cooperation and Development (OECD) uses the figure of 50 per cent of the national median income in order to compare poverty rates within OECD countries (UNICEF, 2012). However, UNICEF (2012) puts forward the case that the concept of relative poverty does not succeed in convincing politicians or the public that poverty is in fact 'real' and that the focus should centre on updating and monitoring poverty to reflect living standards of the society as a whole. As an example, the child deprivation index offers a view of poverty based on a household's ability to provide at least twelve of fourteen items; items include: three meals a day, regular leisure activities, a quiet place with enough room and light to do homework, and some new clothes (i.e. not all second-hand) (UNICEF, 2012). Such lack of items will be experienced by children and young people living in poverty, and, in the context of education, such an absence has the potential to impact negatively on both well-being and educational attainment (Ridge, 2006) so affecting future life chances. Education is acknowledged as a protective factor against the adverse effects of disadvantage (EPPSE, 2012; Duncan Smith, 2015; CPAG, 2015; NCB, 2012) and yet poverty serves to marginalise, and to exclude, even within the educational context.

In their report into secondary schooling in the UK, EPPSE (2012: 134) highlighted the importance of the 'school behavioural climate' and 'support for learning'. They found, however, that pupils from low-income families, in receipt of free school meals (FSM), tended to study at schools with poorer 'climates' with less learning support, so exacerbating an already recognised risk of poor educational attainment and subsequent life chances. The report also identifies the importance of homework in consolidating learning and in developing capacities for achievement; in light of the child deprivation index (UNICEF, 2012), it can be seen that not all pupils may experience similar opportunities, notwithstanding additional responsibilities within poorer families to care for siblings or ageing relatives, or to perform domestic chores before and after the school day. Indeed, the weight of responsibility may fall heavily upon such pupils as over two-thirds of those living in poverty today, in the UK, are recognised as living within waged families where one or both adults are in paid employment (Joseph Rowntree Foundation, 2012; Lansley and Mack, 2015), so adding to the stressors of family life. The effects of poverty on parenting are acknowledged (Gupta and Blewett, 2008; Pugh, 2010), whereby the anxiety of having to refuse children the possibility of attending school trips, of how to afford school uniform and of the purchase of other sundry items to give an air of 'fitting in' to normative child and adolescent lifestyles (Ridge, 2006) all make for stressful living, in addition to long hours of work for low pay. The competing tensions of earning a wage sufficient to be lifted out of poverty and of providing an emotionally nurturing and stimulating learning environment at home

(Pugh, 2010) remain the constant strain on parents living in poverty. After all, poverty has been recast since the introduction of the concept of 'social exclusion', in the late 1980s, and while historically seen as a failure of policy to include, it is now constituted as a responsibility of the individual (Lansley and Mack, 2015; Procacci, 2007); that is, the poor have only themselves to blame.

The recognition of poverty within the UK in the twenty-first century as not entirely 'real' (UNICEF, 2012) seems to be reflected in the public imagination; the silent shame of our own 3.5 million children living in poverty seems to pass us by. We remain complicit in their existence and yet relatively unmoved to collectively lift them out of such impoverished conditions from within our Westernised, industrialised and seemingly affluent society. This is despite the dominant protectionist discourse around young children in particular, and the need to eliminate all manner of risks. Furedi's (2008) exhortation of parental fears of 'everything' is compounded by Palmer's (2006) declaration that this is the first generation to have been 'reared in captivity'. And yet, the risks of living in poverty are not openly acknowledged in the same way as other risk-taking behaviours. To what extent children living in poverty should be added to the 'children at risk' register (Corby, 2006) may be a question worth asking if indeed the day-to-day effects, and long-term life chances, are to be more fully acknowledged. While the Child Poverty Act (2010) introduced a target to eliminate child poverty by 2020, the Coalition government was quick to distance itself from the income-based poverty measure (Lansley and Mack, 2015) when it took office in 2010, and more recent political moves have indicated a 'scrapping' of the Act's targets in favour of measurements around 'worklessness' and 'educational attainment' (Duncan Smith, 2015). The Chief Executive of the Child Poverty Action Group, Alison Garnham, reacted by saying: 'Lacking money or being in work will mean you no longer count as poor.... This is public policy going through the looking glass. Nothing will be quite what it seems' (Garnham, 2015). Indeed, current austerity measures in the UK are predicted to see 4.7 million of our children living in poverty by 2020 (CPAG, 2015), a very long way from promised targets. If inclusion is to be effected for all sectors of society, then hiding the social processes which produce poverty, such as low wages, is not helpful: 'marginalisation puts poverty further apart from the whole of society' (Procacci, 2007: 3).

✎ **Individual/group task**

How might you, as a current/future practitioner working with children/young people and their families, seek to influence professional practices to take account of the effects of poverty?

The status of marginalisation is one heralded by those living in poverty. Issues to do with being judged by others, isolation, depression, low self-esteem and lack of choice – about such decisions as which school to attend or where to live – are cited as just some of the ongoing complexities affecting day-to-day living (Gupta and Blewett, 2008; Ridge, 2006). In their study of service users ('family members') contributing to a social work training programme, Gupta and Blewett (2008: 465) note the term of 'povertyism', which is employed by the group to offer an understanding of the 'poverty-blind' approach taken by professionals, in particular, the lack of recognition of the strengths that have necessarily been deployed by poor families in surviving as long as they have done. This deficit framing (Petriwskyj, 2010) of those living in poverty is worrying. Since success at school is measured against attainment targets, the tension between including those pupils who may struggle – and so be more difficult to teach (Rouse, 2008) – is an extant challenge, and one which depends on the resolve of individual teachers and schools. The concept of inclusive education (Booth and Ainscow, 2004; Stubbs, 2008) is part of a wider strategy to fulfil the demands of human rights so that all people might contribute fully to society. It is important, then, not only that instrumentalist measures are put in place – through policies and procedures – but also that attitudinal perspectives of professionals, and indeed the general public, are revisited in order to emphasise values of acceptance, respect and dignity: 'Education, safety, freedom from oppression, and support can help people uphold and practise these higher values ... Inclusion ultimately has to be seen in this wider context' (Stubbs, 2008: 53).

'Hard-to-reach' families: acknowledging diversity and complexity

Parents and carers play a significant role in the overall educational attainment of children and young people. Strand (2011) states that parenting practices have the strongest impact on the achievement of the young. Washbrook (2010) endorses this, stating both parenting and the home environment are the most important contributors to inequalities in educational attainment. Therefore, the effectiveness of any strategy that seeks to ensure that all children and young people receive a fully inclusive education must rely on the active participation of both the children and their families in all decision-making processes.

However, the culture and ethnicity of families can contribute to potential barriers which hinder engagement and prevent individuals from contributing to the formation of processes that impact on them. Those families in greatest need of support tend to be those least likely to engage (Ghate and Hazel, 2002) and without engagement there is no consultation. Therefore, it is essential that professionals place all their efforts on removing the barriers.

The term 'hard-to-reach' in relation to families can be problematic as it can mean different things to different people. For instance, a practitioner's professional discipline may determine what or whom is defined as 'hard-to-reach'. Other influential factors that may impact on the understanding of the term might be past experience, the accessibility of individuals, perceived barriers to engagement and the availability of resources to meet the needs of a specific group. The last factor may have caused you to question how it is that 'they' can be deemed hard-to-reach, if it is 'us', our inadequacies, that may have created the barrier(s) in the first place. Who then is actually 'hard-to-reach': the families or indeed the professionals?

✎ **Individual/group task**

How would you define the term 'hard-to-reach'?
What do you think has influenced your understanding of the term?

Brooks-Wilson and Snell (2012: 3) propose that the term 'hard-to-reach' should be (re)conceptualised as 'accessible when approached', which may offer a more candid appreciation of the term. The UK government in 2004 defined 'hard-to-reach' as those persons who are 'inaccessible to most traditional and conventional methods for any reason' (HSE, 2004: 8). However, it could be argued that strategies judged to be 'traditional and conventional' by the UK government may be anything but that to those they seek to engage. Indeed, a lack of sensitivity to the differing cultural beliefs of individuals within minority groups is cited as a common reason for the lack of engagement from certain parts of the community (Treise and Shepherd, 2006; Van Cleemput, 2007; Greenfields, 2008).

A further issue when seeking to delineate the term is that of categorisation. An internet search of the phrase shows a recurrence of specific classifications: black and minority ethnic groups, disabled people, Gypsies and travellers, the socio-economically disadvantaged and those who cannot read, write or speak English. However, this type of 'broad-based grouping' (Doherty *et al.*, 2004) of individuals can result in a loss of identity and individuality when the assumption is made that all persons within that group have the same needs and will experience the same challenges. Indeed, it was not too many years ago when a common interview question for those wanting to work in any care-related profession would read: *How would you ensure equality when working with this particular group?* With the correct answer, at the time being something akin to: *By making sure that all persons, regardless of age, sex, disability, race or gender, are treated the same.*

How wrong we were. Not only do the needs of groups differ but the needs of individuals within groups also differ. A brief examination of some of the main categorisations of those deemed to be 'hard-to-reach' allows us to see how inclusion can become exclusion if the diversity within groups is not recognised.

When we speak of the black and minority ethnic group (BME) we refer to all persons who are of 'non-white descent'. This would therefore include those non-white persons who descend from, amongst other places, the Caribbean, Africa and Asian countries such as Bangladesh and Pakistan. These persons may be 'first-generation' immigrants who may have been born abroad and have now relocated to the UK and taken up residence here. On the other hand, they may have been born in Britain and may be third- or even fourth-generation descendants of immigrants. Individuals within this group may be classified as asylum seekers – that is, they may have left their country of origin and be seeking residence within the UK – or they may have had their applications for asylum accepted (refugees). Regardless of the circumstances, however long these individuals have resided in the UK and whatever their command of the English language, all would be placed within this same grouping. However, if we unpick the BME group further, it becomes apparent that there are disparities that result in differing sets of needs.

Using education as an example, within this group there are wide disparities in academic attainment. In 2013/2014, pupils from a black background were the lowest-performing group, with 53.1 per cent achieving five A*–C GCSE grades, including Maths and English (DfE, 2015). However, the highest performing group overall also falls within the same BME category: 74.4 per cent of pupils of Chinese origin achieved the same result, well above all other pupils (DfE, 2015). This means there is a 21.3 percentage point difference between the two groups, with further differences amongst other groups within this category. This is further complicated by the sub-categories that exist within the groups themselves; for instance, the term 'black' includes, amongst others, those of black-Caribbean or black-African heritage, but again there are disparities in the attainment of these groups, totalling in excess of 10 percentage points in 2011/2012 (DfE, 2013a). It is clear from these data that any strategy that relied on the perceived needs of the BME group as a whole would be flawed.

Gypsy, Roma and traveller families are another distinguishable group defined as 'hard-to-reach', but here too there is a lack of uniformity. They certainly constitute a minority group: in the 2011 census, 58,000 people or 0.1 per cent of the population identified themselves as Gypsy or Irish traveller (ONS, 2014). Whilst this figure does not account for those members of the traveller community who are from other ethnicities and is therefore likely to be lower than the true percentage, it is still significantly lower than the numbers of other minority ethnic persons in the UK. This may or may not be the reason for the apparent exclusion of Gypsies and travellers in policy initiatives and strategies designed to promote inclusion (Cemlyn *et al.*, 2009). Individuals within this group may originate from England or other European countries, such as Romania (Roma) or Ireland. Families may live in houses (bricks-and-mortar dwellings), static caravans, or they may travel around the country. According to the ONS (2014) ethnic groupings guidance, these families are white. However, there are distinct differences in the experiences and attainment of these individuals in comparison to the experiences of other white groups. For instance, there is little evidence of discrimination against other white groups in the UK, and any intolerance of other minority groups is largely hidden. However, hostility, racism and prejudice towards members of the Gypsy/Roma community are reportedly common and seemingly tolerated in a way that is unique only to this group (Cemlyn *et al.*, 2009). There are further inequalities in health and education. With regard to health, within this community there is a prevalence of neonatal deaths, miscarriages, respiratory problems such as asthma and bronchitis, and arthritis (Parry *et al.*, 2007). Using educational attainment again as an example, 56.2 per cent of white pupils achieved 5 A*–C GCSE grades (or equivalent) including Maths and English in 2014 (DfE, 2015). However, only 8.2 per cent of Gypsy/Roma pupils achieved this. Further inequalities exist, such as higher rates of suicide and poverty and lower rates of employment in comparison to other groups (Cemlyn *et al.*, 2009).

✎ **Individual/group task**

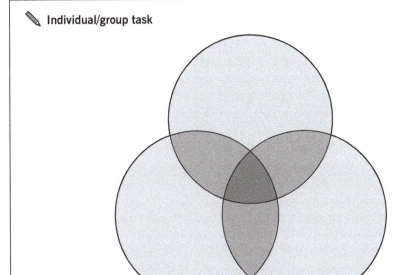

Choose three groups that are considered 'hard-to-reach'. Draw three concentric circles, as above, and label them according to the three groups chosen.

In each circle, list the inequalities and/or discrimination that this group may face. In the centre of the diagram, list the inequalities and discrimination that all the groups might share.

Whilst it is evident that there are widespread differences within BME groups, there are further complexities where individuals have multiple minority identities and therefore may face an even greater level of exclusion. Gillborn (2015: 278) describes the notion of 'intersectionality' whereby 'multiple forms of inequality and identity inter-relate in different contexts and over time'. So, for instance, a black woman may face inequalities on account of race but also on account of gender; a gay man from the traveller community may face discrimination on account of his sexuality and also his cultural differences, whilst a non-English-speaking asylum seeker may face challenges on account of race and language barriers. Any of these persons could also present with a disability or health issue, adding to the complexity of need. The intersectional identities of individuals can lead to them feeling excluded and overlooked when strategies that claim to focus on them only account for one part of who they are.

Whilst the evidence shows that there are commonalities within the BME group, such as economic deprivation, we can deduce that families with such an expanse of backgrounds, race, cultures and experiences will inevitably have their own, specific issues that affect them and may contribute to their ability to reach us, or our ability to reach them. Therefore, when considering inclusion, the practitioner needs to accept and adopt the attitude that no single value or principle 'be it inclusion, individuality or autonomy … can guide and determine what is considered to be worthwhile' (Norwich, 2002: 483) but rather work from a premise whereby full inclusion is gained by accepting, and addressing, the multiple values that make up the individual.

A further issue is the assumptions that are made when developing programmes that target the 'hard-to-reach'. Katz *et al.* (2007) speak about the lack of available research that examines why families might not engage with services, stating that families deemed 'hard-to-reach' by services appear also to be 'hard-to-reach' for researchers. This lack of credible knowledge as to why specific groups remain distant has a direct impact on the evidence base upon which programmes are built. A lack of clarity means that different services and organisations develop their own definitions and categorisations of 'hard-to-reach' and this, in turn, determines how they interpret the needs of individuals within these groups, which then impacts on service delivery (Doherty *et al.*, 2004). The result is often the formation of programmes designed in ways that ensure all persons at which the programme is aimed be considered alike. This in turn results in individuals who remain excluded and discriminated against with their 'voice' eliminated from matters that concern them, and families left feeling even more disconnected from their children's education than before. Therefore, a first true step to inclusion when working with those deemed 'hard-to-reach' is to ensure that we hear the voices of those we seek to engage.

True inclusion is not only empowering for the families involved, but there is also the plurality of re-education or 'transformation' (Young, 2000) whereby those who are otherwise silenced are able to use their voice to question and challenge the thoughts and misconceptions that others may have about them. In order to enter into democratic discussions with families, professionals must be open minded and have a willingness, and the means, to act in some part according to the preferences of these individuals, taking into account their respective needs and differences. At the heart of the democratic process is the 'give and take that often leads to compromise' (Young, 2000: 5). Therefore, an inclusive strategy can be achieved so long as all parties are given a voice and enter into the debate with a willingness to listen.

Individual/group task

When working with families, how might you ensure the voices of those families are heard?

Why is parental participation in service shaping important?

This final section discusses parental engagement and presents real-life examples where the user voice has facilitated and successfully shaped the design and delivery of services for families where one or more young children are experiencing a disability.

The professional role in supporting families whose children experience disability aims to enhance care and education through provision of specialist support, including information, advice and guidance. The shape and nature of specialist support is most effective when parents have authentic involvement in its inception, design, continuation and review. This is referred to as *service shaping*. In the Greater Wirral study (2009), the primary beneficial impact of service shaping was found to be experienced by parents rather than children. This was demonstrated through improved self-confidence, suggesting an overall enhancement to individual value and self-worth may be achieved through participation. Therefore, we can conclude that parents were empowered through service shaping (Pemberton and Mason, 2009). Professionals should believe, unless evidenced otherwise, that parents are the experts on their children, possessing the best understanding of their needs, wishes and well-being. Therefore, an inclusive partnership approach to service shaping with professionals is advocated, where parents have confidence to participate and voice their opinions to meaningfully enhance the quality of service provision for children. Where services are specialist, in particular for disabled children, participation in service shaping can improve inclusivity.

The first robust empirical evidence linking empowerment and parental participation in early years programme development is from the 2005 National Evaluation of Sure Start (Melhuish *et al.*, 2005). This study revealed that children's centres where the whole programme was successfully implemented, including parental involvement as service shapers, had more impact on children's well-being than those that were less able to do so. Crucially, a specific finding was that increased parental empowerment secured through participation in service shaping resulted in improved parent/child relationships, which directly increased early educational outcomes through more stimulating home learning environments for three-year-olds (Belsky *et al.*, 2007). The National Evaluation of Children and Families with Special Needs and Disabilities in Sure Start Local Programmes (Pinney, 2007a) found that it was the way Sure Start Local Programmes delivered services to all families, providing more of them, in more accessible settings with more flexible responses to what parents wanted that made it possible for families with additional needs to participate. Where programmes provided services specifically designed for children with special educational needs and disabilities, like Portage and special playgroups, they were more able to reach children with more complex needs. Parental participation in service shaping can, therefore, be beneficial for both parents and children, enabling professionals to provide services which are desired, needed and utilised.

Individual/group task

Parents are described as *experts* within this section. Do you agree/disagree, and why?

A case study example of effective consultation with parents of young children who experience disability

The case study summarises research by a Sure Start children's centre programme to help engage more families with disabled children and to ensure that the type of service provided is the most appropriate for their needs. Sure Start statutory guidance (DfE, 2013b) requires children's centres to take account of the views of local families and communities in deciding what constitutes sufficient children's centre provision. The core purpose of Sure Start children's centres is to provide accessible, integrated early childhood services for all parents-to-be and families with young children, placing an emphasis on reducing inequalities. Specifically, Sure Start aims:

> to improve outcomes for young children and their families, with a particular focus on families in greatest need of support in order to reduce inequalities in:
>
> - Child development and school readiness
> - Parenting aspirations, self-esteem and
> - Parenting skills; and child and family health and life chances.
>
> (DfE, 2013b: 7)

Sure Start targets families in greatest need of support, including disabled children for whom links with specialist services should be provided. The most recent Sure Start definition, established in the Practice Guidance (2002), of a young disabled child is a child under five experiencing significant developmental delay in one or more of the following developmental areas: cognitive, physical, communication, social, emotional, adaptive, or if they have a condition which has a high probability of resulting in developmental delay (Pinney, 2007b).

Findings from the study

Satisfaction

Parents expressed high levels of satisfaction with services available, valuing the *as and when* intervention of professionals to provide specialist support which enhanced their parent-led group. This flexible, drop-in approach, as discussed earlier by Pinney (2007b), to session attendance minimised pressure felt by parents who often experienced highly scheduled lives to attend other child-related appointments. The ease and comfort of parents is best emphasised in their own words:

> When I walk into the group I feel the weight of the world lift from my shoulder.
> My little boy has come on leaps and bounds by coming to the group.
> It's great to see smiley faces and a warm welcome walking into the room.
> There are children of all ages and all abilities, so I don't feel my little girl is so different.

Parents articulated a desire to celebrate this good example of parent-led provision through sharing experiences with other local parents and children's centre programmes. They were keen that promotion of the service could be made to multi-agency professionals to showcase the value of the activities available to them, including establishing links with the local special school to support transition. In relation to professionals, parents emphasised the requirement to ensure that children with disabilities, parents and carers felt welcomed, comfortable and confident in all groups. This genuinely inclusive approach could be achieved through ensuring staff have training and skills in how to talk to a child, and/or parent, with a visible complex need or disability, and children with behavioural difficulties.

Clarity and transparency

Parents were concerned that clarity and transparency should be improved, both strategically and operationally. They felt the Sure Start brand held a false perception that children's centres are not universally available or of value to families of all socio-economic backgrounds. This may have been exacerbated by the evolution of the original Sure Start Core Offer into the Core Purpose in 2011, following a change in political leadership in 2010. The new requirement of the Core Purpose is to focus service provision upon targeted groups, shifting from the universal service provision previously initiated by New Labour. Families with disabled children did not categorise their needs in this way, and felt uncertain whether they could access services. In particular, they often waited months or even years for formal diagnosis of their child's disability to be confirmed and felt that as children's centres focus on early intervention and prevention no formal diagnosis should be required to access services. Therefore, there is controversy surrounding the Sure Start Core Purpose (DfE, 2012), which outlines the specific definition of a young, disabled child who requires access to services. If parents are authentically perceived as experts on their children, parental concerns regarding their child's well-being should initiate access to services where diagnosis has not been confirmed.

Accessibility

Accessibility could also be developed through introducing different media forms, such as email and social media, to improve the flow of communication, ensuring information is relevant and current, including instructions on how to access services. This can involve development of online registration procedures. Parents felt the introduction of home visits to precede first visits to the centre when a disability or additional need is identified could be beneficial, providing a named person to meet and greet. Within centres, parents requested more information and training about communication and signing, and suggested that display boards contain information about certain conditions and disabilities to raise general awareness as not all disabilities or complex needs are visible. Positive images and photographs of children with a range of disabilities would enhance the inclusiveness of visual displays.

Existing services could be more accessible and inclusive through the development of a resource pack with signposting links to further service provision, which supports the Sure Start Core Purpose (2012), discussed earlier, to promote access to specialist services for families experiencing disability. Development could include the sensory room so its utilisation would increase, providing a sensory room manual to explain how sensory equipment can be best utilised.

Individual/group task

Reflect upon and review accessibility to services within your setting/organisation/placement. Develop an action plan to improve two identified key areas to promote access.

Recommendations for practice

In order to support the expressed interest in further participation of planning and service delivery for disabled children, that is to say *shaping services*, it is recommended that the children's centre works collaboratively with parents to establish a forum. The forum should have strong parental representation to analyse, monitor and review this research and associated action planning. This can include consideration of knowledge, availability, criteria, demographic data, analysis of trends, strategic priorities, performance information, financial planning and evaluating current commissioned service contracts to ensure the needs and opportunities for disabled children are fully understood and met. For this particular local authority, it would also publically and formally acknowledge the empowerment which has taken place through this initial consultation, and provide organisational commitment which enables parents to become more involved in managing the services they and their children access. Continuing participation through structured parent forums where user voice is heard, listened to and initiates change possesses the potential for empowerment to develop within families, concurring with Pemberton and Mason's 2009 study regarding the growth stimulus of service shaping as a tool for empowerment.

Parental participation has recently been recognised in the Children and Families Act (HMG, 2014), where a duty is placed on local authorities to formalise parental and child/young person participation relating to choice of their individual care and also in the shaping of services. Practice recommendations for collective voice include utilisation of parent/carer forums in the design or commissioning of services to ensure that those services are successful in meeting local needs. Parent/carer forums can access central government grant funding to contribute to the additional work they are undertaking with local authorities, which creates increased potential of a rise in status and recognition for parents as equal partners with professionals to influence service provision. These findings and recommendations demonstrate the potential breadth and depth of parental participation, and how harnessing these skills, knowledge and expertise can improve outcomes for disabled children and their families.

Conclusion

This chapter has explored the variety of ways in which inclusion, and its corollary of exclusion, might be experienced by a range of children, young people and their families. No single lived experience is the same, despite public and professional attitudes, and policy initiatives that may seek to persuade otherwise; as such, strategies to foster inclusion and well-being need to focus upon the individuality of families and the specific needs of their members. The concept of 'service shaping' is based on the active participation of persons – service users and professionals – to tailor services to better meet those needs. It is, however, heavily reliant upon the skills and confidence of professionals; the prerequisite communication skills to elicit, and to listen to, the viewpoints of individuals, as well as the humility and willingness to take seriously what is being offered. Subjective knowledges (Gupta and Blewett, 2008) of those experiencing exclusion are often overlooked and undervalued in favour of more dominant professional discourses whereby suitable interventions are constructed within knowledge bases deemed more credible. Discussion provided within this chapter points unequivocally to the need to value families – both parents and their children/young persons – as worthy partners in the way forward to effect positive changes; to work within a rights-based approach whereby the voices of those traditionally silenced, or unacknowledged, are genuinely solicited, listened to and acted upon. In the context of education, it is important that teachers and schools do not 'compound the effects of existing disadvantage with lower expectations for individuals' (EPPSE, 2012: 133); in the context of society as a whole, it is vital that the wider strategy for inclusion is developed in order to sustain hope and optimism for the future (UNICEF, 2012) and to maximise the opportunities for all to contribute to the social, emotional and material wealth of the nation.

Summary points

- Recognition of poverty within the UK, and the potential for damaging present and future life chances, are not taken seriously enough and are compounded by a range of complex and contradictory definitions.
- Deficit framing of children, young people and families living in poverty deny the existence of strengths that have been used to survive and can lead to a poverty-blind approach to professional engagement.
- There is no final definition of what constitutes 'hard-to-reach' in relation to families. Our understanding of the term is shaped by who and what we are and our experiences.
- There is no 'one size fits all' when seeking to engage with families; our efforts should be targeted at individuals and not at any group as a whole.
- There is a significant need to ensure the voice of those seeking to be engaged is obtained; no-one is better able to inform professionals about their needs than the families themselves.
- Parent voice can yield rich and productive recommendations in relation to improving inclusive service provision for young disabled children and their families.
- Parental participation in service shaping in the early years has the potential to improve outcomes for parents and children.

Further reading

Gaine, G. and George, R. (1999) *Gender, 'Race' and Class in Schooling*. London: Falmer Press.

Goodman, A. and Gregg, P. (2010) *Poorer Children's Educational Attainment: How important are attitudes and behaviour?* York: Joseph Rowntree Foundation.

Kay, E., Tisdall, M., Davies, J.M., Hill, M. and Prout, A. (Eds) (2006) *Children, Young People and Social Exclusion*. Bristol: Policy Press.

Lansley, S. and Mack, J. (2015) *Breadline Britain: The rise of mass poverty*. London: Oneworld Publications.

Thompson, N. (2012) *Anti-Discriminatory Practice Equality, Diversity and Social Justice* (5th Edn). Hampshire: Palgrave Macmillan.

Whalley, M. (2007) *Involving Parents in their Children's Learning* (2nd Edn). London: SAGE.

References

Belsky, J., Barnes, J. and Melhuish, E.C. (Eds) (2007) *The National Evaluation of Sure Start: Does area-based early intervention work?* Bristol: The Policy Press.

Booth, T. and Ainscow, M. (2004) *Index for Inclusion: Developing learning, participation and play in early years and childcare.* Bristol: CSIE.

Brooks-Wilson, S. and Snell, C. (2012) 'Hard to reach' or 'accessible when approached'? Sustainable development discussions with marginalized pupil groups. *Children, Youth and Environments*, 22(2), 1–24.

Cemlyn, S., Greenfields, M., Burnett, S., Matthews, Z. and Whitwell, C. (2009) *Inequalities Experienced by Gypsy and Traveller Communities: A review.* Manchester: Equality and Human Rights Commission.

Child Poverty Action Group (CPAG) (2015) *Child Poverty Facts and Figures.* [Blog entry]. www.cpag.org.uk/child-poverty-facts-and-figures (accessed 17 July 2015).

Corby, B. (2006) *Child Abuse: Towards a knowledge base* (3rd Edn) Maidenhead: Open University Press.

DfE (2012) *Core Purpose of Sure Start Children's Centre Programme.* London: DfE.

DfE (2013a) *GCSE and Equivalent Attainment by Pupil Characteristics in England.* London: DfE.

DfE (2013b) *Sure Start Children's Centres Statutory Guidance for Local Authorities: Commissioners of local health services and Jobcentre Plus.* London: DfE.

DfE (2015) *GCSE and Equivalent Attainment by Pupil Characteristics, 2013 to 2014 (Revised).* London: DfE.

Doherty, D., Stott, A. and Kinder, K. (2004) *Delivering Services to Hard to Reach Families in On Track Areas: Definition, Consultation and Needs Assessment.* [Online]. http://webarchive.nationalarchives.gov.uk/20110220105210/rds.homeoffice.gov.uk/rds/pdfs2/dpr15.pdf (accessed 2 July 2015).

Duncan Smith, I. (2015) *Iain Duncan Smith's Statement – Summary.* [Blog entry]. www.theguardian.com/politics/blog/live/2015/jul/01/reaction-as-davies-report-says-new-runway-should-be-at-heathrow-politics-live#block-5593eb33e4b08f71d0eba490 (accessed 16 July 2015).

EPPSE (2012) *Effective Pre-School, Primary and Secondary Education 3–14 Report (EPPSE 3–14): Final report on the Key Stage 3 phase: Influences on students' development from 11–14.* [Online]. www.ioe.ac.uk/KS3_final_report.pdf (accessed 16 July 2015).

Furedi, F. (2008) *Paranoid Parenting.* London: Continuum.

Garnham, A. (2015) While the government officially abolishes child poverty, things are getting worse. [Blog entry]. www.newstatesman.com/politics/2015/07/while-government-officially-abolishes-child-poverty-things-are-getting-worse (accessed 16 July 2015).

Ghate, D. and Hazel, N. (2002) *Parenting in Poor Environments: Stress, support and coping.* London: Jessica Kingsley Publishers.

Gillborn, D. (2015) Intersectionality, critical race theory, and the primacy of racism: Race, class, gender, and disability in education. *Qualitative Inquiry*, 21(3), 277–287.

Greenfields, M. (2008) *A Good Job for a Traveller? Exploring Gypsy and Travellers' perceptions of health and social care careers: Barriers and solutions to recruitment, training and retention of social care students.* Guildford: Aim Higher South East.

Gupta, A. and Blewett, J. (2008) Involving services users in social work training on the reality of family poverty: A case study of a collaborative project. *Social Work Education: The International Journal*, 27(5), 459–473.

Health and Safety Executive (2004) *Successful Interventions with Hard to Reach Groups.* London: HSE.

HMG (2014) *Children and Families Act 2014.* London: The Stationery Office.

Joseph Rowntree Foundation (2012) *Monitoring Poverty and Social Exclusion 2012.* [Online]. www.jrf.org.uk/sites/files/jrf/poverty-exclusion-government-policy-summary.pdf (accessed 16 July 2015).

Katz, I., La Placa, V. and Hunter, S. (2007) *Barriers to Inclusion and Successful Engagement of Parents in Mainstream Services.* York: Joseph Rowntree Foundation.

Lansley, S. and Mack, J. (2015) *Breadline Britain: The rise of mass poverty.* London: Oneworld Publications.

Melhuish, E., Belsky, J. and Leyland, A. (2005) *Early Impacts of Sure Start Local Programmes on Children and Families National Evaluation of Sure Start Research Report 013.* London: HMSO.

NCB (2012) *Fair Society, Healthy Lives: The Marmot Review.* [Online]. www.ncb.org.uk/media/42195/marmotreview_vssbriefing.pdf (accessed 16 July 2015).

Norwich, B. (2002) Education, inclusion and individual differences: Recognising and resolving dilemmas. *British Journal of Educational Studies*, 50(4), 482–502.

ONS (2014) *Gypsy or Irish Travellers Smallest Ethnic Minority at 58,000*. [Online]. www.ons.gov.uk/ons/rel/census/2011-census-analysis/what-does-the-2011-census-tell-us-about-the-characteristics-of-gypsy-or-irish-travellers-in-england-and-wales-/sty-gypsy-or-irish-travellers.html (accessed 15 January 2016).

Palmer, S. (2006) *Toxic Childhood: How the modern world is damaging our children and what we can do about it*. London: Orion Books.

Parry, G., Van Cleemput, P., Peters, J., Walters, S., Thomas, K. and Cooper, C. (2007) Health status of Gypsies and Travellers in England. *Journal of Epidemiology and Community Health*, 61, 198–204.

Pemberton, S. and Mason, J. (2009) Co-production and Sure Start Children's Centres: Reflecting on users' perspectives and implications for serviced delivery, planning and evaluation. *Cambridge: Social Policy & Society*, 8, 13–24.

Petriwskyj, A. (2010) Diversity and inclusion in the early years. *International Journal of Inclusive Education*, 14(2), 195–212.

Pinney, A. (2007a) *The National Evaluation of Children and Families with Special Needs and Disabilities in Sure Start Local Programmes*. London: DfES.

Pinney, A. (2007b) *A Better Start: Children and families with special needs and disabilities in Sure Start Local Programmes*. London: DfES.

Procacci, G. (2007) Genealogies of poverty: From inclusion towards exclusion. *Development*, 50(2), 26–30.

Pugh, G. (2010) Improving outcomes for young children: Can we narrow the gap? *Early Years: An International Research Journal*, 30(1), 5–14.

Ridge, T. (2006) Childhood poverty: A barrier to social participation and inclusion. Participation for what? In E. Kay, M. Tisdall, J.M. Davies, M. Hill and A. Prout (Eds) *Children, Young People and Social Exclusion*. Bristol: Policy Press.

Rouse, M. (2008) Developing inclusive practice: A role for teachers and teacher education? *Education in the North*, 1(16), 1–20.

Strand, S. (2011) The limits of social class in explaining ethnic gaps in educational attainment. *British Educational Research Journal*, 37(2), 197–229.

Stubbs, S. (2008) *Inclusive Education: Where there are few resources*. [Online]. www.eenet.org.uk/resources/docs/IE%20few%20resources%202008.pdf (accessed 16 July 2015).

Treise, C. and Shepherd, G. (2006) Developing mental health services for Gypsy Travellers: An exploratory study, *Clinical Psychology Forum*, 163, 16–19.

UNICEF (2012) Innocenti Research Centre. Report Card 10. *Measuring Child Poverty: New league tables of child poverty in the world's richest countries*. [Online]. www.unicef-irc.org/publications/pdf/rc10_eng.pdf (accessed 16 July 2015).

Van Cleemput, P. (2007) Health impact of Gypsy sites policy in the UK. *Social Policy and Society*, 7(1), 103–117.

Washbrook, E. (2010) *Low Income and Early Cognitive Development*. London: Sutton Trust.

Young, I.M. (2000) *Inclusion and Democracy*. Oxford: Oxford University Press.

Part II
Inclusion through the stages of learning

6 Inclusive practice in early childhood education

Zeta Brown and Ioanna Palaiologou

Introduction

> It has been argued that early education at its best *is* inclusive education – perhaps because of its emphasis on individual needs, developmentally appropriate practice and intrinsic involvement of parents.
>
> (Nutbrown, 1998, cited in Nutbrown and Clough, 2004: 303)

In the last two decades, the field of early childhood education and care in England has been transformed and is still witnessing changes. Central to all the changes in the field was the creation of 'joined-up' thinking where a varied range of services such as nurseries, pre-schools, child minders and social workers aimed to work in a multi-agency, multi-departmental way in order to allow all children and their families to get the best start in life. There was also an attempt to ensure that all the changes in the field at policy and curriculum level were aimed at achieving equality of opportunity for all children and their families as well as ensuring anti-discriminatory practice so that all children are included and supported. In that sense, Nutbrown's quote reflects the core element in early childhood education and care for an inclusive provision. However, Nutbrown importantly stated that only *at its best* is early years inclusive practice possible. This is because inclusive practice is complex: it cannot simply be considered ideologically and instead tensions need to be considered that may exist in practically implementing inclusion in the early childhood.

In this chapter, we start by discussing the complexity involved in defining inclusive practice, especially in early childhood. We deliberately avoid discussing the historical development of inclusion here as this is detailed at the beginning of Chapter 7. Instead we consider Nutbrown's (1998) three areas of early childhood practice: the emphasis on individual needs, developmentally appropriate practice and involvement of parents/carers. When discussing these areas of practice, we consider tensions that may exist between the philosophies of inclusive practice and its practical implementation. These include the influence of practitioners' perspectives and the need to consider both inclusion and social inclusion in early childhood. Case studies from early years advisers and Ofsted are used as examples of practice.

Individual/group task

Before you read the rest of this chapter, consider Nutbrown's statement on inclusive practice in relation to your observed or researched knowledge of early childhood practice.

Do you think inclusive practice is able to be fully implemented in today's early childhood education?

Complexity in defining inclusion

Despite multiple policies such as the Children Act 2004 and Every Child Matters, the Race Relations Amendments Act 2002, the Children's Plan 2007 and academic writing about inclusive practice in early childhood education, there remains confusion about what 'inclusion' means. There are multiple definitions present in publications that range from focusing on children being placed in early childhood provision to considering changes made to provision in order to accommodate children's educational needs. As Nutbrown *et al.* (2013: 8) state, 'there are as many "versions" of inclusion as there are early-years settings – or, indeed as individuals who make up those particular cultures of living and learning'. For the purpose of this chapter, inclusion is considered as 'the unified drive towards maximal participation in and minimal exclusion from early years settings, from schools and from society' (Booth *et al.*, 2006: 8). In this sense, all children should be provided with the opportunity to be included in early childhood education. This form of social inclusion encourages a participatory approach where all families feel welcome and all children feel belonging as valued learners. However, in order to be fully inclusive early childhood settings need to adapt their provisions, resources, methods and implementation of the curriculum to accommodate the needs of all children (Frederickson and Cline, 2009). These principles of inclusion are comparable with the *Index for Inclusion* in early childhood (Booth and Ainscow, 2004: 4). That definition of inclusion focused on a need to value all pupils and view difference as a resource to support development and learning. The *Index for Inclusion* provides a detailed list of how inclusion should be implemented in practice:

- Increasing the participation of children and young people in, and reducing their exclusion from, the cultures, activities and communities of local settings.
- Valuing equally, all children, young people, parents/carers and practitioners.
- Viewing the differences between children as resources to support play and learning, rather than as problems to overcome.
- Acknowledging the right of children to good-quality education and childcare in their locality.
- Making improvements for practitioners as well as children.
- Reducing barriers to play, learning and participation for all children, not only those with impairments or those who are categorised as having 'special educational needs'.
- Learning from attempts to overcome barriers for children whose play, learning and/or participation is a focus of concern, to make changes that benefit children more widely.
- Emphasising the development of community and values, as well as achievements.
- Fostering mutually sustaining relationships between settings and communities.
- Recognising that inclusion in early education is an aspect of inclusion in society.

This approach to inclusive practice moves away from normative methods of categorising children and instead provides differentiated pedagogies that consider the varied characteristics of learners. Nutbrown and Clough (2009: 193) state:

> Inclusion is a social and political struggle where individual identity and difference has prominence. In early childhood achieving an inclusive setting means change for the entire setting and *all* practitioners who work there … it's important to recognise that issues of inclusion are part of the core of current UK governmental agenda applying to *all* children, not 'only' to children identified as having particular and identified learning needs.

Because inclusive practice encompasses all children, exclusion becomes focused on barriers that hinder its practical implementation (Booth and Ainscow, 2004).

 Individual/group task

Consider the *Index for Inclusion*'s definition of inclusive practice. Reflect on your time in practice. Can you remember incidences where these inclusive strategies have been used in your settings?

Emphasis on individual need

The Early Years Foundation Stage (EYFS) states:

> practitioners must consider the individual needs, interests and stage of development of each child in their care and must use this information to plan a challenging and enjoyable experience for each child in all of the areas of learning and development.
>
> (DfE, 2014: 8)

This emphasis on individual need encourages practitioners to consider the nature of each and every child as a unique person. The process of considering individual need in this way would be considered as inclusive practice, as it is not associated with categorising children into specific marginalised groups. Instead, all children's needs, stage of development and interests should be considered to plan for their learning and development. Considering children's learning styles is also important in early childhood, with the EYFS promoting the awareness of characteristics of effective learning. These include:

- playing and exploring (engagement)
- active learning (motivation)
- creating and thinking critically (thinking).

These characteristics are seen to support the development of children's prime areas (personal, social and emotional development, communication and language, physical development), specific areas (literacy, mathematics, understanding the word and expressive arts and design) and development

(Early Education, 2012). However, Siraj-Blatchford (2004: 182) states that settings can vary in the impact they have on children's learning and development outcomes. Inequality may occur through 'the implementation of differential policies, adult interactions, the use of displays, or through variations (or lack of variation) in the planning, curriculum or programme that the staff offer to individuals or groups'. An inclusive setting, according to the *Index for Inclusion*, develops continuously and, while full inclusion may be desirable, Booth and Ainscow (2004) state that it could never be fully achieved. This is because of exclusionary pressures that are either persistent or present in new forms over time.

Corbett and Slee (2000) consider there to be three levels to inclusion. The first is surface inclusion, which is led by policy; the second is focused on changes accommodated in practice; and the third, deepest, level considers areas such as values and acceptance by practitioners to implement inclusive practice. Petriwskyj (2010: 1) states 'this suggests a shift in philosophies of inclusion that encompasses more positive images of diverse children and goes beyond surface adjustments'. Nutbrown (1996, cited in Nutbrown and Clough, 2009: 192) states respectful educators will include all children,

> not just children who are easy to work with, obliging, endearing, clean, pretty, articulate, capable, but every child – respecting them for who they are, respecting their language their culture, their history, their family, their abilities, their needs, their name, their ways and their very essence.

However, in research on inclusion as an 'agenda', practitioners' and teachers' perspectives on inclusion are commonly pragmatic (Avramidis and Norwich, 2002; Croll and Moses, 2003). This means that they believe in the ideological concept of inclusion, but consider there to be barriers to its full practical implementation.

Barriers to inclusive practice in early childhood may include 'practical, attitudinal and policy issues that require resolution if deep level inclusion is to be a reality' (Petriwskyj, 2010: 2). Guralnick (2001, cited in Petriwskyj, 2010) considers that the stigma associated with difference needs to be reduced in some early childhood settings. Staff confidence in implementing inclusive practice and the need for more professional development opportunities appear to resonate in a number of studies as barriers to inclusion (Nutbrown and Clough, 2004). Siraj-Blatchford (2014: 182) says that children can be disadvantaged in early childhood education, 'on the grounds of diversity in ethnic background, gender and socioeconomic class in both intentional and unintentional ways'. Siraj-Blatchford goes on to also state the disadvantage that can be present for children with special educational needs (SEN). For instance, children with emotional and behavioural difficulties (EBD) can prove a challenge to implementing inclusive practice as their behaviour may threaten the social order of the setting (Nutbrown and Clough, 2004). Thomas and Loxley (2007: 48–49) contend that the categorisation and stereotyping that can be present in identifying EBD in children continue to be a 'powerful subtext that the real causes of difficult behaviour lie in deficit and deviance in the child'. Therefore, the differences present in children may be seen as the reason for exclusion, which contradicts the principles of inclusive practice and instead focuses on a normative deficit model (known as the medical model).

Thomas and Loxley (2007: 147) state 'one can suggest that the alienation and exclusion experienced by students are constructed largely out of comparison of each student herself or himself with others and the institutional endorsement of such comparison by teachers and other professionals'. Inclusive practice is about celebrating difference and the unique nature of all children. Booth and Ainscow (2004: 4) state:

> in respecting difference this means we avoid creating hierarchies based on such differences. To include any child we have to be concerned with the whole person. This can be neglected when inclusion is focused on only one aspect of a child, such as an impairment, or a need to learn English as an additional language ... we have to avoid thinking in stereotypes.

This means there is a variety of ways to include children in early childhood provision; however, the right methods need to be considered for every individual child. The case study below details an example of a child with characteristics that could be perceived as being part of two marginalised groups and the inclusive approaches that were put in place to meet her learning needs.

Case study from an early years adviser

A child was brought to the attention of an advisor during a routine support visit as causing concern. She had recently joined the pre-school at age three with EAL and was attending for all five morning sessions.

The main concern raised by the setting staff was around behaviour, with the child frequently hiding in some very creative places. Staff knew she was safe as their environment was secure but it was often difficult to find her. She also found it difficult to share space with other children and join in activities, even for a short period of time. This resulted in frequent noisy outbursts from the child and upset for other children around her. As she had very little understanding or use of English, the setting staff initially felt this was the cause of her challenging behaviour.

To work towards meeting this child's needs, her key worker was tasked with noting careful observations to look for possible triggers for her behaviour and to consider appropriate support. Evaluation of these observations led to staff questioning whether EAL was indeed the root of the issue. With parental permission, advice was sought from the local SEYS (Specialist Early Years Service). Following observations and assessments, it became clear that the child had significant learning difficulties and speech and language delay in her home language. This led to specialist support both on-site and through the local SALT (Speech and Language Therapy) team. This sensitive work with the child's family, and early intervention by appropriate specialist support, enabled the setting to better understand and work towards helping her to enjoy pre-school and meet her needs.

✎ **Individual/group task**

Can you list other groups that are seen as marginalised in early years education? Consider the multiple differing identities children can have when they are considered in relation to more than one marginalised group. From this list, think of some inclusive approaches that could be put in place to meet their individual needs.

Thomas and Loxley (2007) discuss the inclusive need to consider children's belongingness, connectedness and promotion of a community of learners. Ofsted (2013) provides an example of good practice where children in one setting were considered in terms of their individual needs and encouraged to work together to decide on aspects of their learning and development. This is detailed in the below case study.

Case study from Ofsted

Newstead Children's Centre has a children's committee that decides on annual outings. All children in the centre are involved in the committee and often state their choice of outing by using a token system. Children are offered a small choice of settings – for instance, the farm or seaside – and asked to decide which one they would prefer. Before they make their choice, children research the differing venues with the help of adults. Ofsted state that this method of collaborative decision-making provides valuable opportunities to understand 'negotiation, fairness, considering the needs of others and researching the options'. One of the children's centre teachers said 'it is a good lesson for children to learn about compromising and making decisions in a fair way'.

Individual/group task

Make a list of links considering this case study on involving children in decision-making with philosophies on inclusive practice detailed in the definition of inclusive practice and emphasising individual need sections of this chapter.

Once you have completed your list, consider how inclusive this example is. Why is it seen as good practice? Do you have any ideas of how this activity could be extended to further consider children's individual needs?

Inclusive practice, therefore, can be seen to educate practitioners in considering equality, diversity and children's rights. This in turn provides a richer learning experience for all children (Frederickson and Cline, 2009). As Siraj-Blatchford (2014: 181) states:

> [in] modern, diverse societies, and a world that increasingly recognises the realities of global interdependence, it is essential that children learn social competence to respect other groups and individuals, regardless of difference. This learning must begin in the earliest years of a child's education. Learning is thus culturally and socially influenced by the context of the child's development.

Developmentally appropriate practice

In 2008, the EYFS curriculum established the English standards for early childhood providers. These standards specifically focused on children from birth to five years of age (DfE, 2008). The framework is mandatory for all early childhood providers and was revised in 2014 (DfE, 2014). The four guiding principles of the current EYFS are as follows (DfE, 2014: 5–6):

- Every child is a unique child, who is constantly learning and can be resilient, capable, confident and self-assured.
- Children learn to be strong and independent through positive relationships.
- Children learn and develop well in enabling environments, in which their experiences respond to their individual needs and there is a strong partnership between practitioners and parents and/or carers.
- Children develop and learn in different ways and at different rates. The framework covers the education and care of all children in early years.

 Individual/group task

Consider these four principles in relation to the philosophies of inclusive practice detailed so far in this chapter. In your opinion, how inclusive are they?

The EYFS curriculum uses developmentally appropriate practice, which can be defined as 'curriculum and pedagogy based upon agreed stages of children's development. It is a framework of principles and guidelines for best practice in the care and education of young children...' (Bredekamp and Copple, 1997: 24). However, there are tensions that exist in its use; as Gipps and MacGilchrist (1999, cited in Petriwskyj, 2010: 197) suggest, the definition of quality in early childhood is a contested issue. They state 'the traditional schooling focus on effective content delivery and the traditional early childhood focus on developmental play have both been challenged by child-responsive, but educationally focused pedagogies located in socio-cultural understanding about learners and learning'. Since the introduction of the EYFS curriculum in 2008, Nutbrown and Clough (2009) state its content can be described as considering issues of citizenship. It is apparent that the EYFS considers issues of inclusion as it seeks to provide quality and consistency for all learners, a secure foundation for all learners and partner working (between practitioners and with parents/carers), and to promote equality of opportunity and anti-discriminatory practice.

There is, however, also a focus in the curriculum on readiness for primary school and assessment of children's learning, assessing children against developmentally appropriate criteria. The EYFS states:

> Assessment plays an important part in helping parents, carers and practitioners to recognise children's progress, understand their needs, and to plan and support. Ongoing assessment (also known as formative assessment) is an integral part of the learning and development process. It involves practitioners observing children to understand their level of achievement, interests and learning styles, and to then shape learning experiences of each child reflecting those observations. In their interactions with children, practitioners should respond to their own day-to-day observations about children's progress and observations that parents and carers share.

(DfE, 2014: 13)

There are also three key assessments in early childhood that are applicable for all children. The first is when children are aged two to three, known as the 'Two Year Old Progress Check', which, in September 2015, was replaced with the Integrated Review, where practitioners review their progress and provide a short written summary to their parents. The summary is focused on development in the three prime areas. The second assessment – Baseline – is the most recent to be established and was piloted from September 2015. Children entering reception may undertake a screening test to support their progression in primary education and predict their outcomes at the end of each key stage. At present, schools are able to choose the screening test they would like to use from a collection of recognised assessments for this age range. Moreover, the third and final assessment is in the final term of the year before children enter Year 1 in primary schools. This is the Early Years Foundation Stage Profile (EYFSP), which is completed to provide 'parents, and carers, practitioners and teachers with a well-rounded picture of a child's knowledge, understanding and abilities, their progress against expected levels and their readiness for Year 1' (DfE, 2014: 14). Children need to be assessed against the early learning goals and practitioners need to indicate whether children are meeting expected levels of development.

However, the assessment processes against developmental targets of the EYFS in England raise issues around the inclusive nature of such a developmentally related approach to assessment. It is now statutory for all children to meet what the politicians and policy makers consider as academic or developmentally appropriate achievements for formal education and schooling. It is assumed that children's learning is 'universal' and that all children's learning can be achieved at a certain age by a legislated curriculum which describes in detail the type of knowledge and learning that is considered worthwhile for our society. Yet, again, reflecting on the opening quote by Nutbrown, early childhood is a multicultural environment with children from a number of ethnicities, languages, cultures, beliefs and values, so the remaining issue is how a developmentally appropriate approach to assessment meets the 'needs' of the individual child, which is core to inclusive practice.

Nutbrown and Clough (2009) note the difficulty that can be presented when practitioners are trying to raise achievement and at the same time promote inclusive practice. At their best, early childhood settings will endeavour to promote inclusive practice at the same time as effectively supporting every child's learning and development. However, what is seen as appropriate development can be contested. It is disputed whether a national curriculum is inclusive because of its use of set developmental criteria that may disadvantage children who are not developing age-appropriately. For instance, some children with SEN cannot always meet nationally age-appropriate standards (Bines, 2000). Armstrong (2005) argues that inclusion is a normative concept, conceptualised in terms of conformity with existing standards and objectives, and in effect provides children with SEN with an 'opportunity to conform'.

To conclude, although EYFS promotes inclusion of all children, the creation of a 'universal' 'correct' developmental line to measure children's progress can become problematic in the creation of an inclusive environment. Emphasis on developmentally appropriate assessment modes can be limited and leaves no space for the child as a learner. Instead, the environment creates the 'performer child', where the performativity, outcomes and outputs are observable and measurable (Palaiologou, 2012a). Consequently, the creation of an inclusive environment might be at risk.

✎ **Individual/group task**

Study the current version of the EYFS in England, then compare it with the Wales Foundation Stage, and the Scottish early childhood curriculum and the Northern Ireland one. Here
are some useful web links to help you access the information you will need:

>   Northern Ireland early childhood provision: www.deni.gov.uk
>   Scotland early childhood provision: www.educationscotland.gov.uk
>   Wales early childhood provision: http://gov.wales/topics/educationandskills/?lang=en

Critically consider whether consideration of standards and inclusion can be implemented at
the same time, by either researching literature on this area or reflecting on observations in
practice.

Intrinsic involvement of parents and carers

Research such as the Effective Provision of Pre-School Education (EPPE) project has highlighted
the importance of attending early childhood provision, especially for disadvantaged children (Sylva
et al., 2004). In terms of inclusion, it is important that children and parents/carers feel that they
can participate in early childhood settings. The *Index for Inclusion* (Booth and Ainscow, 2004)
outlined the importance of the setting, staff, children and parents belonging to a community of its
members. As Cross and Walker-Knight (1997, cited in Frederickson and Cline, 2009: 90) state,
'inclusive settings must emphasise building a community in which everyone belongs and is
accepted and supported by his or her peers and other members of that community while his or her
educational needs are being met'. At its best, all children and their families should have access to
early childhood education and be involved in their child's development.

The theory of social capital, developed by noted theorists such as Bourdieu and Putnam,
intrinsically links to this form of inclusion. According to Putnam, social capital is 'the connectedness amongst people, the social networks and the norms of reciprocity and trustworthiness that
arise from them' (cited in Thomas and Loxley, 2007: 149). Nutbrown *et al.* (2013) note that early
childhood education is largely participatory in the sense that parents are encouraged to be intrinsically involved. However, parental involvement can be interpreted in various ways by differing practitioners and settings.

Ideologically it would be desirable to think that all families are equally included in early childhood provision. However, in reality this is not always the case. Nutbrown and Clough (2006, cited
in Nutbrown and Clough, 2009: 195) give a non-exhaustive list of reasons why families may be
excluded from early childhood education (Table 6.1).

The reasons for exclusion and families seen as hard-to-reach in early childhood directly
compare to Chapter 5 in this book on inclusion for families. The case study below also provides an
example of one early childhood setting which ran an inclusion programme for families who have
English as an additional language (EAL).

Table 6.1 Reasons why families may be excluded from early childhood education (Nutbrown and Clough, 2006, cited in Nutbrown and Clough, 2009: 195)

Age	Language
Achievement	Location
Challenging behaviour	Mental health
Disability	Obesity
Disaffection	Physical impairment
Educational qualifications	Poverty
Emotional and behavioural difficulty	'Race'/ethnicity
Employment	Religion
Gender	Sexual orientation
Housing	Social class
Illness	Special educational need

Case study from an early years adviser

As part of a project focusing on parent partnership, we worked with a school who wanted to find a way to engage with parents prior to their children joining their maintained nursery.

The families were predominately of Asian origin with little English spoken by the mothers. Opportunities to come into school prior to entry were rarely taken up, resulting in children arriving on their first day with no preparation and consequently many were upset and found it difficult to settle in.

Two advisers and a member of staff from the school organised a stay and play session, with refreshments, and invited families of children due to start nursery the next term to join us. Six families took up the offer from a cohort of thirty.

Engaging with the families at this very informal event we found they were interested in learning English nursery rhymes as they had few traditional rhymes to share with their children. They agreed to join us for an afternoon each week for the last half term of the school year. The meetings took place in a section of the nursery unit to help the children and families become familiar with the environment and meet nursery staff.

At each session we learnt a new rhyme together, shared food and explored craft materials. At the end of each session, they took some craft materials home to continue exploring together. During the last session, we produced a DVD with all of the rhymes we had learnt on, giving a copy to each family so they could carry on singing the rhymes together at home.

To evaluate impact, we revisited the school after the children had started nursery. Staff reported that the children who had attended the sessions had settled well with few issues. Parents said they felt confident to leave their children, were very pleased with their start in school and were telling other families that it was a good idea to go to sessions that the school offer.

Following on from this, the school offered the same opportunity to the next cohort and had so much demand they had to run several sessions a week to fit everyone in. Very quickly this induction process became expected by their families and supported positive first experiences for the children.

Conclusion

Throughout this chapter, we have attempted to discuss and problematise key issues of inclusion in early childhood. As has been demonstrated in other chapters, inclusion is a complex social construct that, despite any legislation, is difficult to achieve in practice. In the field of early childhood, and in the light of the United Nations Convention of the Rights of the Child, the dominant construction of childhood is as children who are active citizens and agents, of having voice and who can participate actively at all levels of their lives. In this participatory context that is strongly promoted in early childhood, inclusion as a concept becomes even more complex as all children have the right to be included and participate in all aspects of their lives. However, for some children, due to socio-economic factors (poverty), cultural factors (the right not to participate) or individual differences (such as lack of linguistic articulation due to disability), this right might not be accessible. We argue, extending the *Index of Inclusion*, that the key elements for inclusion in early childhood are:

- the partnerships with parents and communication with them
- listening to the 'hundred languages' (Malaguzzi, 1993) that children use to communicate
- informal assessment and documentation of children's work as the starting point for the discussion among staff, children and parents, and
- the physical environment that is important for the emotional stability of the children (Palaiologou, 2008).

In such an environment, the child can be seen as a co-constructor of knowledge and identity as s/he appears to be an equal partner in the pedagogical practices and inclusion can flourish.

Creating autonomous learners and placing them in active control of their learning process requires certain pedagogical practices, ones enabling and empowering children in their development and learning process and becoming the facilitator of their own learning. This process can lead children towards embracing an embedded cultural relativism and provide core elements for an inclusive practice.

We suggest, therefore, that an inclusive environment in early childhood is one that creates opportunities for the empowerment of the children, their families and practitioners and respects the individual's own rhythm of development. Moreover, inclusion requires a shift from the non-participant child to a child as a social actor, an individual who enacts agency, as well as a demand for the inclusion of the voices of children. This shift creates a space in which children are considered valuable experts in their culture, as beings who have knowledge and insight to offer, and therefore as integral partners in the pedagogical process (Palaiologou, 2012b). The child, and consequently childhood, appears to be a social construct in an inclusive environment in early childhood education.

Another influential element for inclusion in early childhood is the reciprocal relationships among child, family and community, characteristics that allow dynamic interactions between all stakeholders in early childhood education and provide the basis for understanding all involved. In that sense, inclusion should not be limited only to the development of children and their learning outcomes, but should be broadened to the social, cultural, localised contexts where learning episodes are situated in children's behaviours and identities as learners. Early childhood inclusive environments should seek to explore the notion that children should participate 'on the basis of who they are, rather than who they will become' (Moss, 2002: 6). In other words, they are considered social citizens in their own right, rather than future citizens in waiting.

Consequentially, it is argued that to achieve inclusive curriculum practice the child should be viewed as co-constructor of knowledge, identity and culture. Children should be recognised as a social group in their own right, a group who shares with others a place in society. The child should be perceived as socially constructed and embedded within a local context, recognised as being a social actor, having agency, belonging to a unique culture and engaged in worthwhile, meaningful social relationships. Children's voices should be the catalyst for engagement; thus, early childhood pedagogy should aim to alter its method so as to place the child in position of knower (Palaiologou, 2012b).

Summary points

- Inclusion is a complex construct and there are a number of factors that impact on creation of inclusive environments, such as economic, policy, cultural differences, children's needs and assessment processes.
- The limitation on fixed standards around development and learning allows no space for autonomous, creative and constructive inclusive early childhood practice. It is important for the early childhood education to be able to allow space so that children, families and practitioners are able to express their voices. Inclusive environments should focus on each context and consider what works in each setting.
- To be achieved, inclusion needs a number of conditions with policy makers, practitioners, professionals and teachers valuing the importance of the localised context. We need to start with understanding of the stakeholders of early childhood education in order to empower our practice with reflection and critical examination.
- Examining the context of inclusion, which is framed by political, economical, social and pedagogical demands, it is concluded that inclusion in early childhood education does not, of course, happen in isolation. There are strong influences from the establishment, policy and curriculum to which all of us need to work in compliance.

Further reading

Booth, T. and Ainscow, M. (2004) *Index for Inclusion. Developing learning, participation and play in early years and childcare.* Bristol: CSIE.

Frederickson, N. and Cline, T. (2009) *Special Educational Needs, Inclusion and Diversity* (2nd edn). Maidenhead: Open University Press.

Nutbrown, C., Clough, P. and Atherton, F. (2013) *Inclusion in the Early Years.* London: SAGE.

Siraj-Blatchford, I. (2014) Diversity, inclusion and learning in the early years. In G. Pugh and B. Duffy (Eds) *Contemporary Issues in the Early Years* (6th edn). London: Sage Publications.

References

Armstrong, D. (2005) Reinventing 'inclusion': New Labour and the cultural politics of special education. *Oxford Review of Education*, **31**(1), 135–151.

Avramidis, E. and Norwich, B. (2002) Teachers' attitudes towards integration/inclusion: A review of the literature. *European Journal of Special Needs Education*, **17**(2), 129–147.

Bines, H. (2000) Inclusive standards? Current developments in policy for special educational needs in England and Wales. *Oxford Review of Education*, **26**(1), 21–33.

Booth, T. and Ainscow, M. (2004) *Index for Inclusion. Developing learning, participation and play in early years and childcare.* Bristol: CSIE.

Booth, T., Ainscow, M. and Kingston, D. (2006) Cited in C. Nutbrown, P. Clough and F. Atherton (2013) *Inclusion in the Early Years.* London: SAGE.

Bredekamp, S. and Copple, C. (1997) Cited in C. Nutbrown, P. Clough and F. Atherton (2013) *Inclusion in the Early Years.* London: SAGE.

Corbett, J. and Slee, R. (2000) An international conversation on inclusive education. In F. Armstrong, D. Armstrong and L. Barton (Eds) *Inclusive Education: Policy, contexts and comparative perspectives.* London: David Fulton.

Croll, P. and Moses, D. (2003) Special educational needs across two decades: Survey evidence from English primary schools. *British Educational Research Journal*, **29**(5), 731–747.

DfE (2008) *Statutory Framework for the Early Years Foundation Stage. Setting the standards for learning, development and care for children from birth to five.* London: HMSO.

DfE (2014) *Statutory Framework for the Early Years Foundation Stage. Setting the standards for learning, development and care for children from birth to five.* London: HMSO.

Early Education (2012) *Development Matters in the Early Years Foundation Stage.* London: The British Association for Early Childhood Education.

Frederickson, N. and Cline, T. (2009) *Special Educational Needs, Inclusion and Diversity* (2nd edn). Maidenhead: Open University Press.

Malaguzzi, L. (1993) For an education based on relationships. *Young Children*, November, 9–13.

Moss, P. (2002) From children's services to children's spaces. Paper presented at *ESCR* seminar *Challenging Social Inclusion: Perspectives for and from children and young people*, University of Stirling.

Nutbrown, C. and Clough, P. (2004) Special educational needs and inclusion: Multiple perspectives on pre-school educators in the UK. *Journal of Early Childhood Research*, **2**(2), 191–211.

Nutbrown, C. and Clough, P. (2009) Citizenship and inclusion in the early years: Understanding and responding to children's perspectives on belonging. *International Journal of Early Years Education*, **17**(3), 191–206.

Nutbrown, C., Clough, P. and Atherton, F. (2013) *Inclusion in the Early Years.* London: SAGE.

Ofsted (2013) *Involving Children in Decision-making: Newstead Children's Centre.* [Online]. www.gov.uk/government/uploads/system/uploads/attachment_data/file/392153/Newstead_20Children_27s_20Centre_20_20good_20practice_20example.pdf (accessed 26 August 2015).

Palaiologou, I. (2008) *Achieving Early Years Professional Status: Childhood observation.* Exeter: Learning Matters.

Palaiologou, I. (2012a) Introduction: Towards an understanding of ethical practice in early childhood. In I. Palaiologou (Ed.) *Ethical Practice in Early Childhood.* London: SAGE.

Palaiologou, I. (2012b) *Child Observation for the Early Years* (2nd edn). London: Learning Matters.

Petriwskyj, A. (2010) Diversity and inclusion in the early years. *International Journal of Inclusive Education*, **14**(2), 195–212.

Siraj-Blatchford, I. (2014) Diversity, inclusion and learning in the early years. In G. Pugh and B. Duffy (Eds) *Contemporary Issues in the Early Years* (6th edn). London: Sage Publications.

Sylva, K., Melhuish, E., Sammons, P., Siraj-Blatchford, I. and Taggart, B. (2004) *The Effective Provision of Pre-School Education (EPPE) Project* (2nd edn). Nottingham: DfES.

Thomas, G. and Loxley, A. (2007) *Deconstructing Special Education and Constructing Inclusion* (2nd edn). Maidenhead: Open University Press.

7 Primary teachers' perspectives on implementing the inclusion agenda

Zeta Brown

Introduction

This chapter considers the inclusion agenda in UK mainstream primary schools. There have been multiple pieces of legislation and policy on inclusive practice since the development of inclusive practice in 1997. Inclusion in primary schools is seen as an ideological concept where all mainstream educated children will one day be included in every aspect of the schooling experience. However, inclusion is not the only priority in primary schools and this chapter investigates how inclusion can be implemented alongside the competing standards agenda. The standards agenda has been developed since education legislation was established from 1988 to instil achievement and accountability in schools. These policies generated the National Curriculum, Statutory Assessment Tests (SATs) and league tables to ensure that teachers and schools were accountable for their actions. The chapter will detail the development of these agendas simultaneously and draw on recent findings that will consider whether inclusion and standards can be implemented in tandem.

 Individual/group task

Before you read this chapter, consider what inclusive practice means to you.

Do you think inclusive practice is able to be fully implemented in today's primary education system?

The Warnock Report and the development of integration

The great social changes of the 1960s and 1970s, fuelled by Labour's socialist consensus, prompted a significant development in attitudes towards disabled people alongside other oppressed groups. In the early 1970s, there was a radical re-examination of disability, which encouraged a move away from focusing upon children's medical needs towards considering their needs from a societal perspective (Hodkinson and Vickerman, 2009). Disabled children's segregation from mainstream schools was addressed in the Education (Handicapped Children) Act (1970), which determined that all children were educable and supported the view that a greater range of pupils should be educated in mainstream settings. More children should be offered mainstream places if it was practical, if their education was compatible with mainstream education and if it was within a reasonable amount of public expenditure (Thomas and Vaughan, 2004).

The Warnock Committee started working on integration strategies from the government a few years after the Education Act (1970). The Warnock Report (1978) developed a number of key concepts which are still impacting today's schools, and generated a new terminology that remains intact in educational discourse. The report investigated the use of integration and found three types used in varying degrees across mainstream schools. First, there was 'locational integration', where separate units were used inside mainstream schools for children with special educational needs (SEN); 'social integration' with children from these special units included eating and playing alongside their mainstream peers; and 'functional integration', where children with SEN had classes or activities alongside their peers, either part- or full-time. The Warnock Report endorsed all of these types of integration, and in doing so integration appeared to address only the placement of children with SEN into mainstream settings (Slee, 1997).

The Warnock Report changed the terminology used to describe children with SEN and this was linked to encouraging an increase in integration. Mary Warnock (author of the report) stated that teachers must be willing to accept a wide concept of SEN, where 5–6 children per class would have an SEN that required temporary or permanent support. However, at the same time the use of new terms detailing generalised educational needs led to children already mainstream-educated being assessed as having an 'SEN'. The Warnock Report also expanded on the assessment process, attempting to move away from clinical assessment. Instead it had three criteria for entry to mainstream schools: children were assessed to determine whether they would cope in mainstream, whether it would be a good use of resources and whether integration would hinder the education of their peers (Northway, 1997). This criterion highlighted that children with SEN would be entering an education system designed primarily for their peers. Only those closest to their mainstream peers could be successfully integrated and would then struggle in an established mainstream system. Nevertheless, for teachers and schools, this led to a decade of increased diversity within their classrooms but without clear guidance about what they should do once children with SEN had entered their class.

 Individual/group task

From the information provided on integration, can you define the term 'integration'?
   How do you think this is different from the term 'inclusion'?

The development of the standards agenda

In the mid-1970s, there was an economic recession which saw high inflation and low economic growth undermine Labour's socialist consensus. There was a growing influence of trade unions and an influx of strong criticisms came from leading industrialists and employers. These criticisms blamed the education system and Labour's socialist perspective for the lack of skilled employees in the workforce (Chitty, 1989). Labour Prime Minister James Callaghan (1976–1979) famously gave his Ruskin speech emphasising the need for teacher accountability and a central control of the curriculum. However, it was the Conservative party, elected in 1979, that developed the standards agenda in education. The Conservatives' answer to the growing educational concerns was to change education into a marketable commodity. In doing so, Prime Minister Margaret Thatcher wanted to increase the power of the 'consumer' and reduce the power held by the 'producers' (Whitty, 2008).

The Education Act (1988) decentralised power from local education authorities (LEA) and centralised control whilst empowering the parents' role. In effect, the schooling system became 'privatised', accountable to an external audience, the general public. For the first time, LEAs had to acknowledge parental choice, and schools henceforth had to appeal to parents. Consequently, this developed the first phase of a new competitive ethos amongst schools, promoting a market-led change in the education system. The education system was redesigned to enable greater centralised control. Both LEAs and teachers by this point had had their autonomy reduced by the government and their trust damaged within society; they were positioned as not responding to the needs of the consumer (Strain and Simkins, 2008).

The Education Reform Act (1988) consolidated these changes further, reducing teachers' responsibility for designing their curriculum and using their professional judgement with regard to standards. The Act sought to develop a national curriculum where all mainstream pupils were to benefit from the same knowledge. The government proposed to provide a nationally accredited curriculum that not only developed each child spiritually, morally, culturally, mentally and physically, but also targeted their educational development for adult employability.

In 1991, the Parents' Charter was introduced, which gave parents the right to information about their local schools based upon their performance. The target for parental knowledge became two-fold: in the use of public assessment process and also inspections of individual schools. Summative assessment results at the end of each key stage, named Statutory Assessment Tests (SATs), were used to develop a national form of assessment. For primary schools this meant English, Maths and, initially Science tasks (subsequently changed to teacher assessment for Science) in Key Stage 1 and SATs in English, Maths and Science in Key Stage 2. In 1992, these results became publicly available in national league tables, where schools were ranked according to the number of children who achieved the desired 'national average'. The publication of the SATs results in league tables prioritised the SATs process as high-stake tests for schools. The results produced by the SAT process were used to judge school and teacher success. The Education Act (1992) also instituted the Office for Standards in Education (Ofsted). Following this act, schools were subject to inspection every four years to ensure they were adhering to the standards objectives (Chapman 2002).

✎ **Individual/group task**

Consider what impact the introduction of the standards agenda may have on children with SEN.

The impact of the standards agenda on children with special educational needs

The Education Act (1981) was developed from the Warnock Report (1978) and specifically focused on children with SEN. This Act established the statementing process to assess children with SEN and their suitability for mainstream schooling; but this became an assessment of the severity of a child's SEN. Throughout the development of the standards agenda, teachers remained responsible for differentiating the curriculum to meet individual needs. In extreme circumstances, teachers could avoid the National Curriculum criteria entirely for children with SEN, if the child's needs meant the curriculum was not appropriate. It took time for the government to focus on this group of children and separate policies for SEN started to emerge, such as the Code of Practice 1994. There appeared from these developments to be more acknowledgement of the need to consider diversity in mainstream primary education. However, children with SEN were still viewed separately from their peers (Armstrong, 2005).

The combination of the standards agenda with the new concept of inclusion

In 1997, New Labour embraced the need for educational marketisation as society's best route to prosperity. New Labour acknowledged the need to control the work undertaken by teachers and increased standards conformity (Strain and Simkins, 2008). The party's sights were set firmly on schools being accountable through the national league tables and schools were left to focus further on summative assessment, such as SATs. Children with SEN were considered in the same context as their peers for existing objectives, such as the National Curriculum and the SATs process, designed for pupils who can achieve the 'national average' (Bines, 2000). In 1998, the p-scale system was introduced to produce an add-on system to the National Curriculum for children with SEN. The p-scales were put in place to measure levels of attainment lower than the first level of the National Curriculum.

New Labour emphasised a commitment to increasing equity and social justice by enhancing the quality of education for all within the schooling system. Fundamentally, integration became inclusion, where schools needed to 'accommodate' the needs of children with SEN and adapt educationally to meet their needs (Hodkinson and Vickerman, 2009). Inclusion became an ideological concept that envisaged an ongoing process of development that worked towards all children being fully included in the schooling experience. As Clough and Nutbrown (2006) explain, inclusion is a platform for social justice, dependent not only on structural changes of provision and support, but also educating schools and professionals on inclusive practice for equality, diversity and the rights of all children.

Significantly, throughout the multiple legislation and governmental documents there has been no fixed definition of 'inclusion'. Clough and Nutbrown (2006) consider inclusion to be operational as opposed to conceptual, due to the many present versions of inclusion. There are policies that are specifically associated with children with SEN and inclusive practice, including the *Excellence for all Children: Meeting Special Educational Needs* paper (DfEE, 1997b) and the 2001 Special Educational Needs and Disability Act (Armstrong, 2005). In contrast, *Excellence for all Children* (DfEE, 1997a; Bines, 2000) and the 2000 *Index for Inclusion* (Booth *et al.*, 2000) are some of the policies that consider inclusive objectives to be relevant for all children. This implies a broader concept of the inclusion agendas objectives.

Since the Coalition government was formed in 2010 through a Conservative and Liberal Democrat collaboration, there has been a revision of the National Curriculum. This revision encouraged teachers to use the National Curriculum as an outline of core knowledge. Teachers were said to have autonomy to plan exciting, engaging lessons from the National Curriculum's outline. However, there was also a continued emphasis placed on standards. This includes the refocusing of Ofsted inspections and the aim to improve educational standards to make UK schools more internationally comparable. The Coalition government's focus on inclusion had been on identification and assessment to inform initial placement and to provide early intervention of provision for children with SEN. Interestingly, in the revision of the National Curriculum there was great emphasis on teachers' planning to ensure inclusion for all pupils. The revision highlights the importance placed on the 'right teaching' and identification of individual needs in order to include children in the National Curriculum. With effective planning, it is stated in these revisions that there would then be a minority of children with SEN who would need additional resources.

 Individual/group task

List three differences between the development of the inclusion and standards agendas.

Do you believe that they can be implemented simultaneously?

This book was written for publication as the Conservative government won the general election in 2015. Since this time, has there been additional legislation developed on inclusion and standards that influence practice in primary education?

Considering the collective development of the inclusion and standards agendas

The inclusion and standards agendas have been introduced and regulated in very different ways. The inclusion agenda has developed from a time of almost complete segregation of disabled children through an era of integration, and now has not only grown to incorporate the placement of children with SEN, but also extended to consider provisions and barriers present in the classroom. However, there are inconsistencies with the definition of inclusion and whether inclusion is meant solely for children with SEN or all mainstream pupils. The standards agenda does not include such complex inconsistencies. To date, it has retained its original objectives of accountability and achievement. In doing so, the focus has remained to provide criteria for teachers, schools and LEAs that they must meet. Parental knowledge has been at the forefront of the standards objectives, using methods such as the SATs process for over a decade to publicly compare school success.

The inclusion agenda provides objectives which are flexible in today's education system with a projected ideological plan for the future of education, while the standards agenda holds objectives that have become increasingly prescriptive since the Education Act (1980). The objectives for the standards agenda are designed for day-to-day classroom implementation and are of great importance for the measurement of both teacher and school success. However, the introduction of the inclusion agenda did not change the existing standards objectives. Instead, add-on systems were put in place, such as the p-scale system and the requirement to adapt both the curriculum and assessment processes to 'accommodate' children with SEN (Hodkinson and Vickerman, 2009). It is therefore questionable whether inclusion can only be implemented through the standards agenda objectives.

Teachers' perspectives on practically implementing the inclusion agenda

From 2010 to 2013, the current author (Brown, 2013) researched 26 teachers' perspectives on implementing the inclusion agenda from six different primary schools (from both affluent and low socio-economic locations). These teachers were asked to do a card sort where they compared and contrasted statements on inclusion and standards. They were asked to place these statements on a distribution grid according to whether they agreed or disagreed with the statement. These data were analysed statistically to find commonalities in their perspective. This method is known as Q-methodology. Additionally, eight of these teachers were interviewed in order to further ascertain their perspectives. The remainder of this chapter details relevant findings from this study. These findings do not represent the perspective of all teachers, but instead show a sample of perspectives that relate directly to the practical implementation of inclusion.

The confusion in defining inclusion

Teachers in this study mainly focused on children with SEN when considering the inclusion agenda objectives. This is important as inclusion is meant to have developed from a focus on children with SEN to considering the needs of all children. These teachers also defined inclusion in four differing ways. The following information describes these differing definitions.

Inclusion is the placement of children with SEN into mainstream settings

For ten of the teachers, inclusion focused on the placement of children with SEN into mainstream settings. For most of these teachers, the focus on placement was due to practical difficulties of educating children with SEN alongside their peers. One teacher stated, 'often initiatives look good on paper but when you have a class of 50 children they are not easy to implement successfully – especially SEN issues'. However, this definition outlines integration as it focuses on the placement of children with SEN and does not consider the inclusion agendas objectives.

Inclusion involves the school adapting to accommodate children with SEN

In total, seven teachers believed that the inclusion agenda provides objectives that mean the school should adapt to accommodate educating children with SEN. This perspective is comparable to the objectives of the inclusion agenda. These teachers had the greatest diversity of views on the children that inclusion focuses upon, which did extend beyond a focus on children with SEN.

However, the children included differed amongst them. Three teachers also saw inclusion as focusing upon disadvantaged children. Only two teachers took the agenda to its furthest point and believed all children to be included within its objectives.

The standards agenda determines the implementation of the inclusion agenda

For five of the teachers, the standards agenda dominated their responses to such an extent that their positions on the definition of inclusion were not evident on their individual card sort. Only one of these teachers detailed in their card sort children who they think are included within inclusion. The rest of these teachers placed all of the statements referring to which children are included in the negative (disagreeable) part of their distribution grid. Therefore, it was difficult to fully ascertain the positions of these teachers solely on the inclusion agenda. For these teachers, it appears that inclusion objectives for them are implemented through the standards agenda objectives.

Inclusion can be implemented effectively

Only two of 26 teachers believed that inclusion could be fully implemented to accommodate their children's needs. For these teachers, inclusion is focused upon children with SEN and the school is able to adapt to accommodate their educational needs. However, they each held a belief in the effectiveness of inclusion that was apparently different from the other teachers. These teachers stated within their card sort that they believed full inclusion was indeed possible for children with SEN. In fact, they were the only teachers who whole-heartedly believed solely in the benefits of inclusion for children with SEN and that they could fully include children with SEN alongside their peers.

  Individual/group task

Consider these findings in relation to your perspective of inclusive practice.

Teachers' pragmatic positions on implementing inclusion in practice

All teachers in this study held what is known as a 'pragmatic' position on inclusion; however, there were three differing pragmatic perspectives. These perspectives all believed in the ideological concept of inclusion, but they did not believe its objectives are fully possible to implement practically. The following information details each differing pragmatic perspective; the title focuses on the commonalities in these teachers' perspectives.

'I would if I could, but in a standards-driven system it's practically impossible'

In total, seven teachers, mainly from affluent locations, teaching Year 3 upwards held this per-spective. For these teachers, the implementation of the standards agenda dominated their work and affected the implementation of the inclusion agenda. These teachers held a pragmatic position on inclusion because they felt the flexible objectives were too easily lost in such a standards-driven system. Moreover, they felt they had little autonomy in their actions and believed that practically they had to prioritise the objectives of the standards agenda.

'I feel a moral obligation towards inclusion, even though I struggle with the practical barriers I face'

In total, seven teachers, ranging in school locations and years taught, mainly from schools in less affluent locations, held this perspective. Teachers based their perspective on their core beliefs; these teachers embraced the concept of inclusion and actively attempted to implement the agen-da's objectives as much as possible. These teachers' pragmatic perspective derived from the bar-riers they encountered that prevented full implementation of the inclusion agenda's objectives. For these teachers, the practical barriers they faced influenced but did not define their position. These barriers included the standards agenda, the time allocated to implement inclusion and a lack of sufficient funding available for inclusion.

'Inclusion sounds lovely in theory, but it has practical consequences for children with SEN and the education of the rest of the class'

In total, nine teachers across schools in differing locations and ranging in years taught, mostly having over ten years' experience, developed this perspective. Teachers had a combined position on inclusion that incorporated parts of the first two perspectives. These teachers believed in the ideological concept of inclusion, but, in contrast with the second perspective, they felt less moral obligation to implement it. Their pragmatic perspective also saw the standards agenda and vari-ables directly associated with inclusion, such as lack of funding and training, prevented inclusion from being a practical possibility. However, this perspective highlighted that implementing inclu-sion can be consequential for children with SEN and their peers. Critically, they hold inclusion as an externally driven agenda accountable for problems they foresee in educating children with SEN and their peers simultaneously.

 Individual/group task

List three barriers that you think may be present in practically implementing the inclusion agenda.

Barriers to implementing the inclusion agenda

There were five barriers identified in these teachers' card sorts that were highlighted as barriers to practically implementing inclusion. Each of these barriers identified externally appointed resources, support or objectives that compounded the practical negotiation of inclusion objectives. The most stated barrier was funding, and nine teachers claimed that a lack of funding presented a barrier towards inclusion. One teacher said, 'There is generally speaking never enough funding within school to implement any initiative to the best effect'. Six teachers also felt that there is a lack of support from their LEA to effectively implement inclusion. Five teachers reported that they did not have enough training to implement inclusion. One teacher explained: 'I don't feel I have the right, correct amount of knowledge to teach children with SEN. If inclusion is to be successful this support must be provided by schools/LEAs.' Four teachers also believed they did not have enough resources to implement inclusion. Finally, seven teachers indicated that they needed more time to implement inclusion effectively.

The standards agenda and its impact upon the inclusion agenda

For all of these teachers, the constraints of the standards agenda appeared to be seen as a barrier to inclusion. However, a selection of teachers crucially detailed the dominance of the standards agenda in relation to inclusion in further depth. One teacher explained that the dominance of the standards agenda influenced the entire education system. She stated, 'Statutory assessment results are published; the public views schools according to these ... the results of such tests remain the focus point for schools'. Another teacher detailed the pressure she feels specifically to implement the standards agenda: 'Because I feel a pressure to follow all the initiatives and to meet the "good" teacher criterion. There feels more pressure to do this than to help children to achieve their potential.' One teacher explains that 'there still seems to be a feeling that whatever a child's ability, skills, interests they are failing if they do not achieve a certain level by the end of Key Stage 2...'. Comparatively, some of these teachers stated the importance placed upon academia within the standards objectives. One teacher mentioned an imbalance that now exists between academic and vocational/practical skills. Moreover, another teacher stated 'too much attention is on league tables, it doesn't consider that some children in some schools will never reach expected standards'. For these teachers, it appears that the standards agenda objectives dominate their practice. In doing so, children can only be included if they can meet the standards objectives.

 Individual/group task

Considering these teachers' perspectives, has this influenced your perspective of the practical implementation of these agendas in tandem? Do you think it is an impossible mission?

Implementing the inclusion and standards agenda in tandem: mission impossible?

The teachers in this study considered the inclusion and standards agendas' objectives as separate entities. Whilst the findings indicated that the standards agenda was dominant over the inclusion agenda, it was necessary to determine whether the objectives of both agendas can be implemented at the same time. When asked in interview whether the objectives of the inclusion and standards agendas can be implemented together, three of the teachers interestingly questioned the possibility. One of the teachers stated 'they think it is', indicating that theoretically the government believes it is practically possible. Additionally, one of the teachers stated, 'I wouldn't know where to start'. Therefore, for these teachers the inclusion and standards agendas are implemented separately as their theoretical objectives clash on a practical level.

For the six teachers who went into more detail on practically implementing these agendas together, the standards agenda was seen as non-inclusive. Two teachers stated that the government would need to focus more on the child's individual development than on national standards. An important finding for this study suggests that these teachers appear to practically battle between these agendas, fluctuating between concentrating on either the inclusion or the standards agenda. It would appear that the agendas in place would need to be changed to include all children, including children with SEN. One teacher in this study commented on the possibility of taking inclusion to its furthest point. She perceived her practical implementation of these agendas as a 'balancing act you have as a class teacher because you have got thirty-two whole children … I think if you pursue inclusion to its logical conclusion, then you would have thirty-two children who were special and needed including'. It is essential that inclusion is considered theoretically and in practice in its broadest sense to be related directly to the objectives of the standards agenda.

Conclusion

The inclusion agenda provides objectives which enable teachers the freedom to decide upon their own views and in turn how they can implement the objectives within their classroom setting. Teachers within this research held complex views of what inclusion means in mainstream settings. Teachers held differing definitions of what inclusion entails, detailing a focus on aspects of integration, such as placement in mainstream or school adaption for children with SEN. By providing such autonomy within the objectives, these teachers have developed their own concept of inclusion that is influenced by their professional experience. This 'practical' inclusion focuses on disability, highlighting essentially the need to include children with SEN as much as possible into mainstream schools. Therefore, they have adapted the concept of inclusion from having an inclusive system for all in the 'purist' sense, to providing specialist provisions in order to include children with SEN.

Idealistically, the inclusion and standards agendas should be compatible. Inclusion entails children being able to fully be included in all aspects of their education, as well as ensuring standards. Comparatively, the standards agenda holds teachers accountable for their actions and, in doing so, considers the achievements of all children. However, teachers in this study highlighted the dominance of the standards agenda and the impact this has on the implementation of inclusion. As such, these teachers view these agendas as separate entities, where inclusion is focused only on children with SEN.

Summary points

- Inclusion in primary schools is seen as an ideological concept where all mainstream-educated children will one day be included in every aspect of the schooling experience.
- The objectives of the inclusion agenda are flexible in today's education system.
- There is confusion associated with the definition of inclusion; this is due to multiple legislation and policy that define inclusion in differing context. Inclusion is meant to have progressed to include the needs of all children.
- In this study, teachers held complex views of what inclusion means in mainstream primary settings that focused on children with SEN.
- Idealistically, the inclusion and standards agendas should be practically compatible. To be inclusive, all children should appear within the standards agenda and, for all children to achieve, they should all be considered in the inclusion agenda.
- The teachers in this study highlighted the dominance of the objectives of the standards agenda as a barrier to inclusive practice. As such, these teachers view these agendas as separate entities, where inclusion is focused on children with SEN.

Further reading

Clough, P. and Nutbrown, C. (2013) *Inclusion in the Early Years*. London: Sage Publications.
Farrell, M. (2010) *Debating Special Education*. Abingdon: Routledge.
Frederickson, N. and Cline, T. (2009) *Special Educational Needs, Inclusion and Diversity: A textbook*. Buckingham: Open University Press.
Hodkinson, A. and Vickerman, P. (2009) *Key Issues in Special Educational Needs and Inclusion*. London: Sage Publications Ltd.
Thomas, G. and Vaughan, M. (2004) *Inclusive Education: Readings and reflections*. Maidenhead: Open University.

References

Armstrong, D. (2005) Reinventing 'inclusion': New Labour and the cultural politics of special education. *Oxford Review of Education*, **31**(1), 135–151.
Bines, H. (2000) Inclusive standards? Current developments in policy for special educational needs in England and Wales. *Oxford Review of Education*, **26**(1), 21–33.
Booth, T., Ainscow, M., Black-Hawkins, K., Vaughan, M. and Shaw, L. (2000) *Index for Inclusion. Developing learning and participation in schools*. Bristol: Centre for Studies on Inclusive Education.
Brown, Z. (2013*) 'We Just Have To Get on With It': Inclusive Teaching in a Standards Driven System*. (Unpublished PhD Thesis) Wolverhampton: University of Wolverhampton. [Online]. http://wlv.openrepository.com/wlv/bitstream/2436/311413/1/Brown+PhD+thesis.pdf (accessed 3 September 2015).
Chapman, C. (2002) Ofsted and school improvement: Teachers' perceptions of the inspection process in schools facing challenging circumstances. *School Leadership and Management*, **22**(3), 257–272.
Chitty, C. (1989) *Towards a New Education System: The victory of the new right*. Lewes: Falmer Press.
Clough, P. and Nutbrown, C. (2006) *Inclusion in the Early Years*. London: Sage Publications.
DfEE (1997a) *Excellence in Schools*. London: The Stationery Office. [Online]. www.educationengland.org.uk/documents/wp1997/excellence-in-schools.html (accessed 10 January 2013).
DfEE (1997b) *Excellence For All Children: Meeting special educational needs*. London: HMSO.
Hodkinson, A. and Vickerman, P. (2009) *Key Issues in Special Educational Needs and Inclusion*. London: Sage Publications Ltd.

Northway, R. (1997) Integration and inclusion: Illusion or progress in services for disabled people? *Social Policy and Administration*, **31**(2), 157–172.

Slee, R. (1997) Imported or important theory? Sociological interrogations of disablement and special education. *British Journal of Sociology of Education*, **18**(3), 407–419.

Strain, M. and Simkins, T. (2008) Continuity, change and educational reform – questioning the legacy of the Education Reform Act 1988. *Educational Management Administration and Leadership*, **36**(2), 155–163.

Thomas, G. and Vaughan, M. (2004) *Inclusive Education: Readings and reflections.* Maidenhead: Open University.

Whitty, G. (2008) Twenty years of progress? *Educational Management Administration and Leadership, Journal of In-Service Education*, **26**(2), 281–295.

8 Inclusive practice in secondary education

Gavin Rhoades

Introduction

This chapter considers the challenges of implementing inclusive practice in UK mainstream secondary schools. The process of development from segregation to inclusion within education will be discussed, with inclusion considered in its widest sense; the nature of the different groups of secondary school pupils who are at risk of being excluded will be explored. Issues of 'othering' and labelling will be examined for their potential to exclude vulnerable pupils. The potential impact of 'pupil voice' and 'education for inclusive citizenship' provides ideas for future developments.

Chapter 7 provided an overview of important historical and socio-political developments related to inclusion in the UK, and considered key issues and concepts relating to inclusion in primary schools. Many of these issues also apply to secondary schools, and it is recommended that Chapter 7 should be read first.

 Individual/group task

'Inclusion is making someone feel that they are included'.

Consider the above statement and discuss the extent of its effectiveness as:

- a practical definition of inclusion
- a theoretical definition of inclusion.

What differences might there be between these two types of definitions?

From segregation to inclusion

If the history of education in England is examined to consider how disabled pupils have been treated over the years, it can be seen as a journey from segregation through to integration and finally to inclusion. The Education Act (1870) introduced compulsory elementary education. The Elementary Education (Defective and Epileptic Children) Act (1899) empowered school authorities to establish special schools and required parents of 'certified mentally defective children' to cause their children to attend such schools if within reach of their homes. By 1918, these powers had been converted by later Acts into duties and compulsory provision covered all categories of handicapped children recognised at that time, although provision for blind and deaf children was variable for many years, with charities making great contributions to the education of these pupils (Gillard, 2011).

The Mental Deficiency Committee (1929) published the Wood Report, which conducted the first national survey and found a ratio of 8.5 'mental defectives' per 1,000 of population (approximately 300,000 nationally). Rural numbers were significantly higher than urban areas, and boys were 30 per cent more likely to be found to be mentally defective than girls. It recommended manual labour and vocational trades as occupations for boys, and domestic skills to be the focus for girls.

Chapter 7 discussed the enormous impact of the Warnock Report (1978) and the increased movement from segregation to integration. Many of the report's recommendations were incorporated into the Education Act (1981), which amongst other developments introduced 'statementing' of special educational needs. A statement is a formal document that describes a child's learning difficulties and the support they should receive. Previous categories of disability based on a medical model approach were abolished in favour of the educationally focused description of 'children with learning difficulties', or 'special educational needs' (SEN). The report estimated that up to 18 per cent of pupils in mainstream schools may experience learning difficulties because of their SEN (compared to the Wood Report [1929] estimate of 0.85 per cent).

Chapter 7 also explored how, since the 1990s, schools have faced competing demands from the standards agenda and the inclusion agenda. These dual priorities of inclusion and accountability for academic standards have had the consequence that some secondary schools can be reluctant to accept children with SEN because they are worried about the potential for low academic achievement and behavioural problems that might negatively impact the school's examination results (Frederickson and Cline, 2002). Dyson *et al.* (2004) investigated and found a small negative correlation between levels of inclusion in a school and the attainment of its pupils, but they also identified numerous factors which meant that, in their view, it was very unlikely that the relationship between levels of inclusion and attainment was a causative one.

The manner in which very inclusive and high-performing secondary schools manage inclusion varies from school to school, but there are some approaches that appear to be fairly widespread in more inclusive schools. These include some strategies aimed at individuals, such as personalising provision for individual circumstances, a flexible approach to grouping and effective monitoring of individual progress and needs. These are often underpinned by whole-school strategies to increase general levels of inclusion and attainment, together with a strong school ethos to 'do the best for all of the children' (Dyson *et al.*, 2004).

In 1994, the UK government signed the UNESCO Salamanca Statement on the rights of children to an effective and inclusive education, and these principles have informed subsequent policy developments. SEN Codes of Practice published in 1994 and 2001 helped to clarify public bodies' responsibilities to children with different SEN. The Special Educational Needs and Disability Code of Practice (2015) emphasises that the views of the children themselves must be sought and they must be involved in the decision-making process, embracing a social model perspective where the emphasis is on the removal of barriers rather than seeing the child with needs as the problem.

Legislation such as the Equality Act (2010) has contributed to the shift in discourse and policy from a narrow interpretation of inclusion focused on the integration of pupils with SEN to one of real, wider inclusion that considers a range of groups of pupils who are at risk of exclusion. The rest of this chapter considers inclusion in this wider sense and the challenges that secondary schools face in ensuring they are truly inclusive.

Othering, labelling and intersectionality

'Othering' offers a way to conceptualise and analyse different aspects of the social and academic exclusion that can be found both in secondary schools and in the wider world. The concept has developed across a range of fields, including philosophy, psychology and sociology. Its origins can be traced back to the philosopher Hegel in the nineteenth century, with a more structured formulation being expressed by Spivak in the 1980s. Othering is prominent in post-colonial writing, where it was used to justify the marginalisation of the 'Orient' for the benefit of 'Europe', and it is a key concept in gender studies that describes how men are the 'norm' and women are othered (Jensen, 2011).

Human beings are self-aware and once the concept of 'the Self' is recognised, the concept of 'the Other' inevitably emerges. The state of being 'the Other' is fundamentally different from 'the Self' and leads to the formation of identity as either 'like us' or 'not like us'. The process of othering separates out and excludes a person or group of people who in some way are different and therefore do not meet the acceptable 'norms'. The use of language is important in defining an identity by positioning the othered groups of people through the perspectives of a particular ideology. It is the powerful individuals and groups in a community who subscribe to these ideologies and therefore formulate these identities, not the subordinates (Gingrich, 2004).

Importantly, this process renders those who are othered as inferior, often defined by a few stereotypical negative characteristics. In choosing their targets for othering, it can be argued that school bullies are creating standards for what is and is not acceptable amongst their peers. This is an example of normative targeting where pupils who do not meet the requirements of their 'normal' peers may face othering and social exclusion. Vulnerable pupils already at risk of marginalisation are likely to fall into the group of the 'other' who deviate from the 'acceptable' norms. Many of these acceptable norms are subject to frequent and rapid change as fashions and tastes evolve and then die out, but there are some that are more persistent and widely distributed. Departure from physical appearance norms, such as delayed physical development, obesity, disability or severe acne, are strong predictors for bullying and othering, as are norms governing gender and sexuality (Faris and Felmlee, 2014).

Othering can also happen at an institutional level, where the same type of power imbalance can lead to othering of certain groups of pupils through both action and inaction on the part of teachers, administration and support staff. A school's ethos and ideology can shape parents' and pupils' expectations. Schools have clear rules for what is expected from students both behaviourally and academically and pupils soon learn to what degree they belong in the school community. Teachers' choices of pedagogical approaches, assessment formats and learning contexts can make their teaching either more inclusive or more exclusive because different groups of pupils have different learning needs and life experiences. Pupils typically have little or no say about what or how they are taught (Borrero *et al.*, 2012).

Identifying and distinguishing between different groups inevitably requires some form of labelling to enable discussion. Labelling can be positive – for example, where it helps to create a positive identity for marginalised people. In other situations, labelled individuals can come to be defined by a single condition, and the other distinctions that make them individuals can be overlooked. Like othering and identities, vulnerabilities can differ in different local contexts and teachers can have a strong influence over this by ensuring that they are inclusive in their teaching.

Intersectionality developed within feminist studies as a way of analysing how women face multiple dimensions of discrimination, but is now used much more widely. The experience, for example, of being a disabled Indian girl in a secondary school is different from other pupils who are Indian, or are disabled, or are girls. Intersectionality is a way of understanding how multiple factors such as disability, race, gender, ability, age, sexual orientation or socio-economic status can intersect or interact, to the benefit or detriment of the individual concerned. Multiple factors are not merely additive but rather they can compound the impact of discrimination to reveal different types of disadvantage (Cassidy and Jackson, 2007). Appreciation of this concept is important for evaluating the true impact of different types of disadvantage faced by diverse groups of secondary school pupils.

Groups of pupils at risk of exclusion or marginalisation

Treating pupils equally does not mean treating everybody the same. Some pupils need more support than others to remove barriers from their participation and success in education. The identification of groups of vulnerable pupils is a difficult task that secondary schools often address through the use of data. Academic achievement, attendance and exclusion data can provide a picture of how different groups of pupils are faring in their schooling. In this context, the term 'exclusion' means a disciplinary action resulting in a pupil being barred from attending school either for a fixed term or permanently. Analysing these data can help to identify individuals and groups who are either performing below an expected standard, have a higher-than-expected absence rate or are being excluded from school more frequently than other groups of pupils.

These data can indicate the presence of more fundamental underlying issues affecting these pupils and in many cases intersectionality will be evident with pupils facing multiple challenges. These situations can provide potential for othering, both from peers and in some cases from the institutions. Schools need to be aware of these issues in order to provide appropriate support, and ensure that the school and its staff operate as inclusively as possible. Separate from developing an inclusive culture in the school, Ofsted will examine the available data on pupils from these vulnerable groups when it inspects the school, and assess the school's success in meeting its duty to provide an effective education for all of its pupils.

Pupils who have identified special educational needs

Pupils with SEN are significantly over-represented in terms of fixed-term and permanent exclusions from schools. Taken as a whole, pupils who have SEN are eight times more likely to be permanently excluded than their peers without SEN. Statemented pupils are seven times more likely to be excluded than pupils without SEN. Pupils with SEN but no statement are nine times more likely to be permanently excluded (Atkinson, 2012: 12).

The Children and Families Act (2014) replaced statements with new Education, Health and Care Plans (EHCs). EHCs are designed to be a more cohesive system of support that encompasses pupils' health and social care needs alongside educational needs. Local authorities have a duty to prepare and implement EHCs for eligible pupils. No school can refuse to admit a pupil if the school is specifically named in the pupil's EHC. This development is a clear recognition of the wider range of needs for which some pupils require support if they are to be effectively included in mainstream schools.

Inclusion for pupils with SEN has developed considerably in the last few decades but provision across all schools is not always as effective as it could be. In some schools, interaction in classes can be limited to working with a learning assistant and a small number of other peers with their own learning difficulties. Production of work and participation in class activities can be highly variable, with the expectations of teachers playing a major role. Teachers need to have high social and academic expectations of all pupils, including pupils with SEN in order to get the very best out of them. This is often not the case as far as students with learning difficulties are concerned.

Talking to secondary pupils with SEN about their educational experiences, Rose and Shevlin (2004) found clear evidence of informal peer and institutional othering where these pupils still reported ongoing issues with physical access, access to the curriculum, negative peer attitudes and low teacher expectations. They also felt that attempts at inclusion were often ineffective and they were expected to adapt to and assimilate mainstream norms.

Pupils with SEN wanted to be effective partners in a more inclusive education, stating that they could offer clear insights into what would help them and that they could also identify what was not working. They wanted to challenge low expectations of their abilities and deal with the lack of knowledge and awareness amongst their peers and teachers so that they could work towards developing autonomy in their school lives and peer relationships (Rose, 2010). Secondary schools that genuinely encourage pupil voice (a system where pupils are regularly consulted on whole-school issues that affect them) can promote a more inclusive atmosphere and culture that is embedded within the school community.

Black Caribbean boys

Black Caribbean boys have long been recognised as underperforming academically, being over-represented in terms of exclusions from school and being more likely to attend special schools. In 1985, the Swann Report (DES, 1985) found that black Caribbean boys as a group were underachieving in the English education system. The Children's Commissioner for England found that 'Black Caribbean boys were 11 times more likely to be permanently excluded than White girls of the same age in similar schools' (Atkinson, 2012: 13). In terms of academic performance, a DfES report found that only 39 per cent of black pupils achieved 5+ A*–C GCSE grades, which means black Caribbean boys are among the lowest achievers at secondary school level, compared with pupils of other ethnic minorities (Gosai, 2009).

It has been suggested that teacher perceptions of racial stereotypes together with the impact of 'pop culture' influences boys to aspire to black masculine stereotypes which do not value educational success (Sewell, 1997). Black Caribbean boys reported that their teachers had low expectations of them, often ignored their requests for assistance and tended to encourage them to pursue sports or arts instead of core academic subjects (Gosai, 2009).

Pupils living in poverty

In 2011–12, child poverty was 27 per cent, the lowest figure for twenty-five years. This meant, however, that there were still approximately 3.5 million children living in poverty in the UK. Poverty in this context means relative poverty, where the children live in a household where the income is less than 60 per cent of the median national income (Joseph Rowntree Foundation, 2013).

Using free school meals (FSM) eligibility as a proxy for deprivation is a widespread practice in educational research in the UK and data related to FSM are readily available. Families either have to be in receipt of various benefits or have a gross annual household income of no more than £16,190 to be eligible to receive FSM. There are numerous objections and criticisms levelled at this approach, but pragmatically it is the most effective given the data available.

Children eligible for FSM are approximately four times more likely to be permanently excluded from school than their peers who are not eligible for FSM (Atkinson, 2012: 13). Academically, schools in London out-perform the rest of the country, with 40 per cent of their pupils eligible for FSM going on to higher education aged 18 or 19, compared to no more than 20 per cent in other regions (Joseph Rowntree Foundation, 2013). Pupils eligible for FSM are much more likely to lack the basic equipment they need for lessons, miss out on extra-curricular enrichment activities and attend school without having eaten any breakfast before leaving home. Many schools and teachers do what they can to support and include these deprived pupils, but funding is a real issue in the majority of situations.

The 2010 Coalition government introduced the 'Pupil Premium' in April 2011 to provide additional support for looked-after children and those from low-income families. Money is provided to schools based on the number of eligible pupils on their roll. The Pupil Premium was found to be most useful when schools used the money in an inclusive and targeted manner. Where the extra money was spent specifically to address the needs of eligible pupils, rather than on general school expenditure, it was found to be effective. A key issue for success was where schools did not confuse eligible pupils for low-ability pupils, and made sure that support was provided with high expectations of what pupils could achieve (Ofsted, 2013a).

White working class pupils

In this context, white working class pupils means those white pupils whose families have been eligible for FSM within the previous six months (Education Committee, 2014). Ofsted (2013b: 30) reported that 'white British children eligible for free school meals were now the lowest-performing children at age 16, with only 31 per cent of this group achieving five or more GCSEs at A*–C including English and Mathematics'. Importantly for secondary schools, the gap between working class white pupils and their non-FSM peers already exists at age five and continues to grow as the children get older. Eligibility for FSM varies from ethnicity to ethnicity but 'although a smaller proportion of white children are eligible for free school meals than some other ethnicities, white British children still constitute the majority (64 per cent) of the FSM group – some 55,000 children per year' (Education Committee, 2014). FSM pupils are approximately four times more likely to be permanently excluded, and approximately three times more likely to be excluded for a fixed term than their non-FSM peers (Atkinson, 2012: 13). It should be noted that these figures do not take ethnicity into account.

Effective and inclusive secondary schools can have a very powerful impact on the achievement and life chances of white working class children. When white working class children attend outstanding schools, they are twice as likely to gain five good GCSEs than similar children in schools classed as inadequate. For non-FSM children attending outstanding schools, the figure is only 1.5 times greater than for non-FSM children attending inadequate schools, which demonstrates the impact that can be achieved (Education Committee, 2014).

Roma/Travellers

The rate of exclusions for Roma and Traveller children is similar to that of black Caribbean boys, and 'Gypsy and Roma Traveller and Irish Traveller children were four times more likely to be permanently excluded than was the school population as a whole' (Atkinson, 2012: 13). Despite the general suitability of 'Roma' or 'Traveller' as a label for these communities, Travellers are not a single homogeneous group. Some Traveller children who live with a circus may be travelling for up to 11 months of the year, and moving to a new school as frequently as every week, where other groups and families will stay longer between seasonal moves (DfES, 2004).

Traveller pupils regularly face discrimination, stereotyping and racial prejudice in schools. Together with 'invisible' institutional issues, such as a curriculum not aligned with their needs and a lack of understanding of Traveller history, culture and identity, it is not surprising that Jordan (2001) reports many Traveller pupils suffering from low self-esteem and disaffection with education.

Refugees/asylum seekers

Including children of refugees or asylum seekers can present considerable challenges to schools. English language skills may be limited, the children's schooling will have been disrupted and broken to a greater or lesser extent and, in some cases, children may be traumatised from witnessing the rape, torture or murder of family members (Hek, 2005).

Refugee children can face barriers to integrating into the school community, such as limited support for learning English, isolation, discrimination and othering. Some schools provide separate specialised language tuition, but this needs to be used carefully because of its potential to limit the refugee children's opportunities to socialise with local children. Unfamiliarity with the English education system is also a barrier to making informed choices that may impact on the children's opportunities later in life (Ager and Strang, 2008).

Looked-after children

A child is a 'looked-after child' under the Children Act (1989) if he or she is subject to a care or placement order, or is provided with accommodation by a local authority for more than 24 hours (DfE, 2013a). Looked-after children, the majority of whom are in care through no fault of their own, have poor educational outcomes. In 2013, just 15.3 per cent of looked-after children achieved five or more A*–C GCSEs including Maths and English compared to 58 per cent of non-looked-after children. This is a larger gap than the figures from 2009 (DfE, 2013a).

In 2013, 67.8 per cent of looked-after children had SEN, 6.2 per cent of looked-after children aged 10–17 years old had been convicted or given a final warning and 3.5 per cent of all looked-after children had a recognised substance abuse problem (DfE, 2013a). About half of all looked-after children aged 5–16 years old have been assessed as causing concern in relation to their emotional and behavioural health. Like the statistics on the attainment and exclusion of black Caribbean boys, these data should be cause for concern at a national level.

Schools are required by law to appoint a designated teacher for looked-after children. This should be a senior teacher in the school who can act as a link for multi-agency cooperation, as internal communication with the school's staff, and as an advocate for the looked-after child (DCSF, 2009). Making friends can be difficult given the often chaotic nature of the pupils' living arrangements, and this can often fuel othering from peers. Providing continuity and inclusive lessons can be a challenge for their teachers given the pupils' erratic attendance and often challenging behaviour. Completion of work and revision for examinations can be challenging for all concerned. The school has to have effective monitoring in place to support and guide these pupils.

Other groups

This list of groups who are potentially vulnerable to exclusion is far from exhaustive. Some pupils face severe discrimination, bullying and othering because of their sexual orientation or homophobia from their peers.

Pregnant girls and sick teenagers with long-term illnesses face challenges in receiving appropriate and effective support from their schools to maintain their education during their absence, and to reintegrate into the school community if they return.

Young carers are people under the age of 19 who take some or all of the responsibility for looking after someone else, usually a parent or relative who may be disabled or suffering from addiction (Thomas *et al.*, 2003). Data from the 2011 census showed that there were 177,918 young unpaid carers in England and Wales (ONS, 2013). Carers between the ages of 16 and 18 are twice as likely to be not in education, employment or training (Carers Trust, 2012). It would be hard for a classroom teacher to know that one of their pupils was a young carer unless that information had been disclosed to the school, and therefore they might not be aware of the background to the pupil's absences or lack of homework.

The language of instruction in schools in England is English. Those students learning English as an additional language (EAL) are expected to do so within National Curriculum lessons, and the Department for Education's current position is that they do not offer specialist support for specific groups of learners, relying instead on accountability built into the education system to monitor the situation (DfE, 2013b). There are extensive resources published by previous governments that are now archived online that schools and teachers could use to support and include pupils with EAL.

Pupils identified as gifted and talented can often be overlooked when a school's scarce resources are focused on those at the other end of the ability range who are in severe need of support. If left unsupported or unrecognised, these pupils can begin to display immature or disruptive behaviour due to a lack of challenge in the school curriculum. They may also suffer from social exclusion or othering, and gifted girls in particular face challenges to exceptional performance in science or mathematics because of gender stereotypes. Alternatively, being labelled as gifted and talented has different potential problems, such as pressure to be successful (Heller and Hany, 2004).

✎ **Individual/group task**

How would you know if a school was truly 'inclusive'? What might the indicators be that:

- all pupils in the school receive a 'fair deal'
- the school addresses any barriers to learning for pupils and groups
- the school's values are clearly reflected in everyday practice?

What would you expect to see in classrooms and around the school?

Education for inclusive citizenship

The National Curriculum requires secondary schools to provide pupils with Citizenship lessons. The Citizenship curriculum is primarily focused on issues around growing up to be a responsible citizen, and understanding democracy, legislation and government. These concepts represent a set of shared values that society deems important enough that all young people should learn about them. However, when considering how to create a more inclusive environment in secondary schools the focus could be on the different, more fundamental idea of 'education for citizenship', or 'inclusive citizenship'.

By its very nature, citizenship can be both inclusive and exclusive, as it defines whether a person is a citizen (a member of 'our' group) or not. Used positively, this concept therefore has the potential to strengthen the position of vulnerable groups in a community such as a secondary school through recognition of shared concepts, such as membership, belonging and equality. Inclusive citizenship values such as justice, recognition, self-determination and solidarity can be powerful tools to promote inclusion (Lister, 2008).

In this way, inclusive citizenship offers an effective and self-perpetuating approach to combating othering, by focusing on similarities rather than differences. Unfortunately, the most vulnerable pupils are often the ones who are deprived of exactly these values, particularly self-determination (or agency) or recognition (a voice). A school's shared set of values, culture and ethos of inclusive citizenship can promote respect and community in all of its pupils.

Conclusion

Great progress has been made since the early days of segregation in special education. A growing realisation is that many individuals with special educational needs can craft 'a good life' for themselves. The context, culture and conditions within which they are educated is a key step in democratising education and moving beyond the social model to promote the views of the learners themselves as equal partners in their own, truly inclusive education.

Increasing diversity in multicultural Britain, together with the developing understanding of a modern definition of inclusion that covers many different groups with diverse needs, presents secondary schools with challenges and opportunities. Secondary schools that embrace these challenges and operate in a highly inclusive manner need not fear the demands of the standards agenda because the twin outcomes of effective inclusion and academic success are not necessarily as incompatible as once feared.

Summary points

- Legislation and policy developments over the last few decades have led to wider aware-
  ness of what genuine inclusion needs to involve.
- Secondary schools face competing challenges in trying to implement the standards
  agenda and the inclusion agenda.
- Different groups of pupils have diverse needs and face different challenges. To be inclusive, secondary schools need to address these needs and actively plan for inclusion.
- Education for citizenship offers ways of combating exclusion via othering.
- Some groups, such as looked-after children, are profoundly disadvantaged by the
  current education system.

Further reading

Boyle, C. (2012) *What Works in Inclusion?* Maidenhead: Open University Press.
Cornwall, J. and Graham-Matheson, L. (2012) *Leading on Inclusion: Dilemmas, debates and new perspectives.* Hoboken: Routledge.

References

Ager, A. and Strang, A. (2008) Understanding integration: A conceptual framework. *Journal of Refugee Studies*, **21**(2), pp. 166–191.
Atkinson, M. (2012) *They Never Give Up on You – School Exclusions Inquiry*. Available at: www.childrens-commissioner.gov.uk/publications/%E2%80%9Cthey-never-give-you%E2%80%9D-school-exclusions-inquiry-full-report (accessed 10 August 2015).
Borrero, N.E., Yeh, C.J., Cruz, I. and Suda, J. (2012) School as a context for 'othering' youth and promoting cultural assets. *Teachers College Record*, **114**(2), pp. 1–37.
Carers Trust (2012) *What Is a Carer?* Available at: www.carers.org/what-carer (accessed 10 August 2015).
Cassidy, W. and Jackson, M. (2007) The need for equality in education: An intersectionality examination of labelling and zero tolerance practices. *McGill Journal of Education/Revue Des Sciences De L'Éducation De McGill*, **40**(3). Available at: http://mje.mcgill.ca/article/view/585/467 (accessed 10 August 2015).
DCSF (2009) *The Role and Responsibilities of the Designated Teacher for Looked After Children.* London: HMSO.
DES (1985) *Education for All: Report of the committee of enquiry into the education of ethnic minority groups.* London: HMSO.
DfE (2013a) *Outcomes for Children Looked After by Local Authorities in England, as at 31 March 2013.* Available at: www.gov.uk/government/uploads/system/uploads/attachment_data/file/264385/SFR50_2013_Text.pdf (accessed 10 August 2015).
DfE (2013b) *The National Curriculum in England Framework Document: For teaching 1 September 2014 to 31 August 2015.* London: HMSO.
DfE and Department for Health (2015) *Special Educational Needs and Disability Code of Practice: 0 to 25 years.* Available at: www.gov.uk/government/uploads/system/uploads/attachment_data/file/398815/SEND_Code_of_Practice_January_2015.pdf (accessed 10 August 2015).
DfES (2004) *Aiming High: Raising the achievement of Gypsy Traveller pupils.* London: HMSO.
Dyson, A., Farrell, P., Polat, F., Hutcheson, G. and Gallannaugh, F. (2004) *Inclusion and Pupil Achievement.* London: Department for Education and Skills.
Education Committee (2014) *Underachievement in Education by White Working Class Children*, 18 June 2014, HC 142 2013–14.
Faris, R. and Felmlee, D. (2014) Casualties of social combat – school networks of peer victimization and their consequences. *American Sociological Review*, **79**(2), pp. 228–257.

Fredrickson, N. and Cline, T. (2002) *Special Educational Needs, Inclusion and Diversity: A textbook*. Open University Press: Buckingham.

Gillard, D. (2011) *Education in England: A brief history*. Available at: www.educationengland.org.uk/history (accessed 10 August 2015).

Gingrich, A. (2004) Conceptualizing identities. In G. Bauman and A. Gingrich (Eds) *Grammars of Identity/Alterity: A structural approach*. Oxford: BergHahn.

Gosai, N. (2009) *Perspectives on the Educational Experiences of African/Caribbean Boys*. Birmingham: University of Birmingham. Available at: http://etheses.bham.ac.uk/425/ (accessed 10 August 2015).

Hek, R. (2005) *The Experiences and Needs of Refugee and Asylum Seeking Children in the UK: A literature review*. Available at: http://dera.ioe.ac.uk/5398/1/RR635.pdf (accessed 10 August 2015).

Heller, K. and Hany, E. (2004) Identification of gifted and talented students. *Psychology Science*, **46**(3), pp. 302–323.

Jensen, S. (2011) Othering, identity formation and agency. *Qualitative Studies*, **2**(2), pp. 63–78.

Jordan, E. (2001) Exclusion of travellers in state schools. *Educational Research*, **43**(2), pp. 117–132.

Joseph Rowntree Foundation (2013) *Monitoring Poverty and Social Exclusion 2013*. Available at: https://npi.org.uk/files/9613/8634/5794/MPSE_Findings_2013_FINAL.pdf (accessed 10 August 2015).

Lister, R. (2008) Inclusive citizenship, gender and poverty: Some implications for education for citizenship. *Citizenship: Teaching and Learning*, **4**(1), pp. 3–20.

The Mental Deficiency Committee (1929) *The Wood Report*. Available at: www.educationengland.org.uk/documents/wood/wood1929.html (accessed 10 August 2015).

Office for National Statistics (2013) *Providing Unpaid Care May Have an Adverse Effect on Young Carers' General Health*. Available at: www.ons.gov.uk/ons/rel/census/2011-census/detailed-characteristics-for-local-authorities-in-england-and-wales/sty-young-unpaid-care.html (accessed 10 August 2015).

Ofsted (2013a) *The Pupil Premium: How schools are spending the funding successfully*. Available at: www.gov.uk/government/publications/the-pupil-premium-how-schools-are-spending-the-funding-successfully (accessed 10 August 2015).

Ofsted (2013b) *Unseen Children: Educational access and achievement 20 years on*. Available at: www.gov.uk/government/publications/unseen-children-access-and-achievement-20-years-on (accessed 10 August 2015).

Rose, R. (2010) *Confronting the Obstacles to Inclusion: International responses to developing inclusive education*. London: Routledge.

Rose, R. and Shevlin, M. (2004) Encouraging voices: Listening to young people who have been marginalised. *Support for Learning*, **19**(4), pp. 155–160.

Sewell, T. (1997) *Black Masculinities and Schooling: How black boys survive modern schooling*. London: Trentham Books.

Thomas, N., Stainton, T., Jackson, S., Cheung, W., Doubtfire, S. and Webb, A. (2003) 'Your friends don't understand': Invisibility and unmet need in the lives of young carers. *Child & Family Social Work*, **8**(1), pp. 35–46.

9 Post-16 education and issues of inclusion

Tracey Edwards and Graham Jones

Introduction

This chapter considers inclusion in further education (FE), sixth form and apprenticeships in the UK. The focus will not be limited to those students with special educational needs, but will consider issues around all further education and sixth form students who may be at risk of exclusion or marginalisation. These would include young people such as those currently not in education, employment or training (NEETs) or those who are lower achieving academically. The chapter will explore the topic from the perspective of sixth form teachers and college lecturers examining the challenges they face in trying to implement inclusive strategies in classrooms and work settings. This will include recruitment, planning learning activities and assessment activities for inclusion of marginalised groups. The chapter will reflect on other key issues, such as the tension between promoting inclusive practice and the challenges for schools and colleges.

✎ **Individual/group task**

Before you begin to read this chapter, consider in what way inclusive practice is implemented in today's further education and college system. What does it mean to offer an inclusive education today in post-16 education?

The history of post-16 education

Post-16 education is arguably more important for the economy today than ever. In her first speech after the 2015 election, Nicky Morgan, the Education Secretary, said:

> The question I have asked myself, and the question I will continue to ask, is how I, as Secretary of State, can help to spread excellence throughout the school system, from the early years right through to sixth form, across the whole country?
>
> (DfE, 2015a)

In light of this, it is important to consider how the current system of post-16 provision came to be.

The term 'further education' was first used in Britain in 1906, with the purpose being not dissimilar to today, offering courses aimed at improving the life chances of all ability levels. Bailey and Unwin (2014) list a series of 'classes' (courses) funded by the Board of Education in 1914 that would not look out of place in a modern FE college prospectus. These included elementary, technical and degree-level courses, as well as those offered for disabled students. However, it is debatable whether the course on 'housewifery – for girls' (p. 457) would be considered a good example of inclusive practice in terms of gender equality today!

The 1944 Education Act resulted in the setting up of two different types of secondary schools: grammar schools for the 20 per cent who passed the 11-plus exam, a set of English, Mathematics and intelligence tests for all 11-year-olds, and secondary modern schools for the rest of the population. This division at age 11 largely determined the career paths followed by 16-year-olds. Those in grammar schools took public exams, GCE Ordinary and Advanced levels, with the successful ones going on to university or training in professional posts. Those at secondary modern schools left at 15 to go to work or become apprentices. Thus the divide between children who followed academic or vocational routes was established. Although non-selective comprehensive schools became the most common form of school by the mid-1970s, it was (and still is) common practice to set students by academic ability, with those in lower sets doing more vocational courses. Bol and van de Werfhorst (2013) found that when students are differentiated in terms of expected future employment and allocated to courses to prepare them for this, there is an increased inequality of educational opportunity. An inclusive system would arguably place equal value on different types of courses.

Vocational education has changed over time with various attempts made to increase its perceived value. Initiatives have included Youth Training Schemes (YTS) in the 1980s, General National Vocational Qualifications (GNVQs) in the 1990s and, introduced in 2000, Advanced Vocational Certificates of Education (AVCEs). Currently today's modern apprenticeships and Business and Technology Education Council qualifications (BTECs) form the basis of vocational training. A-levels have remained the most popular post-16 academic route, and were referred to as the 'gold standard' by Education Secretary Nicky Morgan (DfE, 2015a).

The National Qualification Framework (NQF) allocates all qualifications to levels supporting parity between qualifications; A-levels, vocational BTEC Level 3 (L3), the International Baccalaureate, NVQ L3, the Advanced Diploma and others are all examples of the range of qualifications offered at Key Stage 5. In terms of inclusive practice, this allows student choice. However, Pring (1990) argued that A-levels were perceived as more valuable, and suitable for those students of greater academic ability. Bol and van de Werfhorst (2013) found that students from poorer backgrounds were more likely to be channelled into vocational courses, and so the division of students into academic and vocational routes reflects differences in social class as much as in academic ability. This means that post-16 education in practice is not fully inclusive in relation to social class and academic ability.

✎ **Individual/group task**

Is Pring's assertion still true today? Are A-levels valued more highly than vocational qualifications? Log on to the University Admissions website www.ucas.com and look at the range of qualifications accepted at different universities for different degree courses. Do the more prestigious universities prefer A-levels over vocational qualifications?

The culture of inclusion (or exclusion) in 16–19 educational institutions

There have been many studies of the impact of the culture of an institution on the learning of its students. However, there is evidence to suggest that the range of different providers at post-16 is detrimental to a culture of inclusivity at this level, with some students thriving due to attending what they perceive to be an exclusive, academic college.

Although FE colleges provide a range of courses up to degree level, high youth unemployment has led them to provide more low level 'employability' courses for students who have left school with few qualifications (Bailey and Unwin, 2014). On the whole, schools and sixth forms deliver more academic qualifications aimed at entry to higher education, and FE colleges more vocational qualifications (Thompson, 2009).

Hodkinson and Bloomer (2010) found that the plethora of different providers of post-16 education has led to a 'subtle elitism' (p. 192), with A-level providers being seen as more prestigious than providers of other qualifications. A typical town might have a grammar school sixth form, other school sixth forms, a sixth form college and an FE college, with the schools and sixth form college focusing on A-level provision and the FE college focusing on vocational qualifications. This is partly a continuum of the grammar/secondary modern divide between students deemed academically able and those best suited to vocational courses.

In their study of a sixth form college, Hodkinson and Bloomer (2010) found that students viewed the college as being a high-status institution as it offered mainly A-levels and was seen as difficult to get into, with the local FE college being seen as a poor second choice. Inside the college, they found a homogeneous culture with a cohesive set of norms and values regarding studying and learning. Students internalised these values with most of them having the same aspiration of entering higher education. They found that the spirit of elitism motivated students to work hard.

Although this study showed how well the sixth form college benefitted those that fitted in, it also found that those students who failed to conform to the social norms of the college felt unsupported and often dropped out. If the positive effect of identifying oneself as an academic is that A-level study at a sixth form college helps those inside the organisation to succeed, conversely the downside for those not admitted to sixth form college is not achieving academically.

Thompson (2009), using data from the Youth Cohort Study of England and Wales (DCSF, 2008), found that the type of post-16 institution attended was largely determined by social class. He found that higher-achieving students from higher social class backgrounds attended school sixth forms or sixth form colleges, whereas lower achieving students from these backgrounds attended FE colleges. Indeed, he found that FE colleges are perceived by the middle classes as a 'last resort for its own children' (p. 40). For students from lower social class backgrounds, high achievers were more likely to attend an FE college, while low achievers dropped out of education. This self-exclusion of higher social class students from FE colleges serves to prevent a greater academic ethos developing in FE colleges, 'leaving working-class children in one institution without the benefits of middle-class peers' (Thompson, 2009: 38).

Theoretically, this relates to different types of social capital (Putnam, 2000). The success of sixth form colleges, such as the one in Hodkinson and Bloomer's (2010) study described above, is explained by bonding (exclusive) capital. This is where a group with similar identities and interests support each other; in this case an academic identity is reinforced throughout the college, leading to high achievement. Bridging (inclusive) social capital involves connections between hetero-geneous groups. Thompson's (2009) study shows how the lack of bridging social capital denies working class students at FE colleges the opportunity to form an academic identity from socialising with students who are more likely to possess this identity.

 Individual/group task

Compare the prospectuses of a range of post-16 institutions in your local area. Try to rank them from the most inclusive to the least. On what basis did you make your decisions for these rankings?

Further education and training today

The Education and Skills Council legislated through the Education and Skills Act 2008 to raise school leavers' age from 16 to 18 years of age from 2015. Of particular importance at this time was the need to reduce the number of young people categorised as NEETs (Ofsted, 2010). A par-ticular challenge for FE in relation to this policy of widening participation has been to cater for the higher numbers of students who are 'unfocused, low in confidence and burdened with difficult home circumstances' (Edward *et al.*, 2007, cited in Towler *et al.*, 2011: 512).

The government views FE and training as a means to promote social inclusion and economic prosperity (DfES, 2002). Education is seen today as the key to gaining employment and the means to which social inclusion can support individuals and communities out of poverty. This strategy appeared to be working, as a statement from the Department for Education (DfE, 2015b) stated that the number of teenagers in education and training was at an all-time high and the number of those not in education, employment or training (NEET) was at an all-time low. However, Williams (2008) warns against defining social inclusion in terms of attending college or training schemes, as these do not necessarily lead to stable employment or a higher living standard if the economy as a whole is performing poorly.

Inclusion in FE today

Teaching and learning are social and emotional experiences. Vygotsky (1978) suggests that the role of the teacher is to engage socially with the student, providing work that is just beyond their current developmental level so as to provide some challenge, but not too far ahead so that the task is not achievable by the student; this is known as the student's zone of proximal development (ZPD). Carr (2001) argues that, as well as being able to learn, students need also to be in a posi-tion where they feel willing and ready to learn. Therefore, to be truly inclusive, teaching has to involve students as individuals with individual learning plans and targets.

In 1996, the Learning Difficulties and Disability Committee (LDDC) identified the concept of 'Inclusive Learning' as a clear understanding of the students' starting point (Tomlinson Report, 1996). By encouraging active participation from the student and best fit of resources and teaching within FE, successful learning can be achieved. Inclusive learning was at this time defined by the point at which the student's needs and the institutional resources meet for a best-fit scenario (ibid.). However, the expectation placed on the learner for active participation could further suggest a culture of blame, failure to achieve being the fault of the individual student's inability to actively participate with the process.

In 2011, Alison Wolf's recommendations (DfE, 2011) for change in FE delivery facilitated a move towards supporting young people in their transition to adulthood as well as developing their academic and skills-based learning. These changes within the vocational education system were also initiated to support the UK economy through employer-led training. Ofsted (2014) in the Teaching, Learning and Assessment report recommended that providers focus on improvements in teaching, learning and the development of skills, knowledge and attitudes. Ofsted (2014) concluded that improvement in the teaching and learning of skills is linked to the sustainability of employment for many young people.

Concentration on core subjects rather than achievement of qualifications has now become the primary concern of the Education and Training Foundation (DfE, 2011, Recommendation 7). The quality of teaching and delivery of Maths and English has become the primary focus for all FE curricula. Robey *et al.* (2014) offered insight into the views of FE institutions over the changes to the GCSE Mathematics and English curricula from July 2014. Initial findings conclude that motivation, flexibility and workforce development are vital in supporting all learners. However, there are concerns over the contextualisation of the teaching and learning benefits in securing 'C' grades in GCSE for employability. Robey *et al.* (2014) also raised issues of inclusion over the inequity for some young people who find traditional classroom teaching difficult. Enforcements of these regulations for students undertaking new and stretching qualifications in FE could be disadvantaging and jeopardising to future job prospects. This is particularly evident in the current debate over apprenticeships and GCSE equivalencies and currency. Students currently training through an apprenticeship route with GCSEs five years or older are required to complete an equivalency or to retake their GCSEs. Neil Leitch (Chief Executive of the Pre-school Learning Alliance) stated that eligibility criteria had created serious barriers to otherwise suitable learners (Offord, 2015).

✎ **Individual/group task**

Look at the website for your local college or school sixth form. Who is the college attempting to appeal to? Is it appealing to a diverse range of students or does the entry requirement mean it is specialising to appeal to a specific type of student?

Funding for inclusion at 16–19

Any discussion of inclusion also needs to take into account how funding for inclusive practice works. The greater the overall funding for colleges, the more they can spend on inclusive practices. Between 1998 and 2009, education spending rose in real terms by 5.2 per cent, with the increase in spending on the 16–19 sector exceeding this and increasing by 7.7 per cent (Bolton, 2014). This significant investment in education by the New Labour government was curtailed by the 2010 Coalition government's Comprehensive Spending Review, which cut education spending by 3.5 per cent.

Following these cuts, in 2012 funding for students aged16–19 was taken over by the Education Funding Agency (EFA), except for apprenticeships, which are funded by the Skills Funding Agency. At the time of writing, the EFA manages £54 billion of funding a year to support all state-provided education for 8 million children aged 3 to 16, and 1.6 million young people aged 16 to 19 (EFA 2013).

In 2014–15, colleges received £4000 per student per year. For some students, additional funding was made available through three categories:

- students who came from economically disadvantaged backgrounds – colleges received 'additional funds to recognise the additional costs associated with engaging, recruiting and retaining young people from disadvantaged backgrounds' (EFA, 2013: 25);
- young people in or having recently left care generated additional resources;
- those requiring additional learning support – students without Maths or English GCSE grade C generated extra funding.

For each of these criteria, the college received an additional £480. Therefore, if a student was from a deprived postcode, was in care and had neither Maths nor English GCSE, they generated an extra £1920. This money went not directly to the individual student but to the institution, which determined how best to use this money in the support of disadvantaged students. (Note that students with 'High Needs', such as acute physical disabilities or learning needs, had funding arrangements separate from this.)

In terms of students gaining access to money to support them, there were two types of bursary:

- The vulnerable student bursary: students could access up to £1200 if: they were in or had recently left care; got income support in their own name; had a disability and got support for this (e.g. Disability Living Allowance).
- Discretionary bursaries: colleges set their own eligibility criteria for these and decided what the money was spent on. For the case study (see below), students whose parents received a low family income or income support received help towards travel, lunch, trips, UCAS applications and specialist equipment needed.

In terms of inclusion, colleges that served an economically deprived student body did not see their overall budgets cut as much as other colleges. Offering Level 2 programmes, including Maths and English GCSEs, was also made more attractive by these funding arrangements, meaning that colleges that had previously offered mainly A-level courses now had a financial incentive to offer lower-level courses, widening access to a greater diversity of students.

✎ **Individual/group task**

The figures quoted in this section are from when this book was published. How has funding increased/decreased in the years since? Note: such figures are not as easy to find as you might think!

Case study of a sixth form college

In looking at how inclusive practices work, it is useful to consider the work of a single college. This example is of a medium-sized sixth form college servicing a multicultural industrial city. Its inclusion practices may be seen as typical of colleges in the sector.

Each year the 'Equality and Diversity Annual Report' is presented to the governing body. This document reports on student achievement, retention and progression in regard to ethnicity, gender, qualifications on entry and additional learning support. Areas of strength and improvement are highlighted. This data informs the college-wide 'Single Equality Scheme – Action Plan', which links to a specific 'equality, diversity and inclusion course plan' for each course offered by the college.

At a college-wide level, the action plan includes many items, a few of which relate to:

- ensuring that marketing and promotion materials reflect a diverse community;
- positive images of diversity being displayed around the college;
- liaising with the student guild to celebrate equality and diversity across the college;
- monitoring staff in post and applicants by ethnicity, gender and disability;
- ensuring systems are working in terms of disseminating necessary information to staff regarding student additional support needs.

At a subject level, teachers are required to demonstrate how they promote equality, diversity and inclusion through their teaching, learning and assessment. Examples from course plans include:

- course materials (e.g. plays, music, artists) chosen to reflect the diversity of the student population;
- students being encouraged to choose their own coursework topics;
- differentiated workshops for students of all ability levels;
- class files to contain information on all students requiring additional learning support, with recommendations from the learning support department being followed;
- teaching materials available in advance of class to students via the virtual learning environment;
- virtual learning environment to contain three categories of reading: essential, recommended and extended.

Inclusion is supported throughout the college structure. At a college-wide level, all staff receive equality and diversity training and are made fully aware of the policies and procedures of the college. Specialist pastoral and learning support teams have specific roles in maintaining inclusivity throughout the college.

The pastoral team consists of specialist personal tutors. It used to be that all teachers in this college were responsible for a tutor group of about 20 students. This changed to having 'super' tutors who have no teaching responsibilities but have a number of tutor groups.

(continued)

This splitting of teaching and pastoral staff is becoming more common throughout the sector. Personal tutors act as a first port-of-call for any issues students have, both academic and personal. They liaise with subject teachers, the learning support team, the careers department, the counselling services, as well as providing any references for students. They have an overall picture of an individual student's progress over their time at the college.

The Learning Support Team comprises qualified teachers who specialise in assessing and delivering support to students requiring additional learning support (ALS) and several 'learning mentors', typically graduates that can offer a mentoring support role. The team support students in numerous ways, including:

- Students with additional learning requirements are identified. Many students bring a statement from their previous school; others are assessed during their time at the college.
- The team liaises with class teachers to cater for any specific student requirements, e.g. students often benefit from being given worksheets in advance, not being asked to read aloud, marking that does not penalise students unfairly for poor spelling.
- Some students have a regular weekly time-slot where they see the same mentor to help with their work. Depending on the student, help could be academic, organisational or to help with conditions such as stress or lack of confidence.
- Students can refer themselves or be referred by their teachers for specific help. Between them, the team has a balance of skills so support can be offered in all subject areas.
- Assessments are supported by arranging separate rooming, reading and scribing for individual students.

Doughty and Allan (2008) studied the effectiveness of inclusivity training for teachers at this level and found that, although those attending the training found it useful, there were several barriers to staff development in their colleges. These barriers included staff not receiving the time and funding to attend training; but a larger barrier was a lack of time to disseminate training and share good practice between colleagues. In addition to these structural barriers, they uncovered attitudinal barriers with some staff who do not consider inclusion training to be of relevance to them. They also found that inclusivity strategies were less well received when they were seen as being imposed from above by senior managers rather than coming from the bottom up.

✎ Individual/group task

What are the advantages and disadvantages for inclusive practice of having separate staff working as either teachers, pastoral tutors or learning mentors? Would it be better if all staff taught, had a tutor group and offered learning support?

Planning and implementation of learning activities to suit the needs of all

Hay McBer (2000) was asked by the DfE to investigate what constituted effective teaching in the 16–19 sector and identified several points relevant to the issue of inclusive practice:

- Fairness: students will have entered the sector from different backgrounds and will have different needs and abilities, including some with learning difficulties. It is important to maximise opportunities for progression for all.
- Participation: students need to feel confident to ask questions, offer opinions and explore their own ideas.
- Safety: from emotional and physical bullying. The teacher has a role to create an environment where learners do not feel isolated, lonely or vulnerable.
- Support: the teacher's role is to both support and challenge students. Students need to feel able to try new things, to be prepared to fail and to learn from their mistakes.

Gravells and Simpson (2012) found that the range of student differences was above and beyond that which the Equality Act 2010 observes as protected. Intellectual ability, mental health and domestic circumstances were amongst many factors that could affect a student's potential to learn. In practice, Ofsted (2014) recognised that those teachers with flexibility in their teaching strategies and approaches were able to adapt to the learners' needs and support effective learner progress. *What Works and Why?* (Ofsted, 2014) claims that those teachers that plan clear learning activities and are expert at assessment achieve the best outcomes for their learners. This is done through good training and acknowledgement of the individual rather than just the group needs and delivery of both skill development and knowledge simultaneously. Gravells and Simpson (2012) also agree that inclusive learning is linked to teaching attitudes and the ability to reflect on one's own values and beliefs supported by a positive and inclusive environment. It is, therefore, vital that a teacher should recognise and accept that not all students are the same, and that within any given group of learners there will be a wealth of experience, learning styles and needs. Gravells (2013) suggests that positive and inclusive practice can be seen through the differentiation of resources, materials and teaching strategies.

Inclusion by differentiation is 'crucial in planning for effective 16–19 teaching' (Butcher, 2005: 60). Although being prepared for a common assessment, the teacher must be aware of the different abilities of the students in the class. Chapter 2 of this book offers a discussion on the advantages and disadvantages of differentiated learning, but the view expressed by Butcher is common at post-16 education.

Although teachers may strive to be inclusive in their teaching, they face difficulties that prevent them from always using the best teaching strategies for their students. In a series of interviews with teachers and learners at two FE Colleges, Towler *et al.* (2011) found that when success is measured by the achievement of qualifications, this can be detrimental to high-quality teaching and learning. In order to get through the curriculum and prepare students to pass their assessments, they found that teachers relied on more didactic methods (e.g. direct instruction). Several of the teachers in their sample expressed the view that 'their hands were effectively tied by the stipulations of the qualification routes on which they taught, and that this narrowed the scope for learning' (Towler *et al.*, 2011: 516). This relates also to Ecclestone's (2008: 11) view that students today are 'achieving more but learning less' on many post-16 courses. Towler *et al.* also found that students tended to view learning as something that happened in class and was the responsibility of the teachers, with little independent work being done by the students. This point is echoed by Williams (2008), who argues that, when gaining qualifications is the sole point of education, 'there is no space left for education for enjoyment, for personal development or simply for its own sake' (p. 159).

✎ **Individual/group task**

There are many different ways of achieving differentiation at post-16, including differentiation by outcome, progress, task, enrichment, additional support. Research these types of differentiation. How effective are they are in relation to inclusive practice?

Conclusion

The Wolf Reports (DfE, 2011, 2013) aim to increase the perception of employers on the quality and value of post-16 education. This includes the apprentice route as being the means to learn on the job. Current data suggest that more young people have been offered either an education place or a training place. Indeed, there has been a fall in the number of young people classed as NEET (DfE, 2015b). What seems to be the main and most contentious issue in inclusive practice, however, is the delivery and study of the core subjects of Maths and English, particularly the pressure on students to achieve a 'C' grade to gain meaningful employment opportunities. It remains to be seen, but the possible result of changes in post-16 education could be to make education *less* accessible to many students. If a qualification becomes more 'rigorous' (as is proposed for A-levels), the chances are that it will become less inclusive, with fewer students able to meet entry requirements. Students disaffected with secondary education may find revisiting core subjects arduous and beyond their capabilities, thereby jeopardising future employment prospects.

Contextualising educational experiences is a vital move towards inclusion; more motivation and flexibility for learners' development of vocational skills parallel to the core subjects is needed (Towler *et al.*, 2011; Robey *et al.*, 2014). Post-16 education reforms may in fact be less inclusive than first thought. Issues of social inequality are evident in the widening gap of employment opportunities, particularly in favour of those students who are academically more able (Williams, 2008).

Summary points

- Career advice and support are needed for young people to make the right choice for them regarding post-16 training and education.
- Students studying for Maths and English GCSE parallel to vocational subjects may be under more pressure than academically more able students.
- Due to the plethora of different providers of post-16 education, there is concern over 'subtle elitism' within the qualifications on offer.

- Training for teachers in FE has been highlighted as having significant impact in meeting the needs of the individual. However, the lack of dissemination and sharing of good practice within settings has been seen to be a barrier to the effectiveness of this training.
- Local authority-targeted community support may offer lifestyle stability to young people with greater opportunity to succeed as a learner; however, government cut-backs mean lack of equity amongst local authorities.
- The government agenda of economic growth and focus on NEETs, whilst offering opportunity to some, has created more barriers to success.

Further reading

Huddleston, P. and Unwin, L. (2007) *Teaching and Learning in Further Education: Diversity and change*. London: Routledge.

Wright, A-M., Abdi-Jama, S., Colquhoun, S., Speare, J. and Partridge, T. (2006) *FE Lecturer's Guide to Diversity and Inclusion*. Bodmin: Continuum International Publishing.

References

Bailey, B. and Unwin, L. (2014) Continuity and change in English further education: A century of voluntarism and permissive adaptability. *British Journal of Educational Studies*, 62(4), 449–464.

Bol, T. and van de Werfhorst, H.G. (2013) Educational systems and the trade-off between labor market allocation and equality of educational opportunity. *Comparative Education Review*, 29(2), 285–308.

Bolton, P. (2014) Education spending in the UK. *House of Commons Library* (10 December 2014) SN/SG/1078.

Butcher, J. (2005) *Developing Effective 16–19 Teaching Skills*. Abingdon: RoutledgeFalmer.

Carr, M. (2001) *Assessment in Early Childhood Settings*. London: PCP.

DCSF (2008) *Youth Cohort Study of England and Wales, 2004–2007: Cohort Twelve, Sweep One to Four*. Colchester, Essex: UK Data Archive.

DfE (2011) *Wolf Review of Vocational Education: Government response*. London: DfE. [Online] available at www.education.gov.uk (accessed 23 March 2015).

DfE (2013) *Wolf Recommendations Progress Report. November 2013*. London: DfE. [Online] available at www.gov.uk (accessed 23 March 2015).

DfE (2015a) Nicky Morgan discusses the future of education in England. Delivered on 18 June 2015 at the *Sunday Times Festival of Education*, Wellington College, Berkshire.

DfE (2015b) *Participation in Education, Training and Employment by 16–18 year olds in England*. London: DfE.

DfES (2002) *Success for All*. London: DfES.

Doughty, H. and Allan, J. (2008) Social capital and the evaluation of inclusiveness in Scottish further education colleges. *Journal of Further and Higher Education*, 32(3), 275–284.

Ecclestone, K. (2008) The impact of assessment on pedagogy can have damaging consequences. In I. Nash, S. Jones, K. Ecclestone and A. Brown (Eds) *Challenge and Change in Further Education*. London: Teaching and Learning Research Project.

EFA (2013) *Overview of the 16 to 19 Funding Formula: Funding full participation and study programmes for young people*. Available at www.gov.uk/government/publications (accessed 5 July 2015).

Gravells, A. (2013) *The Award in Education and Training (Further Education and Skills)*. London: Learning Matters.

Gravells, A. and Simpson, S. (2012) *Equality and Diversity in the Lifelong Learning Sector*. London: Learning Matters.

Hay McBer (2000) *Research into Teacher Effectiveness*. Norwich: HMSO.

Hodkinson, P. and Bloomer, M. (2010) Stokingham Sixth Form College: Institutional culture and dispositions to learning. *British Journal of Sociology of Education*, 21(2), 187–202.

Offord, P. (2015) Government U-turn on new childcare apprenticeships hailed a victory for employers. *FE Week*, News, 23 July 2015. Available at http://feweek.co.uk/2015/07/01/government-u-turn-on-new-childcare-apprenticeships-hailed-a-victory-for-employers (accessed 23 July 2015).

Ofsted (2010) *Reducing the Number of Young People Not in Education, Employment or Training: What works and why.* Available at www.ofsted.gov.uk (accessed 11 March 2015).

Ofsted (2014) *Report for Teaching, Learning and Assessment in Further Education and Skills: What works and why.* Available at www.ofsted.gov.uk/resources/140138 (accessed 11 March 2015).

Pring, R. (1990) *The New Curriculum.* London: Cassell.

Putnam, R. (2000) *Bowling Alone: The collapse and revival of American community.* New York: Simon and Schuster.

Robey, C., Jones, E. and Stevenson, A. (2014) *New English and Maths GCSEs in Post-16 Education and Skills: Findings of the call for evidence undertaken on behalf of the Department for Business, Innovation and Skills, and the Department for Education*: National Institute of Adult Continuing Education (England and Wales). Available at http://shop.niace.org.uk/media/catalog/product/g/c/gcse-reform-final-report.pdf (accessed 22 July 2015).

Thompson, R. (2009) Social class and participation in further education: Evidence from the Youth Cohort Study of England and Wales. *British Journal of Sociology of Education*, 30(1), 29–42.

Tomlinson, J. (1996) *Report of the Further Education Funding Council Learning Difficulties and/or Disabilities Committee.* Coventry: FEFC.

Towler, C., Woolner, P. and Wall, K. (2011) Exploring teachers' and students' conceptions of learning in two further education colleges. *Journal of Further and Higher Education*, 35(4), 501–520.

Vygotsky, L.S. (1978) *Mind in Society: The development of higher psychological processes.* Cambridge, MA: Harvard University Press.

Williams, J. (2008) Constructing social inclusion through further education: The dangers of instrumentalism. *Journal of Further and Higher Education*, 32(2), 151–160.

10 From elitist to inclusive higher education

Stephanie Brewster

Introduction

In the United Kingdom and internationally there is a continuing drive to widen participation in university education, to include greater numbers of students from 'non-traditional' backgrounds and 'under-represented' groups. This has been interpreted in terms of social divisions relating to social class, gender and ethnicity and, more recently, disability. Looking at evidence from the UK about recruitment, retention and degree attainment in relation to these various equality strands we see that, despite the mass expansion of UK higher education (HE), differential patterns of access and outcome remain.

Numerous interventions are aimed at addressing various aspects of this inequality, including the provision of support for students thought to be at risk of underachievement. Whether support is universal/mainstream (available to any student) or targeted at specific groups has very real implications for students' identities and their experience of an inclusive ethos. Furthermore, many consider there are tensions between the provision of support and the need to maintain academic standards.

Higher education is widely regarded not only as a societal good, but increasingly it is viewed in terms of the range of benefits it confers on the individual. It can be seen as enhancing social mobility and as a means to social inclusion because of its power to enhance life chances for socially disadvantaged groups (Hinton-Smith, 2012). But who has benefitted most from the transformation of UK HE from an 'elite to a mass system' (Riddell *et al.*, 2005: 157) catering for a diverse student population? And to what extent are universities now fully inclusive environments, where all individuals, with their unique and multi-faceted identities, strengths and needs, will learn and develop, and contribute to the diversity of the student population?

✎ **Individual/group task**

Look around your campus and classes and observe: what proportion of students is from an ethnic minority? How many are mature students? What is the balance between the genders? How many have disabilities? Take care about judging by appearances of course: not all differences are visible. Ask your friends doing other courses or attending other institutions the same questions. How diverse is the student population on your course and how does this compare to other courses and other institutions? In your opinion, to what extent is our current HE provision still an elite one, or an inclusive one? Why?

The context of higher education

> Twenty-one Oxbridge colleges took no black students last year.

So said Jeevan Vasagar, writing for the *Guardian* in 2010, suggesting the possibility of racism within Oxford and Cambridge Universities. Of course the situation is much more complex than the headline suggests but it highlights the emotive nature of issues to do with access to universities. Issues extend to possible sexism too, understandably, considering that Oxford and Cambridge did not formally award degrees to women until 1920 and 1947, respectively. The tendency for non-traditional students to go to newer, less-prestigious universities, rather than accessing the elite institutions of Oxbridge and other older universities (discussed further below) has also fuelled concerns about inequality. Such concerns are based on the assumption that HE benefits individuals in terms of enabling higher earnings, intellectual development, personal growth, access to social networks (Riddell *et al.*, 2005) and so on. We then need to ask: 'Are these benefits equally available to disadvantaged/under-represented groups?' Or in other words, is HE fully inclusive?

✎ **Individual/group task**

What are the benefits and challenges of a diverse and inclusive HE system . . . for you as an individual HE student? . . . for HE institutions? . . . for the economy and for society in general?

The concept of inclusive education is usually applied to compulsory educational provision, where it is concerned with the 'presence, participation and achievement' (Ainscow *et al.*, 2006: 25) of all children and young people. But entry to HE has always been, and remains, selective: it is only accessible to those with *the right qualifications*. It is therefore competitive, unlike most education up to this point, which is accessible to all. Nevertheless there is growing support for more inclusive higher education provision, based on equality for all members of a diverse population of learners. This diversity has arisen from huge changes in the HE sector in recent decades.

With the transition from traditional manufacturing to knowledge-based economies comes an increase in the demand for a differently educated workforce. As a result, there has been a massive expansion of HE over the last 30 years worldwide, with close to 50 per cent of young people in England now going to university (BIS/ONS, 2013). So participation has widened beyond the narrow preserve of middle and upper class males, as was originally the case in European universities. But the incorporation of groups of students who have traditionally been less likely to go into HE has not proved straightforward, and the need for active facilitation to promote their full inclusion has given rise to the Widening Participation (WP) agenda. WP refers to the participation of disadvantaged groups in higher education. Concerns about social class and socio-economic disadvantage have tended to dominate discussions of WP, but the concept has also encompassed other under-represented groups: those who have no history of HE participation in their families, women, black and minority ethnic (BME) groups, mature students and those who have been 'looked after children'. Disability is not always encompassed in conceptions of WP but is increasingly regarded as an equal opportunities issue alongside gender, race, ethnicity, sexual identity and age. Where disability has traditionally been seen as a medical problem or deficit associated with the individual (the 'medical model' of disability), it is increasingly being viewed from the 'social model' viewpoint, in which society is regarded as creating the disabling barriers experienced by the individual. From this perspective, disability then becomes a matter of equality. Of course, the multi-faceted nature of identity means that any individual will belong to various groups; this makes for a very complex picture indeed when trying to get to grips with this field.

Discussions of inequality in HE frequently draw on Bourdieu's concept of cultural capital: differences in cultural capital (social connections, experiences and knowledge) are regarded as accounting for social class differences in HE participation and attainment, and the distribution of students between elite and other institutions. So, for example, a working class potential student may in effect be excluded because they feel as though they would not fit in or belong at university; their cultural capital has not equipped them with the skills and information necessary to gain entry to and succeed in HE. Interestingly, recent research now indicates that the strongest influence of cultural capital is *indirect*, through its effects on school attainment (and hence entry qualifications), rather than *directly* through social class (Noble and Davies, 2009). In other words, a pupil from a working class background finds that their own cultural capital does not fit well with that of the school, and they are therefore at a disadvantage. And as noted above, without the right entry qualifications, you cannot get into university.

So a HE system designed originally for the privileged minority of white, male middle/upper class non-disabled students is now expected to cope with a much more diverse student population. Another contributor to the diversification of the HE student population in recent years is the increasing number of international students travelling to the UK to study, resulting in universities now being multicultural communities. Caruana and Ploner (2010) suggest that two differing agendas – equality and diversity on the one hand, and internationalisation on the other – are in tension. The driver for promoting internationalisation is largely financial: UK HE is big business and institutions may consider that attracting international students will enhance its prestige. The underpinnings of equality and diversity, however, are ethical: the case for inclusion of a diverse population is a matter of social justice. A commitment to fairness and social justice would suggest that universities have a responsibility not only to allow access to this newly diverse population but to meet their complex and differing needs, rather than merely assimilate them into the existing system.

Legal requirements of equality of opportunity continue to be refined and strengthened. For example, in the UK, the Disability Discrimination Act (DDA) (2005) placed on all public institutions a duty to actively promote equality of opportunity for people with disabilities. This obligation includes making reasonable adjustments 'to policies, provisions or the physical environment in order to overcome a disadvantage suffered by a disabled student' (Rickinson, 2010: 4). More broadly, the subsequent Equality Act of 2010 has encompassed and strengthened numerous pre-existing pieces of equality legislation and makes it illegal to discriminate against any student or potential student because of any of the nine 'protected characteristics', including those of disability, age, race and sex. Specific to HE, the Office for Fair Access (OFFA) was set up 'to promote and safeguard fair access to higher education for lower income and other under-represented groups following the introduction of higher tuition fees in 2006–07'. It operates primarily through the monitoring of 'access agreements', which set out what HE institutions intend to do to promote access, such as outreach work and summer schools.

Having provided a little historical and contemporary context regarding HE, the next three sections take Ainscow *et al.*'s (2006) three aspects of inclusion in education – presence, participation and achievement – and apply these to HE.

'Presence': who gets into university?

Increasing numbers of (especially young) people are entering HE and the student population has become more diverse. However, above we questioned whether all groups of society have benefitted equally from this expansion. But what is the evidence of inequality in access? The term 'under-represented groups' was used above, as if this is an unproblematic concept. In fact, considerable debate has surrounded which groups of society are under-represented in HE. Are you more or less likely to go to university if you are male or female? From a particular ethnic group or social class or are disabled? Who counts as 'disadvantaged'? What proportion of HE students is identified as such and how does this compare with the population as a whole? Given that the student population is not representative of the population as a whole (they are more likely to be young, for example), is this a fair comparison? Below we consider several groups in turn, looking at the evidence regarding their representation at university.

Socio-economic status

The Sutton Trust (2008) stated that 'Forty-three per cent of young people from the higher social classes participate in higher education, compared with 19 per cent of those from the bottom social classes'. McCaig and Bowers-Brown (2007) confirm that students from lower socio-economic groups are still less likely to participate in higher education than those from more advantaged groups. Partly this is because students from poor backgrounds are less likely to achieve good enough entry qualifications. As Gorard (2008) points out, 'these prior qualifications are strongly associated with social class and, to a lesser extent, with ethnicity, disability and sex'. But it is worth noting that students with the same entry qualifications have the same chance of being in a position to apply to university regardless of their background. Another possible factor is that selection and interview processes may be biased in favour of those with the right cultural capital (i.e. middle class students).

Gender

While the historic picture of unequal access regarding social class clearly still exists despite having shown some improvement, the picture is different regarding gender. The Higher Education Statistics Agency (2014) reports that 'A higher proportion of female students (56.2 per cent) than male students (43.8 per cent) were studying in HE in the UK' in 2012–13. So males could now be regarded as under-represented in HE – a stark contrast with the exclusively male early higher education institutions.

Of course the simple statistics hide greater complexity, such as the tendency for certain subject areas to attract a majority of one gender or the other; the implications of this for later employment prospects are discussed below.

Ethnicity

If we look at statistics regarding ethnicity, the picture is complex.

✎ **Individual/group task**

Look at Table 10.1. What do the statistics tell you? And, perhaps more importantly, what don't they tell you? Does this offer evidence of under-representation?

Table 10.1 Number of young UK students starting in HE 1996–97 to 2005–06

Starting year	White	Minority ethnic	Unknown	Total	Minority ethnic (%)
1996–97	144,625	18,335	9,540	172,495	11
1997–98	155,245	21,555	10,945	187,745	12
1998–99	153,305	22,385	11,545	187,235	13
1999–2000	157,925	23,775	7,760	189,465	13
2000–01	159,585	26,390	6,885	192,860	14
2001–02	163,375	28,310	8,385	200,065	15
2002–03	171,965	30,095	5,655	207,715	15
2003–04	173,025	31,945	6,750	211,720	16
2004–05	176,775	34,545	4,340	215,655	16
2005–06	190,260	38,360	4,815	233,435	17
2006–07	180,200	39,295	3,970	223,470	18

Source: HEFCE (2010: 8).

The upward trend in participation in HE of BME students is clear and Modood (2012: 19) indicates that 'by 2008, non-whites constituted 20 per cent of HE places offered to new students, this being almost double their share of the population' (but remember some BME students travel from overseas to attend UK universities). However, the statistics mask complex issues. There are considerable disparities between specific ethnic groups in terms of participation rates, patterns of study (e.g. full/part time, under/postgraduate) and degree attainment. In other words, regarding 'minority ethnic' students as a homogeneous group (as in Table 10.1 from HEFCE) can mask much of the disadvantage, which is evident when we identify groups' specific ethnic origins. Furthermore, BME students are still more concentrated in the (typically less-prestigious) newer universities. Modood claims there is evidence of institutional discrimination on the part of pre-1992 universities, whose BME applicants have to perform better in order to secure a place. So there remain important issues regarding fair access in relation to ethnicity.

Disability

Gosling (2009: 127, in Rickinson, 2010: 4) describes the current situation within the sector as follows:

> Students with disabilities are under-represented in higher education. The reasons for this may be to do with underachievement and low aspiration as children at school, but may have as much to do with their social class, or their ethnicity or a combination of these factors. But we

cannot rule out the possibility that prejudice against disabled students and ignorance about what they are capable of, with appropriate support, has also contributed to their under-representation.

This highlights the complex interplay of factors. Added to this is the difficulty with simply counting the number of disabled students. Not all 'disabled' students will have disclosed their disability to their institution or be claiming Disabled Students' Allowance (DSA) – the two key ways of identifying such students. According to the Equality Challenge Unit (Equality Challenge Unit, 2013: 98), 'Over the last nine years, the proportion of students who were disabled steadily increased from 5.4 per cent in 2003/04 to 8.6 per cent in 2011/12'; but is this evidence of continuing under-representation? Take a moment to think about the age profile of the university population: they are mostly young, whereas within the population as a whole, disability is much more common amongst elderly people. And, as with ethnicity and gender, these figures also vary considerably by subject area: 'The proportion of students within a subject area who were disabled ranged from 15.7 per cent of those studying creative arts and design to 4.9 per cent of those studying business and administrative studies' (Equality Challenge Unit, 2013: 95). We will see below how this has major implications for subsequent earning potential.

The examples above (social class, gender, ethnicity and disability) show how evidence of under-representation is complex and sometimes contradictory. Indeed, some have questioned the whole assumption underlying the widening participation agenda, which is 'that potential students are unfairly and disproportionately denied access to higher education in terms of occupation, ethnicity, sex or disability' (Gorard, 2008: 436). Gorard goes on to say 'the two groups most obviously under-represented in HE at present – males and whites – have been largely ignored in concerns about WP'. One thing that is clear is the uneven spread of non-traditional students across the HE sector; they are concentrated in (less-prestigious) newer institutions which emphasise teaching, with relatively lesser growth in numbers in elite institutions which tend to be more research intensive. Hinton-Smith (2012) identifies processes of 'self-selection' by non-traditional students favouring non-elite institutions, because of their financial concerns, and also issues to do with culture and identity; non-traditional students may perceive elite institutions as not providing an environment they would comfortably fit into, in contrast to a more welcoming culture in newer universities, which they recognise as more 'for people like me' (see discussion of cultural capital above). Hinton-Smith also accuses some institutions of discriminatory admissions processes, in which elite universities favour applicants who hold traditional entry qualifications (A-levels).

'Participation': what happens once they get there?

Once a student has been offered a place at university, what happens next? Some groups of non-traditional students show concerningly low retention rates; in other words, a lot drop out during their studies. For example, the Joseph Rowntree Foundation draws attention to 'the disproportionate number of students from disadvantaged family backgrounds who prematurely discontinue their careers in higher education' (Forsyth and Furlong, 2003: 2). There are also disparities between ethnic groups; Thomas and Berry (using data from the National Audit Office, 2007) state, 'BME full-time students (with the exception of mixed race and "other" ethnicities) are more likely to continue into their second year of study than White students' (2010: 14). With financial pressure on institutions to retain as many of their students as possible, universities are keen to understand the experiences of various groups of students. The case study below briefly reports on unpublished research carried out at the University of Wolverhampton, which invited disabled students to discuss their experiences of support in terms of barriers and enablers to their learning.

All students were invited to participate in the survey if they felt they had additional needs (related to a physical, mental, sensory impairment or health condition or a specific learning difficulty such as dyslexia) – whether or not they had disclosed these to the institution.

Case study: disabled students' experiences of barriers and enablers to their learning

Some students underlined how crucial additional support was to their success in HE:

> In my first and second year my personal tutors were amazing constantly checking to see if there was anything that they could improve or help me with to increase my learning.

A wide range of 'reasonable adjustments' (such as 'considerate marking' for dyslexic students) was reported to be used by students, although some had not come forward to access support. There was a variety of views expressed about whether to disclose a disability; for example:

- Anxiety about being told I'm wrong, due to lack of medical attention I have had.
- I had the opportunity to declare, so I declared everything, there was no point me not declaring anything because it wouldn't benefit me if I didn't lay my cards on the table.
- Not something I want people to be aware of on a formal basis.
- It would depend on the need as some of my illness I have disclosed to the University and others I haven't.

Some students felt the implementation of adjustments was inconsistent, and attitudes seemed crucial to this. One individual stated:

> You can get left out by students and staff, it's like you can get brushed aside.

Unfortunately, such attitudinal and cultural barriers are well documented in published literature (e.g. Riddell *et al.*, 2005) and these data reinforce the continuing need to actively promote an inclusive institutional ethos regarding disability.

✎ **Individual/group task**

A significant proportion of respondents in this survey had not disclosed their disability to the university. What factors might an individual student consider when deciding whether to do so? What could be done to encourage disclosure?

'Achievement': students' degree attainment

As a student completes their time at university, we turn next to attainment and specifically the 'attainment gap'. This term refers to any persistent discrepancy of outcome (indicated by such indicators as degree classification or subsequent employment), between different groups of students (such as working or middle class students; white or BME students). The closing of any such attainment gaps is a priority for those concerned with equity in education. The following headline grabbers from the Equality Challenge Unit's 2013 report would suggest there is indeed some cause for concern:

- 8.6 per cent ethnicity degree attainment gap for younger students.
- 26.3 per cent ethnicity degree attainment gap for older students.

✎ Individual/group task

Look at the three tables of data below (Tables 10.2, 10.3 and 10.4) from the HEFCE report *Higher education and beyond: Outcomes from full-time first degree study* (2013). Which statistics do you think give most cause for concern? Can you spot any examples of a 'negative attainment gap' (see below for an explanation of this)?

Table 10.2 Total cohort and percentage of the cohort who achieved each outcome, split by ethnicity

	White	Black	Chinese	Indian	Other Asian	Other/unknown
Starting cohort	181,510	8,465	2,410	10,325	10,835	12,215
Degree-qualified (%)	83.1	73.8	87.2	84.1	77.7	78.4
First or upper second (%)	56.1	31.3	50.7	45.8	35.9	49.2
Degree and employed or studying (%)	72.8	60.5	68.6	70.3	62.3	65.7
Degree and graduate job or study (%)	48.4	37.7	53.2	51.1	42.6	46.2

Source: HEFCE (2013: 8).

Table 10.3 Total number of female and male students, and the percentage of the cohorts who achieved each outcome

	Women	Men
Starting cohort	123,450	102,315
Degree-qualified (%)	84.9	79.2
First or upper second (%)	57.0	48.9
Degree and employed or studying (%)	75.4	66.6
Degree and graduate job or study (%)	49.0	46.4

Source: HEFCE (2013: 8).

Table 10.4 Total cohort and percentage of the cohort who achieved each outcome, split by disability status

	Disabled Students' Allowance	Declared disability	Not known to be disabled
Starting cohort	6,785	9,670	209,310
Degree-qualified (%)	82.8	79.5	82.5
First or upper second (%)	50.6	49.5	53.6
Degree-qualified and employed or studying (%)	69.4	67.2	71.7
Degree and graduate job or study (%)	46.8	45.8	47.9

Source: HEFCE (2013: 8).

Table 10.4, relating to disability status, demonstrates that disabled students receiving Disabled Students' Allowance perform better than disabled students who do not receive DSA and (perhaps surprisingly) better than those students who are *not* known to be disabled. This is one of several examples above of a negative attainment gap (ECU, 2013) – in which a potentially disadvantaged group tends to out-perform others; but it is worth pointing out that this slender overall advantage masks significant differences in some subject areas. For example, ECU (2013) reports that in medicine and dentistry 23.6 per cent of disabled qualifiers received a first, compared with 32.0 per cent of non-disabled qualifiers (an 8.4 percentage point difference).

Similarly, the overall favourable outcomes for women compared to men disguise differences according to subject area. More women complete less-prestigious degree programmes in the arts and humanities, which tend to lead to less-stable employment and much lower pay, compared to the male-dominated subjects of science, technology, engineering and mathematics, where salaries may be 60–90 per cent higher and employment rates more stable.

What has been done to improve equity?

So far in this chapter we have seen that there is a complex range of possible reasons accounting for patterns of differential access to HE and subsequent outcomes. In published literature, most attention has been paid to socio-economically disadvantaged students, and Forsyth and Furlong (2003) identify the following barriers to HE:

- lack of familiarity with how universities work, subjects, study methods and student finance policies
- lack of good advice and careers information
- low aspirations within their schools and neighbourhoods
- fear of debt (more so than actual debt)
- cultural barriers, with HE being an 'alien concept' for families and friends
- trouble fitting in to the institutional life, especially of more prestigious institutions.

Many of these factors are relevant to students who identify with other under-represented groups too. For example, socio-economic disadvantage is more common among some BME groups, single parents, mature students and disabled students.

✎ **Individual/group task**

Working in a small group, generate ideas for what could be done to address these issues. Some of your strategies may be targeted, some may be universal (see below). Consider how much your strategies might cost and who should pay. Anticipate criticisms from other groups of stakeholders, e.g. middle class families, and how you will respond to their points.

Interventions which aim to address inequality in HE can be directed at two stages in a student's career:

- First, action can aim to raise students' early educational attainment (hence HE entry qualifications) and aspiration so they are better prepared and more likely to apply for and gain admission to HE. There is strong evidence to suggest that raising the school attainment of these young people is likely to have a more powerful effect than later interventions (Noble and Davies, 2009). Gorard (2008: 436) claims that there

> is no simple and consistent pattern of under-representation among socially disadvantaged groups in attendance on HE courses, *once prior qualifications for entry are taken into account* ... This, in turn, suggests that WP activities need to be directed at the earlier life of potential students more than at the point of possible transfer to HE.

  This makes a strong case for outreach activity in schools.
- Second, action may attempt to change the way HE institutions recruit and support students from non-traditional backgrounds once there, to maximise their chances of completing their studies (retention) and achieving highly. For example, international students and those who come under the widening participation umbrella may benefit from orientation programmes to help them adjust to the unfamiliar HE environment while maintaining their sense of identity. Similarly, Foundation degrees and bursaries which provide financial support for many less well-off students might effectively address recruitment, retention and achievement.

Intervention can also be either *targeted* at individuals/groups of students, or *universally available* (to all students). While targeted intervention may seem to provide best use of resources, there is now a growing move towards making higher education more inclusive for *all* students, building on students' identities and cultural backgrounds and individual knowledge (Caruana and Ploner, 2010). Funded targeted intervention projects are notoriously prone to fluctuations in funding and government policy, making it hard to track long-term effectiveness of programmes. An example of one such programme is Aimhigher, which closed in 2011; it

> aimed to widen participation and access in HE by raising awareness, aspirations and attainment among learners from under-represented groups. [...] The programme particularly focused on children in school from lower socio-economic groups and those from disadvantaged backgrounds who lived in areas of relative deprivation where participation in HE was low.
>
> (Higher Education Academy, no date)

McCaig and Bowers-Brown (2007) indicate that Aimhigher made a positive difference 'in raising educational attainment and raising aspirations and awareness of HE among underrepresented groups'; and yet the authors remain critical. They suggest that initiatives such as Aimhigher, while promoting the WP of under-represented groups in HE nevertheless do little to address issues of social justice. Instead of targeting students in most need of additional support (e.g. white working class students), they often target easier-to-reach groups (such as BME students as a whole, rather than the specific ethnic groups which are under-represented) who will more readily enable government participation targets to be reached.

For disabled students also, changes to funding arrangements are planned. Disabled Students' Allowances are highly targeted government grants which help meet the extra costs faced by students as a result of a disability or specific learning difficulty. Forthcoming reductions in DSA will put greater financial responsibilities on individual HE institutions to ensure their disabled students are able to participate on an equal basis with other students. Unsurprisingly this is raising concerns about whether universities will indeed 'pick up the tab', although ideologically this move would appear to support an inclusive ethos. This is because it will create incentives for universities to work towards more mainstream practices that are fully inclusive, resulting in a situation where DSA funding (in theory) is no longer needed. This more fully inclusive environment should address staff concerns over fairness (identified by Riddell *et al.*, 2005) arising from many students, e.g. international students, or those from working class backgrounds being recognised as having needs and yet not 'qualifying' for additional help.

How can academic standards be maintained?

As the proportion of people going to university is increasing, entry qualifications have dropped, and honours degree classifications have risen (Yorke, 2012). This gives rise to the common perception of 'dumbing down' or the lowering of academic standards. This is often linked to assumptions about certain groups of students lacking the necessary skills and capital to succeed in HE, and therefore needing additional resources (Hockings, 2010). This deficit view of 'non-traditional' students (which emphasises and labels them according to what they cannot do, rather than what they can) is widely held but also contested by many, who argue there is no evidence of a drop in academic standards as a result of widening participation. Changing curriculum and assessment practices that recognise a wider range of skills and a new emphasis on employability (Yorke, 2012) are some of the factors helping to maintain academic standards, but as we have seen above, much progress is yet to be made before success in higher education can be said to be equally within reach of all groups.

✎ **Individual/group task**

Simplistic assumptions about non-traditional students being deficient in skills and abilities ('deficit model' thinking) can be damaging for individuals; what can be done to promote more positive images?

Do you think that requirements to widen participation in HE have led to the 'dumbing down' of standards or reduction of academic rigour?

Conclusion

A fully inclusive university is one where all individuals, with their unique and multi-faceted identities, strengths and needs, will learn and develop, and contribute to the diversity of the student population. In the evolution away from an elite, to a more inclusive system of HE, May and Bridger (2010: 2, in Rickinson, 2010) have observed an ongoing 'shift away from supporting specific student groups through a discrete set of policies or time-bound interventions, towards equity considerations being embedded within all functions of the institution and treated as an ongoing process of quality enhancement'.

Despite significant progress towards more inclusive higher education, there remains much to be done, and widening access to HE continues to be high on the agenda in many countries. Recent global recession has threatened this, however, with many countries cutting education budgets; this has had a disproportionate effect (according to many critics) on underprivileged students (Hinton-Smith, 2012), whose fear of debt incurred by university acts as a disincentive for students from low socio-economic status backgrounds. In contrast, the Office of Fair Access claims that: 'The introduction of higher fees in 2006–07 has not had a detrimental effect on participation of students from low income and other under-represented groups.' Whatever your own view, there is a clear tension in current UK policy regarding student tuition fees and the WP agenda – a tension that is unlikely to be resolved any time soon.

 Individual/group task

Research your own higher education institution's mission statement and policies and provision regarding widening participation and equality. How do they reflect current legislation and theories of equality, diversity and inclusion?

Summary points

- Historically, access to university was reserved for a narrow elite of the population (white, male, middle/upper class).
- Nowadays arguments based on equality of opportunity form the basis of the widening participation agenda for all sectors of the population.
- Almost half of young people in the UK now attend university and many are from groups that have been traditionally less likely to attend university ('under-represented' groups).
- These groups relate to characteristics such as socio-economic status and social class, gender, age, ethnicity and disability.
- Despite significant progress towards a fully inclusive system, there remain differences in access to HE and in degree attainment, and progression into careers and jobs.
- Disagreement remains about how to address this inequality; increasingly issues of equity and inclusive practice are being embedded in all higher education functions.

Further reading

Basit, T. and Tomlinson, S. (Eds) (2012) *Social Inclusion and Higher Education*. Bristol: Policy Press.
Smith, E. (2012) *Key Issues in Education and Social Justice.* London: Sage.
TeachInclusive (2008) Anglia Ruskin University. http://web.anglia.ac.uk/inclusive_practice/index.html (accessed 8 July 2015).

References

Ainscow, M., Booth, T. and Dyson, A. (2006) *Improving Schools, Developing Inclusion*. London: Routledge.
BIS/ONS (2013) *Participation Rates in Higher Education: 2006 to 2012.* London: BIS/ONS. www.gov.uk/government/statistics/participation-rates-in-higher-education-2006-to-2012 (accessed 1 July 2015).
Caruana, V. and Ploner, J. (2010) *Internationalisation and Equality and Diversity in Higher Education: Merging Identities.* Leeds: Equality Challenge Unit, Leeds Metropolitan University. www.ecu.ac.uk/wp-content/uploads/external/internationalisation-equality-diversity-in-he.pdf (accessed 27 June 2014).
Equality Challenge Unit (2013) *Equality in Higher Education: Statistical Report 2013 Part 2: Students*. London: Equality Challenge Unit. www.ecu.ac.uk/publications/equality-in-higher-education-statistical-report-2013 (accessed 22 September 2014).
Equality and Human Rights Commission (2010) *Equality Act 2010*. London: EHRC. www.equalityhuman-rights.com/private-and-public-sector-guidance/education-providers/higher-education-providers-guidance (accessed 18 May 2015).
Forsyth, A. and Furlong, F. (2003) *Losing Out? Socioeconomic Disadvantage and Experience in Further and Higher Education*. York: Joseph Rowntree Foundation.
Gorard, S. (2008) Who is missing from higher education? *Cambridge Journal of Education Volume*, 38(3), 421–437.
HEFCE (2010) *Student Ethnicity: Profile and Progression of Entrants to Full-time, First Degree Study*. Bristol: HEFCE. www.hefce.ac.uk/pubs/year/2010/201013/ (accessed 22 September 2014).
HEFCE (2013) *Higher Education and Beyond: Outcomes from Full-time First Degree Study*. Bristol: HEFCE. www.hefce.ac.uk/pubs/year/2013/201315/ (accessed 22 September 2014).
Higher Education Academy (no date) www.heacademy.ac.uk/enhancement/themes/retention-and-success/widening-access-programmes-archive/aimhigher (accessed 2 March 2016).
Higher Education Statistics Agency (2014) *Student Introduction 2012/13*. Cheltenham: HESA. www.hesa.ac.uk/content/view/3129 (accessed 13 January 2015).
Hinton-Smith, T (2012) *Widening Participation in Higher Education: Casting the Net Wide?* Basingstoke: Palgrave Macmillan.
Hockings, C. (2010) *Inclusive Learning and Teaching in Higher Education: A Synthesis of Research*. York: Higher Education Academy. www.heacademy.ac.uk/resources/detail/resources/detail/evidencenet/Inclusive_learning_and_teaching_in_higher_education (accessed 1 April 2015).
McCaig, C. and Bowers-Brown, T. (2007) Aimhigher: Achieving social justice? Paper presented at the British Educational Research Association Annual Conference, Institute of Education, University of London, 5–8 September 2007. www.leeds.ac.uk/educol/documents/168534.htm (accessed 22 September 2014).
Modood, T. (2012) Capitals, ethnicity and higher education. In T. Basit and S. Tomlinson (Eds) *Social Inclusion and Higher Education*. Bristol: Policy Press.
Noble, J. and Davies, P. (2009) Cultural capital as an explanation of variation in participation in higher education. *British Journal of Sociology of Education*, 30(5), 591–605.
Rickinson, M. (2010) *Disability Equality in Higher Education: A Synthesis of Research*. York: Higher Education Academy. www.heacademy.ac.uk/resources/detail/evidencenet/disability_equality_synthesis (accessed 1 April 2015).
Riddell, S. Tinklin, T. and Wilson, A. (2005) *Disabled Students in Higher Education; The Intersection of Social Justice and New Management Agendas*. London: RoutledgeFalmer.
Sutton Trust (2008) *Increasing Higher Education Participation Amongst Disadvantaged Young People and Schools in Poor Communities*. London: Sutton Trust. www.suttontrust.com/wp-content/uploads/2008/10/1NCEE_interim_report.pdf (accessed 22 September 2014).
Thomas, L. and Berry, J. (2010) Understanding widening participation. In D. Weekes-Bernard (Ed.) *Widening Participation and Race Equality*. London; Runnymede. www.runnymedetrust.org/uploads/publications/pdfs/WideningParticipation-2011(Online).pdf (accessed 8 July 2015).

Vasagar, J (2010) Twenty-one Oxbridge colleges took no black students last year. *Guardian*, 6 December. www.theguardian.com/education/2010/dec/06/oxford-colleges-no-black-students (accessed 29 July 2014).

Yorke, M. (2012) Widening participation in universities in England and Wales: Is there a connection with hon-ours degree achievement? In T. Hinton-Smith (Ed.) *Widening Participation in Higher Education. Casting the Net Wide?* Basingstoke: Palgrave Macmillan.

Part III
Inclusive practice

International perspectives

11 Diversity in Greece

Equity, access and inclusion issues

Nektaria Palaiologou and Ioanna Palaiologou

Introduction

Throughout this book, the aim is to discuss issues of diversity and inclusion. In this chapter, we aim to offer an overview of these issues in relation to a country that has an interesting social geography: Greece.

Greece is a country in south-eastern Europe consisting of two mainland peninsulas and thousands of islands throughout the Aegean and Ionian seas – part of the Mediterranean sea – that surround her. Greece entered the European Union in 1982 and in 2001 became part of the Eurozone that adopted the Euro as its official currency. As will be illustrated, the Greek state traditionally has been a monolingual and monocultural society with a strong national identity. For example, until the beginning of the twentieth century the Greek government's education policy was characterised by an almost complete lack of interest in issues of diversity and it was mainly the Greek Orthodox Church that was dominating the education system. This situation did not change substantially until the early 1970s (Anagnostopoulou, 1995) and for many years the Orthodox Church retained an influential role in the organisation of education and curriculum design, especially at primary (six to eleven years) and secondary levels (eleven to seventeen years). Greece was one of the few European countries where the Ministry of Education was the Ministry of Education and Religious Affairs (Noutsos, 1998).

However, during the last three decades Greece has experienced rapid socio-demographic change that has impacted in many ways on daily life, the behaviours of people and the attitudes towards national identity; this has been reflected in the policies and the education system. As will be shown, despite the late response at policy level, the Greek education system is still not keeping pace with the demands placed upon it caused by the changing socio-demographics.

Thus, the chapter aims to focus on policies which are implemented in Greece for diverse students, especially for two main groups: children coming from different national backgrounds and children with special needs. It aims to address the challenges that are caused by the financial crisis and will conclude that, despite the introduction of policies, Greek society and the education system are still a long way off being characterised as inclusive and diverse.

Social geography: Greece, a changing society

In the twentieth century, Greece experienced waves of migration, mainly to countries such as the United States, Great Britain, Germany, Sweden, Canada and Australia. The population which migrated from Greece is known as the *Greek diaspora* or *Hellenic diaspora*, also known as *Omogenia* (Ομογένεια), a term that refers to the communities who migrated from the homeland to other countries seeking a better future for themselves and their families (Clogg, 2000; Rozen, 2008; Tziovas, 2009).

The main reasons for the massive migration were:

1   Economic: The Greek economy at the beginning of the twentieth century was wounded by a series of conflicts to reclaim land after the collapse of the Ottoman empire and the aftermath of World War I, which left the country in a state of political instability; under the Treaty of Lausanne (1923), waves of refugees, mainly from Turkey, were connected with the massive task of incorporating 1.5 million Greek refugees from Asia Minor into Greek society.
2   Population exchange: Greeks that lived in the territory of modern Turkey were forced or coerced into leaving their homes as part of the population exchange programmes under the terms of the aforementioned 1923 Treaty of Lausanne, as a consequence of a common agreement resolving the years of conflict between Turkey and Greece which formalised the exodus and barred the return of the refugees.
3   The Greek Civil War (1946–1949): Many communist Greeks and their families were forced to flee to neighbouring countries, mainly influenced by the ex-Soviet Union regime. Within Eastern Europe and the USSR, numbers of Greeks of the diaspora whose Greek ancestry was 'disowned' for many generations migrated to modern Greece's main urban centres of Athens and Thessaloniki.

As can be seen, Greek society experienced migration from Greece and, as mentioned earlier, Greece was mainly shaped up as a monocultural, ethnocentric society up to the 1990s. In the 1990s, the collapse of communist regimes in the ex-Soviet Union and the countries that were influenced, mainly in the Balkans, opened the borders of these countries and brought a wave of migration to the richest and most prosperous countries. At the time, Greece was considered to be one of the richest and most developed countries in the Balkans, and consequently started receiving illegal immigrants seeking a better financial future for their families, mainly from the poorest countries of the Balkan zone that used to be influenced by the ex-Soviet Union and the communist regime. This wave of immigration continued during the 2000s. The main waves of immigration came from Albania, Bulgaria, Romania and, more recently, Pakistan, Kurdistan, Afghanistan, Iraq and Somalia. In brief, Greece has experienced two waves of immigration:

1   the immigrants that did not have Greek origin;
2   the immigrants that had Greek ancestry and were returning to what they thought was their homeland (repatriation). These were mainly coming from countries that were influenced by the former Soviet Union or from Northern Epirus.

The 2001 census showed an increase in the population of immigrants that lived in Greece and a recorded 7 per cent of non-Greek citizens living in the country. The 2011 census recorded a total population of 10,816,286, of whom 9,904,286 were Greek citizens and 912,000 had come to

Greece from foreign origins. The main nationalities had come from the Balkans: Albanians 4.44 per cent, Bulgarians 0.7 per cent, Romanians 0.43 per cent (ELSTAT, 2011).

As can be seen, Greek society has undergone rapid changes in the last twenty years and currently, when this chapter was being written, a further wave of new immigrants, mainly from Syria and Africa, were arriving on the Greek islands, making the news daily.

 Individual/group task

Reflect on the socio-demographic changes in Greece and:

1   Discuss the difference between the terms: migrant, immigrant, political asylum seeker.
2   Reflect on the socio-demographics of the UK and discuss whether there are any similarities and/or differences between these two countries.

A struggling economy

This rapid change in the socio-demographic landscape of Greece has brought tensions between a traditional society with strong national identity and the newcomers (Spinthourakis *et al.*, 2009). These tensions increased with the economic recession Greece was facing due to the global financial crises. In 2010, the financial situation in Greece led to the acceptance of severe austerity measures and the implementation of a sequence of bailout funding from the International Monetary Fund (IMF) and the European Central Bank (ECB).

Economic instability led in turn to political instability and anxiety in society as to how people would cope with the austerity measures. Greek society started experiencing phenomena of racism and xenophobia, and this was reflected in the rise of nationalist views promoting ethnocentric ideas and winning places even in the Greek parliament.

To conclude, Greece has seen a rapid demographic change from a traditional monolingual, monocultural society to a multicultural society. It has a population that lives outside the homeland (the Greek diaspora), but when some of them repatriated to their homeland they were considered as 'others'. Since the 1990s, and even now, the country has been experiencing waves of immigration, but financial instability has led to issues of affordability in relation to the inclusion of immigration and also social anxieties towards them. These factors contributed to the development of xenophobia and to the rise of the extreme Right party (called Golden Dawn); i.e. a phenomenon where people demonstrate prejudice and fear towards anything foreign and unfamiliar. Xenophobia can lead to discriminatory practices against people from other cultures.

 Individual/group task

Consider the political, economical and social landscape in the UK. Can you draw any similarities between Greece and the UK? Discuss the impact of economic recession in approaching immigration. Try to consider why people become xenophobic.

The impact of social change on education

The rapid changes in the socio-demographics of Greece created a dichotomy in Greek society: the population who were nationals and the 'others' – who were immigrants or repatriates. Consequently this had an impact on the education system on two levels: social attitudes and policy. Studies such as Hatzichristou and Hopf (1993) and Palaiologou (2004) have examined how immigrant and repatriated children are included in the education system, especially when they first arrive. It was evident in all these studies that immigrant or repatriated students entering a new education system have difficulties in adjusting to it and find problems of acceptability from other pupils leading to anti-social behaviours. These include negative comments, bullying, discrimination and racist attitudes, all of which influence the self-esteem of these students. The following sections will explain how Greek politicians tried to address these problems by introducing policies to promote intercultural education. Such policies aimed to promote equality in education for all students, no matter what their origin, religion, language or economical status, and to ensure that the education system was equipped to support all students to meet their full learning potential.

However, as will be shown, the implementation of intercultural education does not result simply from the introduction of new policies. A lack of resources, misunderstanding of cultural diversity in teacher training (Tsigilis *et al.*, 2006), limited collaboration with parents (Doliopoulou, 2005) and personal beliefs, prejudice and stereotypes made the implementation of legislation ineffective in practice.

Diversity in Greece

Among the main concerns of the Council of the European Union (2010) has been that there are differences in the degree of social inclusion achieved by the Member States, indicating that there remains significant scope to reduce inequalities and exclusion in the EU, both through structural changes and through additional support for learners at risk of social exclusion. Equity and excellence are not mutually exclusive but complementary, and should be pursued at both national and European levels. While each Member State's situation is different, European cooperation can help identify ways to promote social inclusion and equity, while not compromising excellence.

With regard to education, the Council of the European Union (2009) has pointed out:

> the key role this has to play not only in ensuring that children with a migrant background can fulfil their potential to become well-integrated and successful citizens, but also in creating a society which is equitable, inclusive and respectful of diversity. Yet many such children continue to fare less well in terms of educational outcomes, and issues relating to racial and ethnic discrimination and to social exclusion are to be found in all parts of the European Union. The presence of significant numbers of learners with migrant backgrounds in many Member States thus presents a number of challenges – but also valuable opportunities – for their education systems.
>
> (p. 3)

In the above statement, *diversity* emerges as the new essential dimension in modern societies, most of which are, or have become, multicultural. European countries allege that the social measures they follow target inclusive policies. Acknowledging diversity, however, seems to be a difficult accomplishment in practice since it has been in accordance with the notions of equity, access and belongingness-inclusion for various social groups.

As shown above, since the 1990s Greece has been transformed from a country from which people emigrate, into one to which people immigrate. As a result of the immigration that has occurred, approximately 10 per cent of the total population currently residing in Greece was not born in the country (OECD, 2012; Palaiologou, 2013). The country 'has seen its demography significantly and irreversibly altered in social, cultural, economic, ethnic, racial and religious terms' (Gropas and Triandafyllidou, 2011: 402). Thus, the most common explication for the term 'diversity' for the Greek case usually refers to the different ethno-cultural groups: the documented migrants, legitimate/regular repatriates – of Greek origin, usually from Northern Epirus or from the former Soviet Union countries – and the irregular, documented and undocumented migrants in accordance with the International Organisation for Migration glossary (n.d.). The content of the term 'diversity' might also refer to other ethnic or linguistic minority groups, e.g. Roma, and also to people with special needs.

The recent economic crisis in Greece has influenced relations between the native population and the large number of national and cultural migrants and religious and ethnic minorities residing in the country. According to official data (Ministry of Interior, 2010), approximately 58 per cent of migrants in Greece come from Albania and the remaining 42 per cent come primarily from Bulgaria, Ukraine, Romania, Georgia, Pakistan, the Philippines, Russia, Moldavia, Iraq and Egypt. The majority of migrants (56 per cent) are young people between nineteen and forty years of age. Some 17 per cent are children of migrants – the 'second generation', up to eighteen years of age (Palaiologou *et al.*, 2010). Among adult migrants, 59 per cent are secondary education graduates and 13 per cent are university graduates (Palaiologou, 2012). Poverty and intolerance, as well as an increase in political extremism, have impacted on the social position of minority groups in Greece (Kakos and Palaiologou, 2013). Some recent studies suggest that, since 2010, Greece is once again becoming an immigration society, since the economic recession has influenced most societal classes – both migrants and natives. Today young people and students facing this difficult climate can be considered an especially vulnerable group, referred to as 'NEETS': not in education, employment or training (Kyridis *et al.*, 2012; Tsatsaroni *et al.*, 2011). Many Greeks have lost their jobs and annual total income has declined significantly, while the unemployment rate has increased. According to the Hellenic Statistical Authority (ELSTAT), the percentage of unemployment was 25.5 per cent in the third term of 2014, and for youths (15–24 years old) the figure reached 49.5 per cent.

As described in the OECD's (2011) report for Greece, this is the first time that native Greeks facing socio-economic disadvantages will be included in the targeted populations. Thus, by exploring notions of equity, access and belongingness for subordinate groups, in this chapter socio-economically disadvantaged persons are also included.

Diverse students but with similar needs

The main sub-groups of diverse students are the following:

a   students coming from socio-economically disadvantaged families;
b   migrant students;
c   Muslim students;

d   Roma students; and

e   students with special educational needs (SEN).

In the section below, the focus will be on migrant students as well on students with special educational needs (SEN).

Education and migrant students

According to the Hellenic Statistical Authority's official data (2013), 206,000 migrant children in Greece attend pre-primary, primary and secondary education. Some 200,000 come from non-European countries: 86 per cent from countries with a high index of development, 13.5 per cent from countries with a medium index of development and 0.5 per cent from countries with a low index of development.

The following data presented in tables depict the distribution of migrant students in modern Greece, suggesting that there is a need for adequate educational policies and provisions. Tables 11.1 and 11.2 show that the societal situation has changed rapidly, with a significant rise in the number of migrant students at primary school level and a decline in the number of repatriates. There is also a significant number of Roma students.

Table 11.2 presents the distribution of migrants and repatriates in early childhood and primary education during the school year 2012–2013. These data indicate that there is a decline in the number of both migrants and repatriates compared to previous years (compare to Table 11.3).

Despite large-scale immigration since the early 1990s, it was not until 1996 that Greece responded officially to the presence of migrant and repatriated students in public schools with legal provisions (Law 2413/96). As mentioned by Palaiologou and Faas (2012):

> Law 2413/96 legitimized the foundation of intercultural schools by invoking cultural diversity. Apart from the normal public curriculum, intercultural schools both in Primary and Secondary Education provide courses on the language and culture of the country of origin of migrant students, up to four hours per week.

(p. 7)

Table 11.1 Distribution of migrants, repatriates and Roma students in primary education, school year 2010–2011

Total number of students (migrants, repatriates, Roma, Greeks)	Number of migrant students (%)	Number of repatriates (%)	Number of Roma (%)
600,926	74,683 (12.42%)	5,607 (0.93%)	10,850 (1.8%)

Source: Ministry of Education.

Table 11.2 Distribution of migrants and repatriates, Greek public schools, school year 2012–2013

Level of education	Number of students (migrants, repatriates)	Number of migrant students	Number of repatriates
Pre-primary school	19,762	18,862	900
Primary school	72,334	68,345	3,989
Total number	92,096	87,207	4,889

Source: Ministry of Education.

Table 11.3 Distribution of migrants, repatriates and Greeks in public schools for the school year 2007–2008

Level of education	Number of students (migrants, repatriates and Greeks)	Number of migrant students	Number of repatriates
Pre-primary school	90,698	8,111	759
Primary school	531,674	58,167	5,909
Gymnasium	271,024	76,267	4,996
Lyceum	181,946	38,438	2,729
Technical-vocational schools	56,531	7,266	2,512
Total number	1,131,873	188,249	16,905

Source: IPODE (in Palaiologou and Evangelou, 2011).

Since 1996, twenty-six intercultural schools have been established across the country – thirteen primary schools, nine gymnasia (first cycle of secondary education) and four Lykeia (second cycle of secondary education). Out of 15,174 state schools, these intercultural schools amounted to 0.17 per cent of the total. Twelve per cent of students with a migrant background (excluding Muslims and Roma children) attend Greek mainstream public primary schools (see Palaiologou and Evangelou, 2011). Following a Presidential Decree in 1999, 'reception' and 'tutorial or support' classes were established. All public schools with a high percentage of migrant students could set up either reception or tutorial classes. A reception class is a 'parallel' class, which migrant students attend during mainstream language lessons. Support classes provide additional support after school (see Palaiologou, 2004).

Unfortunately, in practice, Law 2413/96 and the 1999 Presidential Decree have not explicitly promoted an intercultural policy towards students with different cultural backgrounds. On the contrary, the educational praxis reveals the law's underlying discriminatory approach towards migrant students. The late-arrival immigrant students in particular have encountered obstacles in Greek public schools and in general they are in a disadvantaged position. Unfortunately, the main problem is the lack of educational support measures that would help such children achieve better school grades and develop higher self-esteem (Palaiologou and Evangelou, 2011, 2013).

In addition, three national educational programmes were carried out between 1997 and 2014, in collaboration with Greek universities, supported by the European Social Fund. The aim was to support migrant students to participate in society whilst maintaining their ethno-cultural identities. These initiatives were targeted towards three different groups of students: (1) Muslims of Thrace, (2) Roma students and (3) repatriates and foreign/migrant students. In 2010, the Greek Ministry of Education assigned to university departments the administration and implementation of new intercultural educational programmes aimed at 'migrant and repatriated' students, 'Roma' children and native Greek students. This new phase started in 2010 and was completed in 2014 (Palaiologou and Faas, 2012).

Nowadays, second-generation immigrant students are a key focus group (Palaiologou *et al.*, 2014; Palaiologou and Evangelou, 2013; Palaiologou, 2012). Many among this group of migrant students lack a national identity or a permanent place to live. Those children who were born to migrant families in Greece, and also those who have lived for many years with their migrant parents, are eligible to obtain Greek citizenship if they meet certain criteria (e.g. a certain number of consecutive years of enrolment at Greek schools). It is expected that new policies will be implemented in 2015 after the January election of the leftist SYRIZA government in Greece. This government has proposed measures to address the gap in the Greek constitution related to the naturalisation process for second-generation immigrant children (Bitsika, 2015).

 Individual/group task

Intercultural education ensures that all learners reach their full potential. Discuss how education can promote an intercultural understanding, and what are the strategies that can be adopted for this purpose?

Education and special educational needs

As has been shown in other chapters in this book, a relatively high number of students attend special schools and special classes and this is a sign of mainstream schools' failure to accommodate diverse needs. 'It is a well-known fact that segregation has, historically, been a common institutional response to the management of differences in education' (Baker *et al.*, 2009: 158) and this applied extensively to cases of children (and students and young people) with special educational needs. Besides full integration, encouraged today, practices such as special classes within schools are also considered acceptable, in cases where they are judged necessary. In 2008, 592 children at the pre-primary level attended such special classes, which represents an increase of 67.1 per cent (Tsatsaroni *et al.*, 2011). This increase may indicate a greater awareness on the part of parents of children with special educational needs as to the importance of not keeping their children at home and the importance of enrolling them in pre-primary schools as early as possible. It may also relate to the extension of compulsory education at this end of the system, combined with other factors, such as 'change of the criteria on the part of the school and related agencies as to who attends special classes' (Tsatsaroni *et al.*, 2011: 19).

As far as educational provision for children with special educational needs are concerned, teachers of primary education in Greece have the opportunity to acquire a specialisation in the field of Special Education, following a teacher in-service course that lasts two years, after passing competitive entry examinations. These teachers work in special schools or in special classes. During the period 2000–2010, 1,666 primary school teachers and 392 pre-primary school teachers gained qualifications as experts in special educational needs (op. cit.: 27). In addition, with respect to the education of special needs teachers, the Department of Special Needs at the University of Thessaly offers special education studies to its students. The graduates of this department are the only teachers in Greece who can obtain a university degree in the field of special education. Also, the Department of Educational and Social Policy of the University of Macedonia in Thessaloniki offers a university degree in Persons with Disability and/or with Special Educational Needs (Palaiologou, 2009).

In 2008, of the 150,079 children in total attending pre-primary (public and private schools), 592 attended special classes (0.4 per cent). Also, of the 647,543 children attending (public and private) primary schools, 14,651 (2.3 per cent) attended special classes (Tsatsaroni *et al.*, 2011).

In the field of early and primary education, though, special classes and efforts to promote integration into mainstream schools are widespread. In such cases, the class teacher is expected to cooperate with a special education teacher. However, despite all the legislation, Greek society, and especially the education system, has not yet achieved an inclusive nature and in the current financial crisis in Greece it appears that these issues will not be addressed.

 Individual/group task

After studying Chapters 6–10 on the UK, compare the SEN policies in Greece and with the other countries in this book: Australia, Montserrat and Liberia (Chapters 12–14). How would you rate the issues of inclusion and diversity in Greece?

Conclusion

The educational situation in Greece, as described in this chapter, shows that important steps are still needed to achieve the principles of equity: see Gorski's (2014) 'equity framework'. There is significant need for the engagement of well-trained teachers; those in place tend to work without any additional educational material to support their diverse students and are underpaid (Palaiologou and Dimitriadou, 2013; Palaiologou and Evangelou, 2011). In conclusion, we would suggest that the vulnerable student sub-groups in Greece – as in other European countries – which were presented here do not have equal opportunities to be educated with dignity and to receive high-quality education. This applies in terms of equal chances for progress, equivalent learning conditions, quantity and quality of teaching resources and approaches, teaching staff quality, consideration for students' ethno-cultural and socio-economic backgrounds and finding a good job in the labour market (Demeuse *et al.*, 2001).

The educational policies that have been implemented so far in the direction of supportive classes are considered important steps, but nowadays in 2016 there is a new need for inclusive policies. More steps need to be taken for the effective inclusion of the diverse groups of students in such a way that it promotes living together with mutual respect and helping communities and individuals maintain their first language and culture. There is an urgent need for the educational systems of Southern European countries to find new flexible policies to better educate, assess and integrate all students into public schools, policies that can survive in times of economic crisis given the very limited resources in the education field.

Summary points

- Greece has seen rapid changes in the socio-demographic landscape. There are two main changes in the population: a massive wave of immigration from mainly Balkan countries after the collapse of communism and the ones that were of Greek origin returning to their homeland (repatriates).
- Greek society was not prepared to accept cultural diversity and, in the light of economic instability and the financial crisis, the issues of cultural diversity have not been addressed.

- The education system was not prepared to accept diverse learners and, although policy was introduced, lack of resources, training, personal prejudices and stereotypical views have made the implementation of these ineffective.

- Inclusion and diversity in Greece are still two notions that policy makers, education systems and society have to work with in order to be embedded in the daily life and education system. However, under the pressures of financial austerity these two notions are now taking a secondary role in the daily needs of society.

- Despite existing legislative parameters for the development and implementation of inter-cultural interventional measures, particularly at the school level, the introduction of intercultural education into the Greek educational system requires a constant and sys-tematic approach in order to be effective and to act as a vehicle to bring about the necessary changes in the Greek education system.

- However, schools do not always have the capacity, the skills, the will or the resources to incorporate these changes.

- In order to place multiculturalism at the centre of curriculum and practices in Greek schools, relevant materials must be developed and teachers should be appropriately trained to teach in a multicultural society.

Further reading

Palaiologou, I. (2012) Ethics researching and working with other cultures, in I. Palaiologou (Ed.) *Ethical Practice in Early Childhood*. London: SAGE.

Palaiologou, N. (2004) Intercultural education and practice in Greece: Needs for bilingual intercultural pro-grammes. *Intercultural Education*, 15(3): 317–329.

Palaiologou, N. (2013) The path of intercultural education in Greece during the last three decades: Reflec-tions on educational policies and thoughts about next steps. *International Journal Education for Diversi-ties*, 1: article 61.

References

Anagnostopoulou, E. (1995) *The History of Day Care in Europe*. Athens: Athens University Press.

Baker, J., Lynch, K., Cantillon, S. and Walsh, J. (2009) *Equality. From Theory to Action*, 2nd edition. Basing-stoke, Hampshire: Palgrave Macmillan.

Bitsika P. (2015) Regulation for the naturalization process of second generation migrant children brings the Gov-ernment. *Vima Newspaper*, 27 March (in Greek). www.tovima.gr/society/article/?aid=689304 (accessed 7 April 2014).

Clogg, R. (2000) *The Greek Diaspora in the Twentieth Century*. London: Macmillan.

Council of the Europe Union (2009) *Conclusions on the Education of Children with a Migrant Background*. www.consilium.europa.eu/uedocs/cms_data/docs/pressdata/en/educ/111482.pdf (accessed 9 April 2015).

Council of the Europe Union (2010) *Conclusions on the Social Dimension of Education and Training*. www.consilium.europa.eu/uedocs/cms_data/docs/pressdata/en/educ/114374.pdf (accessed 9 April 2015).

Demeuse, M., Crahay, M. and Monseur, C. (2001) Efficiency and equity, in W. Hutmacher, D. Cochrane and N. Bottani (Eds) *Pursuit of Equity in Education – Using International Indicators to Compare Equity Policies*. Kluwer: Dordrecht.

Doliopoulou, E. (2005) An approach in intercultural education, in *Contemporary Programs for Preschool Chil-dren*. Athina: Tipothito – G. Dardanos (in Greek).

ELSTAT (2011) *ELSTAT Annual Review*. Piraeus: Hellenic Republic Hellenic Statistical Authority.

Gorski, P. (2014) *Reaching and Teaching Students in Poverty: Strategies for Erasing the Opportunity Gap*. New York: Teachers College Press.

Gropas, R. and Triandafyllidou, A. (2011) Greek education policy and the challenge of migration: An 'intercultural' view of assimilation. *Race Ethnicity and Education*, 14(3): 399–419.

Hatzichristou, C. and Hopf, D. (1993) School adaptation of Greek children after remigration. *Journal of Cross-Cultural Psychology*, 26(5): 505–522.

International Organization for Migration (n.d.) *Glossary of Terms*. www.iom.int/key-migration-terms (accessed 9 April 2015).

Kakos, M. and Palaiologou, N. (2013) *Inclusion and Exclusion in Intercultural Citizenship Education in Greece*, Proceedings for the International Conference 'Unity and Disunity, Connections and Separations: Intercultural education as a movement for promoting multiple identities, social inclusion and transformation', 17–21 September 2013.

Kyridis, A., Vamvakidou, I., Petrucijová, J., Zaleskiene, I., Zagkos, C., Ene, C. and Papoutzis, L. (2012) Social responsibility versus social vulnerability: Students propose ways to face the economic crisis – the case of Greece, the Czech Republic and Lithuania, in P. Cunningham and N. Fretwell (Eds) *Creating Communities: Local, National and Global*. London: CiCe.

Law 2413/96 *Greek Education Abroad: Intercultural Education and Other Provisions*. FEK 124, 17/6/1996, Official Governmental Gazette (in Greek).

Ministry of Interior in Greece (2010) *Official Data for Immigrants in Greece*. Athens: Hellenic Government.

Noutsos, M. (1998) Education, research and progress: How can we meet our European neighbours? *SYGXRONOS PAIDAGOGOS*, 2: 22–35.

OECD (2011) *Education Policy Advice for Greece, Strong Performers and Successful Reformers in Education*. Paris: OECD. http://dx.doi.org/10.1787/9789264119581-en (accessed 5 April 2014).

OECD (2012) *Equity and Quality in Education: Supporting Disadvantaged Students and Schools. Spotlight Report: Greece*. Paris: OECD. www.oecd.org/edu/equity (accessed 5 April 2014).

Palaiologou, N. (2004) Intercultural education and practice in Greece: Needs for bilingual intercultural programmes. *Intercultural Education*, 15(3): 317–329.

Palaiologou, N. (2009) Mapping the field of teachers' multicultural special education in Greece: A new era emerges. *The International Journal of Diversity in Organizations, Communities and Nations*, 8(6): 179–193.

Palaiologou, N. (2012) *Intercultural Education in Greece: The Situation with Second Generation Immigrant Students*, International Conference Dialogue of Civilizations and Cross-cultural Cooperation, Moscow City Department of Education, UNESCO Moscow Office, Moscow Institute of Open Education (MIOO) Proceedings of the Conference, 4–7 December.

Palaiologou, N. (2013) The path of intercultural education in Greece during the last three decades: Reflections on educational policies and thoughts about next steps. *International Journal Education for Diversities (IJE4D)*, 1: article 61.

Palaiologou N. and Dimitriadou C. (2013) Multicultural/intercultural education issues in pre-service teacher education courses: The case of Greece. *Multicultural Education Review*, 5(2): 45–63.

Palaiologou, N. and Evangelou, O. (2011) *Intercultural Education*. Athens: Editions PEDIO (in Greek).

Palaiologou, N. and Evangelou, O. (2013) *Second Generation Migrant Students in Greek Education System: Inclusion and School attainments*. Athens: Editions PEDIO (in Greek).

Palaiologou, N. and Faas, D. (2012) How intercultural is education in Greece today? Insights from policy makers. *Compare: A Journal of Comparative and International Education*, 1: 1–22.

Palaiologou, N., Kyridis, A. and Gialamas, V. (2014) The education of second generation immigrant students in Greece: Teachers' views. *Diversity Collection*, 13: 565–575.

Palaiologou, N., Kyridis, A., Gialamas, V. and Evangelou, O. (2010). The education of 'second generation immigrant students' in Greece. Official report submitted to the former Hellenic Institute of Migration Policy.

Rozen, M. (2008) *Homelands and Diasporas: Greeks, Jews and their Migrations*. International Library of Migration Studies. London: I.B. Tauris.

Spinthourakis, J.A., Karatzia-Stavlioti, E. and Roussakis, Y. (2009) Pre-service teacher intercultural sensitivity assessment as a basis for addressing multiculturalism. *Intercultural Education*, 20(3): 267–276.

Tsatsaroni, A., Vrettos, A., Kyridis, A., Katsis, A. and Linardos, P. (2011) *OECD Project 'Overcoming School Failure: Policies That Work'*. Athens: Ministry of Education.

Tsigilis, N., Tsioumis, K. and Gregoriadis, A. (2006) Prospective early childhood educators' attitudes toward teaching multicultural classes: A planned behavior theory perspective. *Journal of Early Childhood Teacher Education*, 27(3): 265–273.

Tziovas, D. (2009) *Greek Diaspora and Migration since 1700 Society, Politics and Culture*. Farnham: Ashgate.

12 Inclusion and inclusive practice in Australia

Catherine Meehan

Introduction

Australia has frequently been called the 'lucky country'. This term is used to refer to the lifestyle, weather and land of opportunities. Television shows such as *Neighbours* and *Home and Away* idealise the Australian lifestyle as an easy-going, laid-back way of life and plenty of sun. Australia, like all nations, is facing many similar challenges to other western countries around the world in terms of the economy, the rise of nationalism, unemployment, poverty, refugees, and the care and education of its citizens. This chapter will present an overview of Australia's approach to the care and education of individuals with disabilities. The Australian government is a signatory (2008) to the UN Convention on the Rights of Persons with Disabilities (2006). The Australian Bureau of Statistics (ABS, 2012a) uses the following statement to define the government's position as a:

> commitment to promoting and supporting the equal and active participation by people with disability in economic and social life. Understanding the prevalence of disability in the Australian population, and the socio-economic characteristics and needs and unmet needs of people with disability, is important in informing policies, planning services, and removing barriers to participation.

Australia's approach to the care and education of individuals with disabilities has meant that changes in policy in recent years have been driven by a desire to ensure that people with disabilities have access to education, health, social care, welfare, employment, justice and housing and this is both a national and state government responsibility. A more joined-up approach will be outlined in this chapter.

As the chapter is alongside examples of other countries, it is critical to explain the context of Australia. Alexander (2014: 1) warns of the dangers of surface comparisons of education systems internationally which lead to 'policy grafting or transplant'. The education system in Australia and the way in which the curriculum has been constructed for Australian children reflect a range of cultural, historical, geographical, economic, social and political factors. As an Australian living in the UK, I have an understanding of both the Australian and the UK contexts. On reflection of my experience as an early childhood teacher in a range of settings, including day care and schools in Australia, I have worked with children, families and other professionals in the care and education of individual children and parents/carers with disabilities. One belief that I hold based on my experiences is that disability is for life, not just about the time children are in school. This view is consistent with the language used historically in Australian literature about inclusion, and in the 1990s and into the twenty-first century Australian authors concentrated on the rights of individuals to an appropriate education rather than a deficit model of 'needs'.

A series of 'snapshots' of Australia are presented in this chapter. They will provide some important background information about Australia and support you in understanding the diversity, complexity and nature of Australian education. It is very different from England, the UK or even Europe, in the size of the country, the range of climates and the population which is spread out across locations in cities, towns and remote villages on islands and in the desert. Of course there are many similarities with the education system in the UK, but the Australian context and its history have shaped the current response to the education of individuals with disabilities.

 Individual/group task

List ten things you know about Australia. What do you know about Australia? What do you know about Australian education? What do you know about Australia's approach to inclusion?

Snapshot: Australia's geographic and climate context

Australia is a land of contrasts. It is the world's largest island, covers four time zones and is divided by the tropic of Capricorn. There are deserts in the centre, with the majority of the population living within 100 km of the coast. The north is remote and sub-tropical and sparsely populated, whereas the south is more temperate, with the majority of the population inhabiting cities and suburban areas. There are many islands that are part of the Australian territory. There are large, densely populated urban areas, compared with remote rural areas where your nearest neighbour is a four-hour drive away. These geographical factors have an impact on the types of services that can be provided for people with disabilities. The distance between some rural locations means that, in some cases, creative approaches using technology need to be adopted to ensure access to services due to affordability issues. For example, the 'School of the Air' was established in 1951 to cater for children living in remote areas of Queensland, Western Australia, New South Wales and the Northern Territory (Australian Government, 2007). Children would talk to teachers at a base school via a radio which was 'pedal powered'. Recent changes in technology, with the use of web cameras and digital whiteboards, have meant that students in remote areas can participate in virtual classrooms.

 Individual/group task

What else can you find out about Australia? How has the 'School of the Air' or distance learning been used with children with disabilities?

Snapshot: Australia's historical, social and cultural context

Australia has been inhabited for more than 20,000 years by the indigenous population of Aboriginal and Torres Strait Islanders. This group continues to live in various parts of Australia, but their traditional lifestyle and practices were interrupted by the invasion of white settlers from Britain who claimed ownership of the newly discovered land in 1788. In some parts of the country – for example, in Tasmania – the indigenous population was exterminated as they were viewed as 'savages'. In Queensland, as late as 1922, it was legal for farmers to shoot aboriginals on their properties. This sad legacy is part of Australia's modern-day history. The 1800s were a period of discovery by the British and settlements grew up across the continent. By 1901, the Federation of Australia was marked with the constitution which united the states and territories into a nation. English is the official language and there are in excess of 200 Aboriginal and Torres Strait Islander languages. Migration has played a key role in the growth of the population. Most Australians or their immediate ancestors are immigrants who have arrived since 1788 from over 200 countries. Some came as free settlers, others as convicts, asylum seekers and refugees escaping conflict in their home country.

The White Australian Policy prevailed from the 1850s to 1949. This policy aimed to allow only European immigrants in order to create a mono-racial society. Following the Second World War, the policy was abolished over a 25-year period and was finally removed in 1973 (Department of Immigration and Border Protection, 2015). The legacy of this policy can be seen in the attitudes of some Australians.

Australia is a country which is attractive to asylum seekers, and has historically welcomed people seeking refuge from war since the 1940s, including Italian, Greek and eastern European refugees, Vietnamese refugees in the 1970s, El Salvadorians in the 1990s and, more recently, refugees from various African and Middle Eastern countries in conflict. Many of these cultural groups have added to the rich social fabric in Australia.

The previous and current Liberal/National Party Coalition governments have taken very strict approaches to asylum seekers or refugees who travel by boat and who are then detained off-shore until processed. Those people who are allowed to settle on the Australian mainland may require additional support in education as they are English as a second language learners and may have suffered post-traumatic stress disorder because of their experiences fleeing from a war-torn area or being detained by the Immigration Service.

 Individual/group task

Investigate some contemporary issues in Australia with regard to migration, refugees and the education system. Are they similar or different from those in the UK/Europe? If so, what are the major differences?

Snapshot: Australia's political and economic context

In order to understand the legislation and policy framework, an appreciation of the Australian constitution and the relationship between the federal, state and local governments and the responsibilities at each level is critical. Australia is a constitutional monarchy and a member of the British Commonwealth. The Queen (Elizabeth II) is the Head of State and she continues to be warmly regarded by many Australians. Australia as a nation is governed as a single federal government. It has six states and two territories. Each state and territory has its own government.

In 1901 the Westminster system of government was adopted in Australia and at the federal level there are two houses. The lower house is the Parliament and the Upper House is the Senate. Currently, the federal government devolves responsibilities to state and local levels. Taxation is based on income tax and goods and services tax; capital gains and similar tax collection is controlled by the federal government. Each year the states come together to form the Council of Australian Governments (COAG) and effectively meet to bid for their share of the funds which cover the state areas of responsibility and are further distributed to local city and shire councils. State and local governments can also levy taxes. Table 12.1 illustrates the portfolios of each level of government in Australia.

For many years, agreement on policy and the distribution of funding between federal and state governments has been an adversarial process. It has typically been the case that, if the federal government was from the Liberal/National Party, most of the states would be Labour, or vice versa. Elections are held every three years in Australia, so that in any decade you could see a lot of change at federal and state levels of government. Under the Gillard Labour government, there were some changes agreed related to education, in particular at the COAG, that have meant a more 'national' approach. With regard to education policy and funding, the adoption of a National Curriculum in 2014 and the establishment of a National Disability Strategy are examples of a more joined-up and strategic approach to responding to current challenges.

The move towards a more universal approach for funding for disability is evident in the *National Disability Strategy, Every Australian Counts* and National Disability Insurance Scheme, all currently being rolled out in Australia. The Australian National Disability Strategy 2010–2020 is a ten-year

Table 12.1 Australian government responsibilities: federal, state and local

Federal	State	Local
Taxation	Health	Parks
Defence	Education	Rubbish and recycling
Social security	Emergency services	Buses
Post-secondary education	Justice – police and prisons	Local road and footpath
Foreign affairs	Consumer affairs	maintenance
Industrial relations	Main roads	Building regulations
Immigration	Public transport (trains)	Town planning
Trade	Forestry	Libraries
Currency	Tourism	Land subdivisions
Airports and safety	Vehicle registration	Infant welfare
Medicare	Public housing	Child-care centres
Post and telecommunications	Community services – adoption, disability, child protections	Public health
	Natural resources – gas, electricity, water, conservation and environment	Recreation facilities, e.g. pools
	State development	

plan for children, adults and families of people with disabilities. There are six priority areas of the plan:

- inclusive and accessible communities
- rights protection, justice and legislation
- economic security
- personal and community support
- learning and skills
- health and well-being.

The National Disability Insurance Scheme (NDIS) is a national scheme to financially support individuals with a disability. The NDIS is a 'rights based, person-centred support system', providing 'targeted support aligned to individual needs' (NDIS, 2015).

 Individual/group task

Review some of the current Australian resources for the education and care of individuals with disabilities policies mentioned in this section. What are the similarities between these and those used in your local area/country?

Snapshot: current education policy

The Australian government signed the United Nations Declaration on the Rights of Persons with Disabilities in 2008. Subsequently, there was a notable shift in the policy related to funding and the curriculum focus for the whole country. This was evident in the Melbourne Declaration on Educational Goals for Young Australians. The outcome of this declaration had two goals: that education in Australian schools provide 'equity and excellence' and that 'all young Australians become successful learners, confident and creative individuals and active and informed citizens' (ACARA, 2013: 4). The COAG agreed a set of propositions that developed into a National Australian Curriculum. ACARA (2013) propositions assume that:

> Each student can learn and that the needs of every student are important; each student is entitled to knowledge, understanding and skills as foundation for lifelong learning and participation in the community; high expectations are set for each student and teachers to take into account the level of learning for individual students and the different rates at which students develop; the needs and interests of students will vary, and that schools and teachers will plan from the curriculum in ways that respond to those needs and interests.

The Australian Curriculum was implemented in January 2014. The curriculum is innovative and reflects the knowledge, skills, abilities and priorities for learners in the twenty-first century. There are three components to the curriculum: learning areas, general capabilities and cross-curriculum priorities. The aims of the curriculum are to enable teachers to facilitate learning environments that meet the needs of all children.

The National Curriculum for Australia is overseen by the Australian Curriculum and Assessment Reporting Authority (ACARA). ACARA have made a clear inclusive statement about the education of learners representing a range of diverse backgrounds. The Australian Curriculum can be adjusted in three ways: via the curriculum and choice and range of subjects taught, through changes to instructional methods and by adjustments to the learning environment (ACARA, 2013).

The stated intention of the Australian Curriculum is that 'All students with a disability are able to participate in the Australian Curriculum on the same basis as their peers through rigorous, meaningful and dignified learning programs' (ACARA, 2013: 10). School-level decisions need to be made by principals (head teachers) and teachers about how each individual child will progress through their education with a personalised plan which requires consultation with families and other specialists to inform the adjustments needed for the child.

Snapshot: schooling system in Australia

The Australian Bureau of Statistics (ABS, 2014a) reported the differences in structures for primary and secondary schools. From 2015, all states and territories, with the exception of South Australia, would have the structure outlined in Table 12.2.

South Australia will continue to have pre-year 1 to year 7 and year 8 to year 12, which was also the former structure for Queensland and Western Australia.

Meehan (2007) described the differences in the names of year before formal schooling and starting age and this highlighted the challenges with each state having its own priorities. The ABS (2014a) confirmed that the pre-year 1, or the first year of primary school, is known as: Kindergarten in New South Wales (NSW) and Australian Capital Territory (ACT); Preparatory in Victoria (VIC), Queensland (QLD) and Tasmania (TAS); Pre-primary in Western Australia (WA); and Transition in Northern Territory (NT). It is known as 'Foundation Year' in the Australian Curriculum. All states had a year before, called 'pre-year 1', but this year is not compulsory and not part of the scope of the Australian Curriculum. There is a mix of community-based and private early childhood care and education provision, including sessional, long day-care (nursery) and family day-care (child minding). The school year usually starts after Australia Day at the end of January or beginning of February and ends early in December. A six-week summer holiday spans the Christmas period.

The starting school age is determined by the state or territory. The ABS (2014a) reported that in all states and territories the compulsory age is six for year 1, with the exception of Tasmania where children start aged five. Typically children in a pre-year 1 class would be five or turning five in that year. Compulsory school attendance has been governed by the National Youth Participation Requirement since 2010, which means that all children should remain in school until the completion of year 10, and those who have completed year 10 should participate in full-time education, training or employment until 17 years of age (ABS, 2014a).

With regard to Aboriginal and Torres Strait Islander (ATSI) children, they are less likely to attend pre-school or primary school than their peers, less likely to complete school to year 12 and less

Table 12.2 Typical schooling structure in Australia

Primary	Secondary
Pre-year 1 to year 6	Year 7 to year 12

likely to go onto further or higher education than their peers (ABS census, 2011). Although the participation rates increased between 2006 and 2011, they still fall behind their peers.

Snapshot: educational provision for individuals with disabilities in Australia

Sharma *et al.* (2012: 12) reported that 'Australia has legislation and policies which emphasise an inclusive model of teaching students with diverse needs in regular classrooms'. It is embedded within some of the teacher registration requirements that have made it mandatory for teachers to undergo study in inclusive education in teacher education programmes – for example, New South Wales and Queensland. The impact has been observed in the curriculum changes at universities and inclusive education has been emphasised in teacher education programmes (Sharma *et al.*, 2012).

Policy in Australia tended to follow the American model, Education for All Handicapped Children Act (1975) and the 1990 Individuals with Disabilities Education Act, with principles including the Least Restrictive Environment and Individualised Education Plans. For many years in Australia there was not a uniform approach; each state and territory developed its own legislation and policy. Unlike the USA, Australia did not have a prescriptive federal model until recently. The policy and practice fitted within an educational service model described by Ashman and Elkins (1998), ranging from specialist services for children, such as full-time residential care, to regular classroom placement. For example, individuals with a disability may require differing levels of care and the decisions about the best placement was one that was considered by the parents/families in collaboration with education, health and welfare professionals.

Australia is a signatory to the Convention on the Rights of Persons with Disability. The preamble of the convention identifies several groups of people with disability who are particularly vulnerable because of the combination of their disability and status. The Convention states concern for:

> the difficult conditions faced by persons with disabilities who are subject to multiple or aggravated forms of discrimination on the basis of race, colour, sex, language, religion, political or other opinion, national, ethnic, indigenous or social origin, property, birth, age or other status.
>
> (ABS, 2014b)

Snapshot: prevalence of disability in Australian populations

The ABS estimates that the current Australian population is 23 million. It is estimated that there are 555,000 Aboriginal and Torres Strait Islander Australians, with a median age of 21 years. New South Wales and Queensland have the highest percentage of ATSI Australians. More than a quarter of the population in the Northern Territory are ATSI Australians.

The *Survey of Disability, Ageing and Carers* (SDAC) (ABS, 2012b) reported that 4.2 million Australians, or 18.5 per cent of the population, had a disability. The definition of disability is: 'any limitation, restriction or impairment which restricts everyday activities and has lasted, or is likely to last, for at least six months' (ABS, 2012b). In 2009, it was reported that 21 per cent of the ATSI population had a disability and that they were 1.7 times more likely to have a disability than non-indigenous peers. ATSI people are more likely to be diagnosed with chronic illnesses such as diabetes and heart/lung diseases. Notably, the prevalence of disability for ATSI children between birth and fourteen years is twice as high as non-indigenous children: 14 per cent compared with 7 per cent (ABS, 2012b).

The SDAC (ABS, 2012b) uses the following definitions to differentiate the different levels of disability.

> A core-activity refers to one of three main everyday activities – self-care (eating, dressing, bathing, etc.), mobility and communication with others. A person with profound core-activity limitation is unable to do at least one of these activities at any time or needs constant help. A person with severe core-activity limitation needs help some of the time with at least one of these activities. The combined measure 'profound/severe core-activity limitation' therefore identifies people at the most severe end of the disability spectrum.

With regard to the Australian population, the SDAC reported that 8 per cent of ATSI people had a profound or severe limitation and that ATSI people were twice as likely to be living with someone with a profound/severe disability.

The ABS (2012b) reported that the majority of children with a disability attend mainstream education provision (65 per cent) compared with 35 per cent who attend a special school or specialist service in a mainstream school. It is estimated that 40 per cent of children with a disability attending a mainstream school had a profound or severe limitation. Table 12.4 highlights the breakdown of males and females with disability and attendance at school. Poorer participation rates in higher education and employment were noted by the ABS (2012b) due to the limitations of the disability.

Table 12.3 Comparison with non-indigenous children in 2011

	Indigenous (%)	*Non-indigenous (%)*
3–5 years attending pre-schools	56	63
6–14 years attending primary/secondary schools	85	93
15–17 years attending secondary school*	61	81
Completed year 12 or equivalent**	25	52
Non-school qualifications – certificate level qualifications	26	49

Source: ABS (2012b).

Notes
*GCSEs or level 2 equivalent; **A-levels or level 3 equivalent.

Table 12.4 Number of students with a disability in Australian schools

	Males (attending school)	*Female (attending school)*	*Males (not attending school)*	*Female (not attending school)*
5–14 years	155,700	80,200	3,700	1,400
15–18 years	29,400	25,200	17,500	7,900
19–20 years	1,000	1,200	15,500	17,700

Source: ABS (2012b).

Classification and prevalence of disability are highlighted in Table 12.5. The two largest groups of disability include students with learning and communication difficulties.

The majority of students between five and twenty years in education have either a severe or a moderate impairment. The profound limitation is 3 per cent of the population, which is double the proportion for mild impairment. This is illustrated in Table 12.6.

The impact of students identified as having an additional need is linked to Table 12.7, which outlines the type of support provided for students according to the categories of communication, mobility and self-care limitations, with the relevant proportion of the population.

 Individual/group task

How do these national statistics about disability compare with your country? Are there any major differences?

Table 12.5 Students by disability type in Australian schools

Type of disability	Profound or severe	Other	Total
Access difficulties	6,000	–	6,000
Difficulty sitting	14,700	3,700	18,400
Hearing or sight problems	7,000	3,700	10,700
Communication difficulties	64,400	13,100	77,500
Learning difficulties	84,800	47,100	131,900
Intellectual difficulties	34,000	3,300	37,300
Fitting in socially	61,000	16,500	77,500
Sports participation	25,600	7,400	33,000
Other difficulties	9,400	3,800	13,200
Total with difficulty	114,400	65,500	179,900
No difficulties	33,200	7,980	41,180

Source: ABS (2012b).

Table 12.6 Students by level of limitation, aged 5–20 years

Level of limitation	Estimates	Proportion (%)
Profound	7,000	3
Severe	113,300	49.2
Moderate	106,800	46.3
Mild	3,400	1.5
Total	230,500	

Source: ABS (2012b).

Table 12.7 Students by type of support given to support participation in education

Type of support	Communication limitation/proportion	Mobility limitation/ proportion	Self-care limitation/ proportion
Specialist equipment	14,100 (11.7%)	18,200 (10.8%)	1,700 (19.7%)
Specialist tuition	69,100 (57.1%)	80,100 (47.3%)	49,400 (57.2%)
Specialist assessment	30,300 (25%)	35,100 (20.7%)	21,900 (25.3%)
Counsellor or disability support person	44,700 (37%)	48,300 (28.5%)	34,200 (39.6%)
Special access arrangements	9,800 (8.1%)	12,400 (7.3%)	10,400 (12%)
Specialist transport arrangements	12,200 (10.1%)	14,600 (8.6%)	13,100 (15.2%)
Other support	2,800 (2.3%)	5,700 (3.3%)	2,100 (2.4%)
Total receiving support	89,800 (74.2%)	108,400 (64.1%)	65,000 (75.2%)
No support received	31,200 (25.8%)	60,800 (35.9%)	21,500 (24.8%)
Total	121,000	169,200	86,500

Source: ABS (2012b).

Snapshot: the Australian Curriculum

Australia's recently adopted 'National' Curriculum is in its infancy. The complexity of administering a National Curriculum lies in the fact that education is a state responsibility, not a national one. Aspland *et al.* (2012) noted that, although every state and territory has signed up to the Melbourne Declaration on Educational Goals for Young Australia (2008) and made a commitment to the Australian Curriculum, there are noticeable differences between states.

A common theme underpinning all states and territories is a commitment to the development of successful, confident learners who will make a positive contribution to wider Australian society. Assessment and the development of common national processes are also features of the new Australian Curriculum. The Australian Curriculum has eight key learning areas: arts, English, health and physical education, modern foreign languages, mathematics, science, social sciences and technology (ACARA, 2012). Aspland *et al.* state that the National Curriculum aims to: 'develop a rigorous and comprehensive system to assess student progress to inform teaching, self-monitoring of student learning and assess student achievement against goals and standards' (2012: 36). Further information about the Australian Curriculum can be found at the Australian Curriculum, Assessment and Reporting Authority website: www.australiancurriculum.edu.au.

Table 12.8 summarises the curriculum review conducted by Aspland *et al.* (2012). It highlights the range of curriculum documents by state and territory, with examples of special needs and inclusion policies. Hyperlinks are included for each document so that you can look at them in more detail or see any recent updates.

Inclusion: challenges in the Australian context

In recent years, the Australian government, both national and state, has made significant progress in addressing its obligations under the UN conventions for individuals with disabilities. The introduction of new policies, funding mechanisms and the curriculum are not without problems.

Table 12.8 Curriculum overview of special needs and inclusion in the Australian states/territories

State/territory and name of curriculum framework/hyperlink	Special needs and inclusion specific policies
Australian Capital Territory Every Chance to Learn: www.det.act.gov.au/teaching_and_learning/every-chance-to-learn/framework	Localised curriculum decisions should ensure that 'all students have access to learning regardless of their race, ethnicity, gender, sexual orientation, ability, disability, physical or intellectual attributes, language, culture, religion, age and social or economic condition' (Aspland *et al.*, 2012: 37). No specific SEN policy.
Northern Territory Northern Territory Curriculum Framework: www.education.nt.gov.au/parents-community/curriculum-ntbos/ntcf	'Inclusivity means all learners, irrespective of culture, language, socio-economic background, geographical location, disability or gender, must be given the opportunity to access a diverse and empowering education. Learners' backgrounds, interests, prior understandings, experiences, learning styles and learning rates should be valued and considered' (Aspland *et al.*, 2012: 37). No specific SEN policy.
New South Wales K-10 Curriculum Framework: http://syllabus.bos.nsw.edu.au/	'One among the many principles is that education must be inclusive of all students attending schools in New South Wales. This is achieved through a Curriculum Framework which takes into account the diverse needs of all students, provides equitable access, participation, and outcomes for all students, enables schools to provide programs that engage each student according to their backgrounds, needs and interests and allows the full range of students to demonstrate achievement' (Aspland *et al.*, 2012: 38). 'Most students with special education needs participate fully in learning experiences and assessment activities provided by the regular syllabus outcomes and content, although they may require additional support, including adjustments to teaching and learning activities and/or assessment tasks' (Aspland *et al.*, 2012: 38).
Tasmania Tasmanian Curriculum: www.education.tas.gov.au/Students/schools-colleges/curriculum/Pages/Curriculum.aspx	In most cases children with disabilities are educated in mainstream schools, and a personalised learning plan is developed across all areas of the Tasmanian curriculum. A whole of life approach is adopted to support children with disabilities beyond schooling.
Queensland Queensland Curriculum, Assessment and Reporting Framework: http://education.qld.gov.au/curriculum/framework/p-12/index.html	All children in QLD are expected to engage with the curriculum. Adjustments to assessment procedures, teaching materials and learning experiences. Decisions about children's learning and programme of study are localised with teachers and schools making decisions about how children with disabilities will be included in the school/class.
South Australia South Australian Curriculum Standards and Accountability Framework: www.sacsa.sa.edu.au/index_fsrc.asp?t=Home	All children from birth have access to a common curriculum which is inclusive for all. Opportunity, access, equity and individualised planning are core principles of this framework.
Victoria Victorian Essential Learning Standards: www.education.vic.gov.au/school/teachers/support/Pages/ausvels.aspx	The VELS Students with Disabilities Guidelines (2014): http://ausvels.vcaa.vic.edu.au/static/docs/AusVELS-SWD-guidelines.pdf

For example, a PricewaterhouseCoopers (2011) study reported that, in spite of the new funding mechanisms, further work is needed to ensure that people with disabilities do not live in poverty. Australia was found to be in the bottom third of the OECD countries for employment of individuals with disabilities. It is hoped that, with the introduction of the NDIS, some of the inequities will be addressed, but those implementing the policies are concerned about the complexities of administering the system.

There have been recent suggestions that Australia is moving to a more segregated special schooling system, contrary to trends internationally (Boyle *et al.*, 2015). The debates about what is right or wrong, or better for children with disabilities, continue (e.g. Sharman, 2015; Boyle and Anderson, 2014; Cologon, 2013, 2015). Commentators seem to agree that a decision about a child's education needs to be based on their individual circumstances, and the devolution of decision-making to head teachers and schools allows for children and families to be involved in decision-making (Boyle and Anderson, 2014; Cologon, 2013).

Debates about the terms 'inclusion', 'exclusion', 'integration' and 'segregation', and how these feature in Australian education, seem to add some confusion due to their interchangeable use in the media and in society. According to Cologon (2015), 'Inclusive education involves supporting each child in belonging, participating, and accessing ongoing opportunities, being recognised and valued for the contribution that he or she makes, and flourishing'. It is therefore the responsibility of government/s, schools and other institutions to minimise the barriers to participation and access.

Conclusion

The current and ongoing challenges for education of individuals with a disability or special need moving forward will have a particular focus on indigenous Australians, refugees and other students for whom English is an additional language. These groups are vulnerable and at risk of further marginalisation and poverty. Like all nations, Australia is attempting to meet the challenges with shrinking budgets. It is fair to say that those teachers, carers, families, charities and other organisations continue to go beyond their role and remit to ensure that individuals with disabilities can enjoy a full life with dignity and fairness.

Summary points

- Australia has developed a unique approach to the care and education of individuals with disabilities.
- A number of national changes have been introduced to improve access to services, funding and more individualised plans in response to UN convention requirements.
- The issues and debates in Australia around inclusion and participation are similar to other countries.
- Schools, teachers, parents and other professionals work together to support children's inclusion in education, which is the most appropriate setting or placement for the child.
- The snapshots provided highlight some contextual factors which are specific to Australia, and can be used as points of comparison as you look at the way in which other countries plan for inclusion.

Further reading

ACARA (2012) *The Shape of the Australian Curriculum Version 4*. Sydney: ACARA. www.acara.edu.au/verve/_resources/the_shape_of_the_australian_curriculum_v4.pdf (accessed 13 August 2015).

Australian Government, Department of Education, Science and Training (2004) *Gifted and Talented Education: Professional development package for teachers*. GERRIC, University of New South Wales. http://foi.deewr.gov.au/collections/gifted-education-professional-development-package (accessed 13 August 2015).

COAG (2009) *Belonging, Being and Becoming: The early years learning framework for Australia, Department of Education, Employment and Workplace Relations*. Canberra: COAG.

Cologon, K. (2015) Inclusive education means all children are included in every way, not just in theory. *The Conversation*. http://thespoke.earlychildhoodaustralia.org.au/inclusive-education-means-all-children-are-included-in-every-way-not-just-in-theory/ (accessed 13 August 2015).

Cook, B., Tankersley, M. and Landrum, T. (2009) Determining evidence-based practices in special education. *Exceptional Children*, vol. 75, pp. 365–83.

Wehmeyer, M., Shogren, K., Palmer, S., Williams-Diehm, K., Little, T. and Boulton, A. (2012) The impact of the self-determination learning model of instruction on student self-determination. *Exceptional Children*, vol. 78, pp. 135–53.

Examples of websites about practice

The following websites may be useful as they provide examples about recommended practice for inclusion in Australian schools. There are examples from a few different locations and phases.

- Australian Curriculum Assessment and Reporting Authority (2015) Illustrations of Personalised Learning. www.australiancurriculum.edu.au/studentdiversity/students-with-disability/view-illustrations-by-primarysecondary (accessed 13 August 2015).

- Victorian Government (2014) VELS Students with Disabilities Guidelines. http://ausvels.vcaa.vic.edu.au/static/docs/AusVELS-SWD-guidelines.pdf (accessed 13 August 2015).

References

ABS (2012a) *Children at School with a* Disability. www.abs.gov.au/ausstats/abs@.nsf/Lookup/4429.0main+features100302009 (accessed 13 August 2015).

ABS (2012b) *Disability, Ageing and Carers, Australia: Summary of findings*. www.abs.gov.au/ausstats/abs@.nsf/Lookup/4430.0Chapter2002012 (accessed 13 August 2015).

ABS (2014a) *Appendix: Differences in Schooling structures*. www.abs.gov.au/AUSSTATS/abs@.nsf/Latestproducts/4221.0Appendix12014?opendocument&tabname=Notes&prodno=4221.0&issue=2014&num=&view= (accessed 13 August 2015).

ABS (2014b) *Profiles of Disability: Populations*. www.abs.gov.au/ausstats/abs@.nsf/Lookup/by%20Subject/4429.0~2009~Main%20Features~Populations~4 (accessed 13 August 2015).

ACARA (2012) *Australian Curriculum*. www.australiancurriculum.edu.au/ (accessed 13 August 2015).

ACARA (2013) *Student Diversity and the Australian Curriculum: Advice for principals, schools and teachers*. Sydney: ACARA. www.australiancurriculum.edu.au/StudentDiversity/Pdf/StudentDiversity (accessed 13 August 2015).

Alexander, R. (2014) *International Evidence, National Policy and Educational Practice: Making better use of international comparisons in education*. Universities of Cambridge and York. www.robinalexander.org.uk/wp-content/uploads/2014/05/Alexander-Jerusalem_Canterbury.pdf (accessed 13 August 2015).

Ashman, A. and Elkins, J. (1998) *Educating Children with Special Needs* (3rd edn). Frenchs Forest: Prentice Hall.

Aspland, T., Datta, P. and Talukdar, J. (2012) Curriculum policies for students with special needs in Australia. *International Journal of Special Education*, vol. 27, no. 3, pp. 36–44.

Australian Government (2007) *The School of the Air and Remote Learning*. www.australia.gov.au/about-australia/australian-story/school-of-the-air (accessed 26 August 2015).

Boyle, C. and Anderson, J. (2014) Disability finding in schools shouldn't be based on state. *The Conversation*. https://theconversation.com/disability-funding-in-schools-shouldnt-be-based-on-state-30018 (accessed 13 August 2015).

Boyle, C., Anderson, J. and Swayn, N. (2015) Australia lags behind the evidence on special schools. *The Conversation*. https://theconversation.com/australia-lags-behind-the-evidence-on-special-schools-41343 (accessed 13 August 2015).

Cologon, K. (2013) Students with and without disability: it's always better when we're together. *The Conversation*. https://theconversation.com/students-with-and-without-disability-its-always-better-when-were-together-21014 (accessed 13 August 2015).

Cologon, K. (2015) Inclusive education means all children are included in every way, not just in theory. *The Conversation*. http://theconversation.com/inclusive-education-means-all-children-are-included-in-every-way-not-just-in-theory-45237 (accessed 13 August 2015).

Department of Immigration and Border Protection (2015) *Fact Sheet – Abolition of the 'White Australia' Policy*. www.border.gov.au/about/corporate/information/fact-sheets/08abolition (accessed 13 August 2015).

Department of Social Services (2011) *National Disability Strategy*. www.dss.gov.au/our-responsibilities/disability-and-carers/program-services/government-international/national-disability-strategy (accessed 13 August 2015).

Meehan, C. (2007) *Thinking and Acting: Early childhood teachers' beliefs and practice with regard to learning, teaching and religious education*. Published thesis, Brisbane.

NDIS (2015) *NDIS Home Page*. www.ndis.gov.au/ (accessed 13 August 2015).

PricewaterhouseCoopers (2011) *Disability Expectations: Investing in a better life in Australia*. Adelaide: PwC.

Sharma, U., Loreman, T. and Forlin, C. (2012) Measuring teacher efficacy to implement inclusive practices. *Journal of Research in Special Educational Needs*, vol. 12, no.1, p. 12–21.

Sharman, R. (2015) Can inclusive education do more harm than good? *The Conversation*. http://theconversation.com/can-inclusive-education-do-more-harm-than-good-43183 (accessed 13 August 2015).

United Nations (2006) *UN Convention on the Rights of Persons with Disabilities*. www.un.org/disabilities/convention/conventionfull.shtml (accessed 13 August 2015).

13 Inclusive practice in Montserrat, Caribbean

Natural disaster experiences

Vernie Clarice Barnes

Introduction

This chapter addresses inclusive education in the context of a chronic or ongoing natural disaster. Natural disasters have been common in the history of Montserrat, a tiny ten-mile-long by seven-mile-wide British Overseas Territory in the Leeward Islands of the Caribbean. The most significant modern-day disasters have been hurricanes: Hugo (1989) destroyed 99 per cent of buildings and claimed many lives. A volcanic eruption in Soufriere Hills has been ongoing since 1995. Such disasters cause disruptions in island life and displacement, which are perhaps the reasons for its consistently small population: currently less than 5,000 due to voluntary evacuation on account of the volcanic eruption. Previously the population was approximately 12,000 and had been in that region since the abolition of plantation slavery in the mid-eighteenth century. From June to October yearly, the island is under threat from hurricanes and tropical storms, warranting major protective preparation. As I wrote this chapter in August and September 2015, there were three which caused anxiety and disruption of services in Montserrat, whilst another tropical storm (Erika) did damage to neighbouring Dominica, where one school was washed away and others became shelters for those made homeless.

Disasters, whatever the causes, are disruptive of the education cycle, traumatising and a major cause of exclusion. UNICEF (2011) estimated that 68 million children are affected worldwide as a result of mass emergencies. The World Education Forum (2000: 24) *Framework for Action* required countries to work towards the objective of education for all, including a commitment to 'meet the needs of education systems affected by conflict, natural calamities and instability'. Continuing disasters are prevalent in the developing world; Montserrat has endured volcanic eruptions for twenty years. The original population (12,000) was dispersed mainly to the UK when three quarters of the island's land space was made uninhabitable by dramatic eruptions that were sometimes potentially cataclysmic.

A teacher's intervention with children who witnessed a pyroclastic flow

---

Case study – reflections of a Montserratian teacher

I have had first-hand experience of observing and working with primary school age children who experienced a sudden volcanic eruption towards the end of their lunch break. It was a pyroclastic eruption that sent a super-heated cloud of fire across the Caribbean Sea within full view of the school. The children know about pyroclastic flows from the daily volcanic forecast. They know that they can burn you up. Their reactions were startling and varied. Some children came together and prayed, asking God to protect them. Others sat quietly looking to their teachers for guidance, while another group charged outside to observe the fearful sight. I had no doubt that all of the children I observed were affected. Through Angel the teddy bear, a usual Circle Time mascot loved by the children, I facilitated their sharing of thoughts and feelings about the horrific event. I made them feel safe, first allowing each child to take a turn in hugging Angel. It made them comfortable as it was they who called the teddy Angel. They voted to do so when they received it as a gift from students in a school in Huddersfield who were concerned about them having to live with an erupting volcano. It had become their common source of hugs and relaxation whenever there were ash clouds or explosions from the volcano.

 Individual/group task

1   What plans and or activities does your school/class or placement have in place for helping students to cope with a critical incident in their school environment?

2   Reflecting on the account of the Montserrat teacher, to what extent are the strategies used to help children talk about their experiences inclusively?

Inclusive education in emergencies

Mindful that an entire generation of children may miss out on basic schooling because of disaster and or conflict, the World Education Forum (2000) asserted that education in emergencies is a fundamental human right. It recommended that 'education in emergency situations should be built into a country's development process and not seen as a 'relief effort' (24). Education is regarded as a beacon for people who have endured the appalling suffering of mass emergencies, crises created by conflict or disaster. For this reason, Margaret Sinclair (2002) suggested that education in emergency should be inclusive and described six guiding principles for planners of emergency education that ensures inclusion. These are: access, resources, activities, curriculum, coordination and capacity-building. Sinclair points out that although these principles are in many respects similar to those that should be considered in planning education generally, appropriating them to the emergency context establishes a standard for determining effectiveness. The Montserrat experience of inclusive education provision following disaster is explored from this perspective.

Notions of inclusion – the Montserrat context

The call for inclusive education was established in the Salamanca Statement, signed in 1994. Since then various concepts and interpretations of inclusion have been adopted across the globe. The concept is widely regarded as context-bound because of the varied conditions that affect its definition, implementation and practice (Makoelle, 2014). Apparently, there is no single perspective on inclusion within a single country or even within a school (Dyson and Millward, 2000). Ainscow and Miles (2008: 17) developed a typology of five ways of thinking about inclusion from an analysis of international research:

- inclusion as concerned with disability and 'special educational needs'
- inclusion as a response to disciplinary exclusions
- inclusion in relation to all groups seen as being vulnerable to exclusion
- inclusion as a promotion of a school for all
- inclusion as education for all.

Miles and Singal (2008: 9) explain further that, not only is there variation in definition, but some governments reduce their provision simply to compulsory schooling for all.

The Caribbean region is often referred to as the original global village and boasts a diverse ethnicity, culture and geography. Montserrat is a British Overseas Territory created out of the so-called 'expansion of Europe' in the sixteenth and seventeenth centuries. Although governed by the English, original settlers were mainly Irish indentured servants and enslaved Africans who worked on plantations typical of the period of the trans-Atlantic slave trade. The influence of the Irish culture was significant for Montserrat to become known as the Emerald Isle of the Caribbean, or the other Ireland.

Small island communities are geographically inclusive by virtue of the tight living space or fishbowl existence where everyone knows everyone and claims to care accordingly. Montserratian folk traditions are illustrative of connectedness through extended family ('all awi a wan') – an all-for-one national identity. This is a communal philosophy emanating from a history of natural disasters, the trauma of plantation slavery and hardships of post-emancipation life. Thus the practice of inclusion is ingrained, but so too is exclusion, which was at the heart of the socio-economic/political system of slavery. Some beliefs about childhood and disability common to the new/post-volcano population of the island are traceable to the plantation labour force, which included 'Pickny gangs' of children as young as four years who weeded and carried out duties perceived to be suitable for their nimble fingers and bodies. Any impairment, illness or weakness which prevented the enslaved from contributing to the labour force could have resulted in abandonment or a death sentence (Donoghue, 2008). Perhaps such traumatic ancestral memories may underlie the belief that a child with impairment should be 'hidden' (Colamarco and Lumpkin, 2013; UNICEF, 2013). Additionally, within Caribbean folk religion, some theologise disability as a bewitched burden, shamefully stigmatising both parents and extended family. Parents and families may attribute a child's impairments to harm done by a living foe or vexed ancestor. In the past, trance dancing and other rituals were resorted to for divination of causes or appeasement, but such practices are now rare.

Phasha and Moichela (2012) argued fervently that discerning the intricacies of the cultural context is critical for planning and implementing any educational change leading to inclusion. They highlighted the importance of this approach from their practice in South Africa, where they called for an equal value to be given to an African philosophy of inclusion, rather than sole reliance on a definition derived from European experience. Makoelle (2014) supported this view, emphasising that cognitive justice is essential to the way inclusion is defined in non-western cultures. Cognitive justice entails recognition of alternative indigenously rooted theorising and conceptualisation of inclusion that enables dialogue without western qualifying standards. For example, Owen (2013) reported from a small survey of teachers and parents in Montserrat that the term 'disability' is not commonly used, and there is hostility to the label. Reference is made instead to the actual impairment, thus avoiding the disability label. It appears that the family and community have their means of assessing needs, providing support and avoiding labelling. This was made obvious in the volcanic eruption, when 'hidden' children and adults with physical and learning impairments excluded by their families from education and other social institutions became visible in the shelters for those displaced by the disaster. Such families had not relied on the pre-volcanic eruption provision by the Montserrat Red Cross of a school and workshop. Although the exact reasons are unknown as to why available provisions were ignored by some and overlooked by the authorities, it could be hypothesised that such actions were perhaps influenced by the limbo/dichotomous view of inclusion and exclusion that is held locally. Definitions and boundaries of inclusion are reliant on country and/or cultural context.

 Individual/group task

Discuss the importance of cognitive justice in defining inclusion for children, young people and families in Montserrat.

Pre- and post-emergency experiences and practices

The education system of Montserrat mirrors that of its colonial administrator. Free, compulsory universal primary education has existed in the territory since the 1950s, and comprehensive secondary education from the mid-1980s. Early Childhood Centres have been established since the mid-1970s (four exist currently) but attendance is not compulsory. However, the Ministry of Education maintains oversight for all facilities. There are four primary schools (population just over 700 at time of writing), two of which (population 464) are government run, as is the one secondary (population 345). The two private primary schools receive minimal funding from the government, which oversees standards for all schools. According to a UNICEF (2013) Eastern Caribbean stakeholder review on disability, there are sixteen children with special educational needs in the 0–18 age range, representative of 1.3 per cent of the child population and 0.3 per cent of the national. Listed disabilities included behavioural, visual and learning, with boys being the largest representation. Revised standards for special education provision are established in an Education Act (2005) and special needs policies have been drafted, modelled on the UK SEN Code of Practice (DfES, 2001), following a collaborative school improvement project with the Isle of Wight Report (Ministry of Education Montserrat, 2008).

This five-year project aimed at sensitising selected Montserrat primary school teachers to the National Literacy Strategy and special needs provision in the UK, first through visits to Isle of Wight schools and second through visits of Isle of Wight teachers to Montserrat to demonstrate best practice and train counterparts (Ministry of Education Montserrat, 2008, 2011). Consequently, SEN, SENCO, SEN Register and other UK standards (DfES, 2001) were adopted as part of the education language in Montserrat. Sensitisation was followed by the specialised training of two primary school teachers in remedial reading for the two government schools, but there is none for private or secondary schooling. This happened in the midst of the volcanic crisis, when students and teachers were of necessity preoccupied with the everyday challenges of living with an exploding mountain. Sinclair (2002: 28) stressed the importance of capacity-building to ensure education for all at the height of an emergency; therefore, the Isle of Wight initiative was timely and fits too with the idea of relying on partnership to achieve this goal (World Education Forum, 2000).

When disasters happen, it is often said that crises are opportunities for change. Openings for experimentation and improvements present themselves. In this vein, the Ministry of Education supported a local educational psychologist in establishing a Pupil Support Unit to address the psychosocial needs of students experiencing the disaster (Pupil Support Unit, 2008). The unit was set up as a child-friendly space within a homely furnished house, providing care for all primary and secondary school children. It was also a base for the training of teachers and guidance counsellors in special education and psychosocial interventions for children experiencing disaster. The topic 'living with the volcano' was included in the Personal, Moral and Social Education Curriculum for the primary and secondary schools, written by the psychologist and counsellors of the unit. A topic on 'transitioning' was also included in support of newly arrived students who had migrated from elsewhere in the Caribbean and who were encountering the volcanic environment for the first time. It was embedded also to assist Montserratians adjusting from long-term residence in public shelters and other issues of internal displacement. Additionally, it was to reduce emerging problems/tensions associated with identity evident in the relationships of children in the new and diverse population. Conflicts between groups of children termed 'national' and 'non-national' reached violent levels. Therefore, the Pupil Support Unit and the Personal, Moral and Social Education Curriculum were means of promoting inclusion and respect for all nations/citizens in the rapidly changing Montserratian cultural landscape. Strategies such as storytelling, drama and Circle Time sharing were utilised in addressing psychosocial needs following 'gang' conflicts, ash eruptions, pyroclastic flows and evacuations, which had become normal in the environment (Pupil Support Unit, 2008).

A teacher's account of using storytelling

Case study – reflections of a Montserratian teacher

Listening to the children tell their stories was amazing. They echoed lots of fear and anxiety. Some children said: 'I saw fire running on the water and I was afraid'; 'I started to pray because I thought the world had come to an end'; 'I sat in my class and cried'; 'My friends and I came together and prayed'; 'The sounds of the volcano scared me'; 'My friends and I were running up and down the school yard screaming'; 'I wanted my mommy to come and get me'. The children repeated their stories over and over...

Individual/group task

1   Imagine that you were a teacher in this situation. Plan a follow-up activity to this initial storytelling session that will offer further help to all students who witnessed the volcanic event.

2   List at least three strategies that you will use to ensure that all students participate in this activity.

3   Why is a storytelling session about a critical incident inclusive?

Changing needs and access to interventions

Views of the needs of children in Montserrat are undergoing rapid change due to the ongoing volcanic eruption and the evacuation 'off' island to the UK and USA of the great majority of the close-knit population. As mentioned earlier, a replacement population has emerged, including migrants from the other parts of the English-speaking Caribbean, Haiti and Santo Domingo. Child protection legislation (grounded in UK standards) and programmes have been initiated to meet the changing needs. There is now a Children's Society with funding from the Lucy Faithfull Foundation. The Children's Society supports early childhood programmes and vulnerable children who are at risk of exclusion from mainstream classes or school. Government-funded fostering is being introduced by the Social Services Department in support. An association of disabled people has emerged too and the Ministry of Education has publicly announced plans to provide English as an additional language support to Spanish- and Haitian-speaking children (Radio Montserrat, February–March, 2015). The Pupil Support Unit is now focused on assessment of reading and remedial interventions for all primary school pupils and support for secondary pupils with profound physical and emotional needs. Advocacy for students, for secondary pupils in the Low Attainment Education Project, is to be included in the mainstream (Interview with Education Psychologist, Pupil Support Unit, September, 2015). Montserrat is blazing with initiatives supportive of inclusion. However, from my observation, notions of inclusion and exclusion remain dichotomous and issues of cognitive justice are ignored in favour of wholesale importation of ideas and programmes from the UK and elsewhere. Also of significance are the financial constraints that planners of inclusive education initiatives may confront in a small island such as Montserrat.

Resources

A key recommendation of special study commissioned as part of the Education for All (EFA) assessment was that 'education in emergency situations should be built into a country's development process from the outset, not seen as a "relief" effort' (World Education Forum, 2000: 24). As an Overseas Territory of the UK recovering from a major disaster, Montserrat relies on its 'mother' nation for financial and technical guidance/support in all areas of development. However, local provision may not always be consistent with those in the UK, even though some policies and practices may appear to be similar. Differences are sometimes due to cultural and internal political decisions. For instance, the Government of Montserrat (2004) Education Act 2004/2008 and supporting policies establish the right to free and compulsory education for all up to secondary level, but constraints are clearly established. 'The Minister shall, subject to available resources, establish and pursue for the education system general and specific goals and objectives' (Part 1, 3.1: 15). With respect to special educational needs, it stated that the Director of Education 'shall, subject to available resources, provide special education programmes for students of compulsory school age who by virtue of intellectual, communicative, behavioural, physical or multiple exceptionalities are in need of special education' (Part 8, 0.1: 53). Further, a student who is entitled to a special programme shall have an Individual Education Plan (IEP). This intent is mentioned in the Education Plan, where the main emphasis is on general improvements of the learning environment. 'A modern, enriching, child-centred learning community, with a nurturing teaching and learning environment, created to respond to the changing and diverse school population' (Government of Montserrat, 2012: 6:36). The extent to which such a provision is actualised is reliant on many factors to include funding, awareness and training. Awareness-building has been done through professional development activities, but the recruitment and maintaining of appropriately trained personnel to work in a disaster environment is a challenge. The greater majority of the trained teaching force left Montserrat at the height of the volcanic crisis; hence there is a reliance on untrained teachers, particularly at the secondary level. Thus, inclusive programming is largely determined by the professional skills available. For example, Pupil Support Unit programmes, popular with students and noted as helpful in improving learning and behaviour, were short-lived. This was the case for interventions such as the Nurture Group (Boxhall and Lucas, 2010), developed and pioneered in the UK specifically to address the unmet social and emotional needs of young children, enhancing their capacity to engage in the social and educational. So it was for other inclusive and school-friendly initiatives, such as the Breakfast Club, and the 'Lunch Time Drop In', which ended when volunteer funding and professional expertise were withdrawn. Education managers faced with the choice of resource allocation to academic programmes, as opposed to social ones, may opt for the former because of pressures to meet targets set around achievement on national and regional exams (Government of Montserrat, 2012: 32). Education and sports received EC$10 million or 7.8 per cent of the recurrent budget, but no new spend for 2015/2016 (Government of Montserrat, 2015: 35). Expenditure on education has increased from 6.8 per cent in 2010 to 7.8 per cent in 2015; but it still remains lower than neighbouring islands, which spend twice as much of their country's total budget on education (Government of Montserrat, 2012: 13–14). Favourable for Montserrat, though, is its high pupil–teacher ratio (Government of Montserrat, 2012: 16:15).

Conclusion

The educational issues highlighted in this chapter are indicative of education planning and practices in a tiny overseas European territory which is subject to natural disasters on account of its geographical location.

Summary points

Using the six points (access, resources, curriculum, capacity-building, activities and coordination) outlined by Sinclair (2002: 28) to assess planning for effective inclusion in emergencies, it was found that:

- Policies, laws, plans and innovations for addressing cultural diversity, SEN and psychosocial needs in emergencies are clearly articulated, but limited financial and human resources may deter provision.
- Planning and delivery of education in emergency provide opportunity for innovative inclusive practice, but issues of sustainability should be carefully considered.
- Issues of cognitive justice and cultural appropriateness of ideas and strategies warrants sensitive consideration as they are important in defining inclusion and inclusive education in a particular locality.
- Emergencies create new and challenging circumstances, which may exacerbate existing vulnerabilities in funding and resources.
- Education systems in overseas territories of Europe have specific issues of inclusion based on their small size and geographical location.
- Specific planning for education in emergencies should be part of all Education Development Plans.

Further reading

Makoelle, T.M. (2014) Cognitive Justice: A Road Map for Equitable Inclusive Learning Environments. *International Journal of Education and Research*, vol. 2, no. 7, July, 505–518.

Sinclair, M. (2002) *Fundamentals of Education Planning – 73: Planning Education in and After Emergencies*. Paris: UNESCO.

References

Ainscow, M. and Miles, S. (2008) Education for All Inclusive: Where Next? *Prospects Quarterly Review of Comparative Education*, vol. XXXVIII, no. I, March, 15–34.

Boxhall, M. and Lucas, S.L. (2010) *Nurture Groups in Schools: Principles and Practice* (2nd Edn). London: Sage.

Colamarco, V. and Lumpkin, G. (2013) *Policies for the Inclusion of Children with Disability: Rights of Children with Disabilities.* New York: UNICEF.

DfES (2001) *Special Education Needs: Code of Practice.* London: DfES.

Donoghue, E. (2008) *Black Breeding Machines: The Breeding of Negro Slaves in the Diaspora.* Bloomington, Indiana: Authorhouse.

Dyson, A. and Millward, A. (2000) *Schools and Special Needs: Issues of Innovation and Inclusion.* London: Paul Chapman.

Government of Montserrat (2004) *Education Act 2004/2008 Revised.* Montserrat: Law Revision Authority.

Government of Montserrat (2012) *Education Development Plan 2012–2020.* www.gov.ms/wp-content/uploads/2011/04/2011-03-22-Montserrat-2012-20-Education-Development-Plan-draft.pdf (accessed 24 September 2015).

Government of Montserrat (2015) *2015/16 Budget Statement – Revive, Build, Restore: Destiny Calls, Let Us Arise.* www.gov.ms/wp-content/uploads/2015/03/Budget-Speech-2015-2016.pdf (accessed 24 September 2015).

Makoelle, T.M. (2014) Cognitive Justice: A Road Map for Equitable Inclusive Learning Environments. *International Journal of Education and Research*, vol. 2, no. 7, July, 505–518.

Miles, S. and Singal, N. (2008) *The Education for All and Inclusive Education Debate: Conflict, Contradiction or Opportunity.* http://disability-studies.leeds.ac.uk/files/library/miles-IJIE-MilesandSingal-resubmission.pdf (accessed 24 September 2015).

Ministry of Education Montserrat (2008) *Isle of Wight Initiative Montserrat Project Report.* Montserrat: Ministry of Education.

Ministry of Education Montserrat (2011) *Montserrat Primary Education Review.* Montserrat: Ministry of Education.

Owen, C. (2013) *Report on Disability in Montserrat.* Unpublished.

Phasha, N. and Moichela, K.Z. (2012) Inclusive Education in South Africa. In A. Bame Nsamenang and T.M.S. Tchombe (Eds) *Handbook of African Educational Theories and Practices.* Cameroon: Human Development Resource Centre.

Pupil Support Unit (2008) *Annual Report.* Montserrat: Ministry of Education.

Radio Montserrat (ZJB) (2015) *News on Support for Non-English Speaking Students*, February/March.

Sinclair, M. (2002) *Fundamentals of Education Planning – 73. Planning Education in and After Emergencies.* Paris: UNESCO.

UNICEF (2011) *Humanitarian Action for Children: Building Resilience.* New York: UNICEF.

UNICEF (2013) *State of the World's Children, Eastern Caribbean Supplement – A Stakeholder Survey: Their Opinions and Perspectives on the Issues and Challenges Faced by Children with Disabilities.* New York: UNICEF.

World Education Forum (2000) *The Dakar Framework for Action, Education for All: Meeting our Collective Commitments.* Paris: UNESCO.

14 Inclusive practice post conflict

An exploration of examples from Liberia

Vernie Clarice Barnes

Introduction

In the prologue to her book *This Child Will Be Great*, President Ellen Johnson Sirleaf described her homeland Liberia as 'a wonderful, beautiful, mixed-up country struggling mightily to find itself' (Johnson Sirleaf, 2009: 1). It is a 43,000-square-mile West African nation with a population of 4.6 million divided into sixteen ethnic groups. Sixteen indigenous languages are spoken alongside English. Recently, it was prominent in the international media for a catastrophic health disaster named 'Ebola'. A decade earlier, the country emerged from a brutal fourteen-year civil conflict in which 200,000 lives were lost, and horrific tales have been told about the experiences of child combatants on both sides of the conflict, which, according to Human Rights Watch (2004), numbered 15,000. The complex social and historical context of this country's development makes it a compelling space within which to study principles and practices of inclusive education, particularly post conflict, which is the focus of this chapter.

Social and historical context

The small-statured Jinna is listed as the original ethnic group to have settled in this area. They were joined by other groups from Central, Western and Northern Africa to include Gola, Mandigo and Kwa. The final group came in the eighteenth century, when British abolitionists advocated the establishment of a colony there for repatriating former enslaved Africans. Thus Liberia was founded in 1822 on the ideal of creating a state within Africa where freed slaves from American plantations could live in dignity. The initial settler group, and those who arrived later, called themselves Americo-Liberians, spoke English and maintained the dress, religion and habits of the American south from whence they came (Johnson Sirleaf, 2009: 5). The country became independent in 1847, but ingrained was a system of social exclusion copied from plantation society and transplanted to the detriment of the local African population. A dualistic system was thus put in place, with the Americo-Liberian settlers building separate and exclusive political, economic and social institutions (International Institute for Educational Planning [IIEP], 2011: 18). It excluded the sixteen indigenous groups, who had to be 'Christianised' by them in order to gain citizenship and own land in the new state, which remains a vexed issue (IIEP, 2011: 27).

Individual/group task

From your reflections on the Liberian social and historical context, identify three issues of inclusion that may arise in the school system.

Post-conflict inclusion practices

Korto (2008) describes the deleterious effects of the protracted conflict on all aspects of the Liberian education system. Education infrastructure was decimated, disrupting the teaching and learning environment. At the end of conflict in 2003, infrastructure, equipment, the management system and the teaching force were all in disarray. Many teachers fled, creating a shortage of qualified and trained teachers. School participation had fallen dramatically as a result of the war, with an entire generation of children having missed the opportunity to go to school, while others (an estimated one in ten) were recruited as soldiers or abducted (IIEP, 2011: 30). A similar proportion was left traumatised having witnessed murders, rapes and other atrocities (USAID, 2014, cited in IIEP, 2011). At the end of the conflict, making primary school education accessible to youth of all ages was regarded as necessary for the maintenance of peace, hope for the rebuilding of shattered lives and successful transition to civilian life. Access to education was regarded as critical; therefore, the government instituted a free and compulsory education policy within the framework of universal primary education (IIEP, 2011). Primary school fees were abolished and, in some secondary establishments, school feeding programmes were established in 2005, as well as a gender unit with policies (IIEP, 2011). The Minister of Education, Joseph Korto, reported at the forty-eighth session of the International Conference on Education that a free Accelerated Learning Program for Positive Living and United Service (ALPP) was rolled out in 2006 alongside the training of a 60 per cent untrained teaching force. It had 21,807 students and was backed by a major portion of the country's annual budget and supported by donor agencies (Korto, 2008; IIEP, 2011). The project, now discontinued in favour of all students receiving the same primary education, was criticised for lacking a technical vocational focus or direct link to livelihood, and for being too concentrated, given that a six-year primary education was condensed into three.

 Individual/group task

Consider the differences in defining inclusive practice in the context of Liberia's post-conflict society. Contrast how you have defined inclusive practice in Liberia's context to that of inclusive practice in England or other countries detailed in this book.

Reflecting on the experiences of former child soldiers

A child soldier is defined as being under eighteen and may have had multiple roles, ranging from spy, cook and girls recruited for sexual services to key fighters (USAID/EQUIP, 2007).

Paul's story

Paul was a well-brought-up boy who joined Taylor to avenge his father, flogged to death by government troops. When asked about his experiences, Paul laughs, slightly embarrassed at his past as a flamboyantly costumed militia. 'I would mark my face, put leaves all around me. It sounds crazy, but it worked. These small boys in the bush; walking, walking into bullets and looking like devils.' Paul compares this masquerade to a man going to a football match. 'Don't he and his friends disguise themselves, paint their faces, to act completely crazy? Then they go home and everything is normal. For some of us, it was like that...'

Paul returns

> I returned to my home village with my AK, the first time since I joined. I was 11, 12 maybe. My mother asked if she could hug me. I said no. She asked if she could shake my hand. I said she should just get me a glass of water.
>
> (Quoted from Young, 2012)

 Individual/group task

Consider Paul's childhood experiences in relation to children who have not experienced conflict. What challenges might Paul present to teachers and other students in his class?

What strategies do you think could be used to ensure that Paul is included in his school?

How could information from Paul's story be used to plan lessons on peace and reconciliation?

An 'Education for All' (EFA) agenda

Ainscow *et al.* (2006: 15) developed a typology of five ways of thinking about inclusion from an analysis of international research. These are:

- inclusion as concerned with disability and 'special educational needs'
- inclusion as a response to disciplinary exclusions
- inclusion in relation to all groups seen as being vulnerable to exclusion
- inclusion as a promotion of a school for all
- inclusion as education for all.

These five ways of viewing inclusive education are reflected in the practices in Liberia, but 'education for all' is a particular post-conflict agenda. President Johnson Sirleaf confirmed this in the Foreword to the 2010–2020 Education Sector Plan (ESP), where she emphasised that: 'Special attention is given to accelerated progress aimed at significant achievement in the achievement in the Education for All (EFA) and Millennium Development Goals (MDGs) for education by the year 2015 despite limited resources' (ESP, 2010–2020: v1). This is consistent in principle with the statement in the Framework for Action of the World Education Forum requiring countries to work towards the objective of Education for All, including a commitment to 'meet the needs of education systems affected by conflict' (World Education Forum, 2000: 24).

Achieving Education for All

Liberia's Education Sector Plan (ESP, 2010–2020) outlays issues pertinent to inclusion. However, it appears that the legacy of social exclusion interferes with, even undermines, current intentions by the political leadership for inclusion to be public policy (IIEP, 2011). For instance, free and compulsory education was legislated for since 2002 and receives an increasing amount of the recurrent budget, but many are excluded from accessing it (ESP, 2010–2020: 7). Poor health and nutrition are recognised as impediments (ESP, 2010–2020: 21). Liberia has many highly prized natural resources (diamonds, gold, timber, rubber); poverty is high nonetheless. The consequence of such poverty is present in the experiences of children in Liberia. There are large numbers of children fending for themselves on the streets of Monrovia and elsewhere. Some actually live on the streets. There is also a significant number of girls who engage in all things possible, prostitution included, to earn enough money to attend school. Apparently the situation is not much better for those who live with parents who resort to using them for commercial purposes. For children living in poverty and those who are not supported adequately, attending school is not a priority (ESP, 2010–2020).

The chapter now considers some of the challenges and barriers to achieving Education for All in Liberia.

Children with special educational needs

The inclusion of children with special educational needs for whom provision is minimal is another disparity:

> Amongst the most vulnerable and under-served groups in terms of access to education are those with special needs and marginalized youth, including vulnerable children. As in many societies around the continent, any deviation from what is seen as 'normal' in a child is viewed as a curse or a punishment. Children with disabilities, therefore, tend to be treated with less love and care than their peers. In fact many are shunned or abandoned. The school is not exempt from the biases of the society.
>
> (ESP, 2010–2020: 60)

With few exceptions, schools are not designed appropriately to the needs of those with physical disabilities; there are only a few trained teachers of the hearing impaired, two schools for the visually impaired and none for children with mental and emotional problems. Further, there is a belief that a significant number of children have undiagnosed emotional and learning difficulties (ESP, 2010–2020).

Rural localities

Barriers to inclusion exist despite the Ministry of Education commitment to Education for All and supporting policies and legislation. The formal school system remains exclusionary because the education system is centralised in Monrovia, the capital city. The other fourteen counties have their capital cities but are essentially rural, some having densely forested interiors. Liberia experiences seven months of heavy rainfall and roads in rural areas are unpaved, making access to school difficult. Some communities have no access to a school. Disparities in access are due also to higher levels of poverty in rural areas.

Gender parity

Gender parity is another significant issue of inclusion as girls still lag behind boys in enrolment, retention and completion at all levels. 'Only 12 per cent of trained teachers are female; the gender parity index is 0.88 at primary level and 0.69 at secondary level' (ESP, 2010–2020: 20). Girls appear to be 7 per cent less likely to be enrolled than boys, and more likely to drop out. Reportedly, gender-based violence against girls in school is said to be high (IIEP, 2011).

 Individual/group task

Consider Ainscow *et al.*'s (2006) typology of five ways of thinking about inclusion in the context of Liberia. Use theory to consider to what extent Liberia is able to address inclusion considered in its fullest extent: Education for All.

Partnerships for inclusion

A number of non-government agencies have partnered the Government of Liberia in improving the quality of education provision and expanded access. UNICEF, the World Food Programme (WFP) and the World Bank are among organisations that have supported interventions relating to health and nutrition, girls' education, infrastructural development and teacher training. USAID and UNHCR rehabilitated and resourced teacher training centres in two key geographical locations, as well as a teacher training programme, following a census report indicating that 60 per cent of all primary-level teachers in Liberia were untrained and only 12 per cent were females who had received training in the emergency period just after the war ended (ESP, 2010–2020). The low level of trained teachers was attributed mainly to the fact that the Rural Teacher Training Institutes (RTTIs), responsible for the training of the great majority of teachers, had not been functioning in some areas of the country since the war (ESP, 2010–2020).

Making teacher training inclusive

William V.S. Tubman University joined in the preparation of teachers at its College of Education. The university is located in the rural south-east of Liberia (Harper City, population 17,837) bordering the Ivory Coast. The mission of the vision of the W.V.S. Tubman University College of

Education is to develop professional educators who are intellectually competent and knowledge-able in content and pedagogy, with critical analytic and problem-solving abilities and compassion, prepared to imaginatively and reflectively provide high-quality instruction and create environments that are transformative for all children in schools in the Republic of Liberia. One hundred and ninety seven students, the great majority males, with 5 per cent females, have enrolled since 2009. Sixty graduated in 2014, of which less than 1 per cent were females. Therefore, the ambitious mission of the college concerning education for all children is not reflected in the sex ratio of teachers in training.

Students all have in common post-conflict traumatic experiences, but very little is done to assess the need for appropriate support or any special educational needs. Less than 2 per cent of students at the college had a physical disability and there were no diagnosed learning difficulties, although many students demonstrated evidence of such in their coursework (Clay, 2014). The absence of a system for assessment of special needs of teachers when registering at the college is highlighted by Clay as a major deficiency of the training programme. So too is the absence of support systems. However, there was recognition that these are sensitive issues demanding careful treatment within a culture where disability is negatively perceived. Clay also indicated that, based on the difficulties observed in students, care should be taken in distinguishing whether the presenting learning problems are a matter of deficiencies in prior schooling and instruction or the effects of severe socio-economic neglect versus cognitive processing differences. These issues are important in preparing teachers for a system advocating education for all. For if teachers are supported in acknowledging that they have special educational needs and that these could be addressed, then perhaps they would deal more sensitively with the needs of the children. Bar Tikva (2008) conducted a study of three teachers with learning difficulties through identification of the professional self by analysing their autobiographic story and reflective feedback. She found that 'personal knowledge' representing the teacher's knowledge is anchored in his/her past experience, in the present where he/she acts and in his/her plan for the future. Put differently, this knowledge links an individual with his/her childhood memories, experiences as a pupil and experiences as a teacher (Bar Tikva, 2002). Toe (2014), a student in training at W.V.S. Tubman University College of Education, attempted to study his difficulties with reading comprehension in this manner and concluded that this is a good and sensitive approach to advancing understanding of how a teacher with such challenges survives within a system that promotes access but does not provide the means for building capacity to cope.

Reflections of a teacher, cited from a teacher's story (June 2014)

I have interest in teaching history but have poor understanding and interpretation of history. Therefore, I copied directly from the book in doing assignments at university and tried to memorise everything. I did the same thing in teaching as I would have my Grade 6 class copy things from the board or directly from the book. Whenever, I tried to explain history to the class I became worried and confused because I could not communicate exactly what I wanted to say. The students realised this and complained to the Principal, which made me feel bad, especially when I was stopped from teaching the subject that I love.

Individual/group task

How could the principal support the teacher and encourage an inclusive ethos amongst the teaching staff?

Conclusion

Education for All is the aim of the Liberian education system. Achieving it is complicated by the geographical, socio-economic and cultural contexts. Parity in access is that influenced by:

1   culturally ingrained social exclusionary practices
2   widespread issues of poverty limiting provision and deterring access
3   a centralised system that disadvantages access to rural locations
4   the slow rate of post-conflict rehabilitation.

Summary points

- Liberia has a complex social and historical context that is experiencing post-conflict inclusive practice.
- Liberia has a dualistic system where Americo-Liberian settlers are separated from the rest of its inhabitants.
- Education for All (EFA) is a particular focus in Liberia's post-conflict agenda. However, whilst Liberia is aiming towards Education for All, there are barriers and challenges to inclusive education, including poverty and childhood experiences, perceptions of special educational needs and disability, the difficulties of living in rural localities and gender parity.
- Gender parity and perceptions of special educational needs and disability are also barriers for teachers.

Further reading

Makoelle, T.M. (2014) Cognitive Justice: A Road Map for Equitable Inclusive Learning Environments. *International Journal of Education and Research*, vol. 2, no. 7, July, 505–518.
Phasha, N. and Moichela, K.Z. (2012) Inclusive Education in South Africa. In A. Bame Nsamenang and T.M.S. Tchombe (Eds), *Handbook of African Educational Theories and Practices.* Bamenda, Cameroon: Human Development Resource Centre.

References

Ainscow, M., Booth, T. and Dyson, A. (2006) *Improving Schools, Developing Inclusion*. Abingdon: Routledge.
Bar Tikva, H. (2002) *Teacher Educators' Attitudes Towards the Inclusion of Students with Learning Disabilities as Teachers.* Paper presented at Ahva Conference, Israel (Heb).
Bar Tikva, H. (2008) *Teachers with Learning Difficulties: Identifying the Professional Self by Analysing the Autobiographic Story and the Reflective Feedback*. Unpublished Thesis. Bath: University of Bath.

Clay, C. (2014) *Interview on the Teacher Education Programme at the W.V.S. Tubman University.* College of Education, Harper Maryland County, Republic of Liberia, June.

Education Sector Plan (ESP) (2010–2020) *Liberia.* Washington: Global Partnership for Education. www.global partnership.org/content/liberia-education-sector-plan (accessed 25 September 2015).

Human Rights Watch (2004) *How to Fight, How to Kill: Child Soldiers in Liberia*, 2 February, A1602. www.refworld.org/docid/402d1e8a4.html (accessed 27 July 2015).

International Institute for Educational Planning (IIEP) (2011) *Education and Fragility in Liberia.* Paris: International Institute for Educational Planning. www.iiep.unesco.org (accessed 27 July 2015).

Johnson Sirleaf, E. (2009) *This Child Will Be Great.* New York: Harper Perennial.

Korto, J.D.Z. (2008) *Inclusive Education: The Way of the Future*. International Conference on Education, 48th Session, 25–28 November. www.ibe.unesco.org (accessed 27 July 2015).

Toe, R. (2014) *My Personal Reflections on Teaching Comprehension in History to Grade 6 Students, Fatima High School*, College of Education, William V.S. Tubman University, Harper, Liberia, undergraduate unpublished study.

USAID/EQUIP (2007) *Role of Education and the Demobilization of Child Soldiers.* Washington: USAID. www.equip123.net/docs/E1-DemobChildSoldiers-IP1.pdf (accessed 25 September 2015).

World Education Forum (2000) *The Dakar Framework for Action, Education For All: Meeting our Collective Commitments.* Paris: UNESCO.

Young, F. (2012) Lost Boys: What Became of Liberia's Child Soldiers. *The Independent*, Friday 13 April. www.independent.co.uk/news/world/africa/lost-boys-what-became-of-liberias-child-soldiers-7637101.html (accessed 26 September 2015).

INDEX